Danish literature from 1000 to 1900

Anne-Marie Mai

Danish literature from 1000 to 1900

Translated by John Irons

UNIVERSITY PRESS OF SOUTHERN DENMARK 2022

University of Southern Denmark Studies in
Scandinavian Languages and Literatures vol. 147
Translation of literary quotations by John Irons if nothing else is indicated.
Photos by Anne-Marie Mai if nothing else is indicated
Cover photo: The Nine Good Heroes in the Church of Dronninglund. Charlemagne and Judas Maccabæus.
Cover by Dorthe Møller, Unisats Aps

Special thanks to Academic Officer Pernille Hasselsteen, SDU,
to Production Manager Erik Tarp and CEO Tine Meyer, Narayana Press
and to the participants of the Uses of Literature research project, SDU

Printed by Narayana Press
ISBN 978-87-408-3100-9

Danish Literature from 1000 to 1900 is published with support from:
The Danish National Research Foundation
DNRF127

University Press of Southern Denmark
55 Campusvej
DK-5230 Odense M
www.universitypress.dk

Distribution in the United States and Canada:
Independet Publishers Group
www.ipgbook.com

Distribution in the United Kingdom:
Gazelle Books
www.gazellebookservices.co.uk

Contents

Introduction 7

From God's time to man's time
1000–1700 13
The age of magic 13
Writing on stone 18
A stone book 21
Runes in verse 26
The end of the world and the power of poetry 29
The new media of the Middle Ages 33
The art of writing 35
Scribes and readers 36
A precious work 40
A major work from Denmark 43
Manuscripts in Latin and Danish 45
God's time and place 47
A world of signs 51
The in-between time 54
Marvellous minds and razor-sharp logic 57
Royal time 63
Man's time and place 71
Realising one's humanity 74
A Royal Daughter of European Fame 78
Restless, dynamic writing 80
From God's time to man's time 86

The century of the Enlightenment
1700–1800 91
Independence and authority 94
The century gets underway 95
Between optimism and a crisis mentality 98
Various terms for the Enlightenment period 101
The habitats of the Enlightenment 104

Author and public 106
The Danish Theatre 109
Freedom of the Press 114
The enlightenment of the sentiments 118
Literary tendencies and positions 123
The modern moment 131
Turning points 139

The ages of longing
1800–1900 141
One century – several ages 143
The modern fairytale – radical Romanticism 151
Romantic longings 157
Impulses from German idealism 168
Goethe divides the waters 172
Three famous figures 179
Modern literary women 188
Modern literature from the fringe 193
Poems for the writing-desk drawer 198
The modern breakthrough 206
More modern impulses 213

Notes
From God's time to man's time 1000-1700 221
The century of the Enlightenment 1700–1800 231
The ages of longing 1800–1900 237

References
Futher works on Danish literary history and biography 247
Works referenced in the notes/especially relevant works 248
Websites 262

Cronological overview 265

Index 269

Introduction

Danish literature from 1000 to 1900 is a literary account of Danish literature from the earliest period to the modern breakthrough of the late 19th century. Together with *Danish literature in the 20th and the early 21st century* this volume forms a complete history of Danish-language literature.

At a time when information about individual authors and works is only a quick click away and constantly updated, it can be an advantage to gather together this myriad of information and place it in coherent order – particularly for readers unable to understand Danish. That is the basis for the two volume on Danish literature, which seeks to help the reader surfing through digital information to gather individual points of reference within some sort of framework.

Internet sources have done an excellent job summarizing individual works, with hypertexts and the use of links between short passages of prose. There is information in English available about Danish literature and authors in this form, through sources like Wikipedia. It is also often possible to visit websites that are run by the authors themselves, by publishers, by critics or by libraries to disseminate their holdings. Studies of single works or authorships have also become extremely prevalent in literary history, especially when it comes to the most recent periods.

But despite the strengths of the single oeuvre portrait, it is not a fully historical genre. As Jon Helt Haarder points out in his book *Portrættets moment* (The moment of the portrait, 2003), it is traditionally used to create an image that synthesizes life, work and historical circumstance. The structure of the portrait, which is rooted in the ideas of the French critic Charles Sainte-Beuve, is not primarily narrative or historically analytic. It seeks to create a single, fixed moment within which the oeuvre can be read. The portrait genre lifts the oeuvre out of history – even out of the processes it comments on. For this reason, career portraits are not the best way to give readers a sense of how a work or oeuvre interacts with complexly unfolding history.

Danish literature from 1000 to 1900 and *Danish literature in the 20th and early 21st century* seek to create a historical framework for the reading of both early, modern and postmodern Danish literature and thereby to supplement the available introductions to and portraits of authorial careers. I carried out the preliminary work for this volume while editing my anthology *Danske digtere i det 20. århundrede* (Danish writers in the 20th century), Vols. I-III, 2000-2001, in my literary history *Hvor litteraturen finder sted* (Where literature takes place), Vols. I-III, 2010-2011, and in *Galleri 66. En historie om nyere dansk litteratur* (Gallery 66. A story of contemporary Danish literature), 2016, The present two volumes are based on these prior works. The inspiration for *Danish literature from 1000 to 1900* and *Danish literature in the 20th and early 21st century* comes from American 'New Historicism', which does not comprise a cohesive school or have a clear theoretical anchorage, but springs from various historical readings from the 1980s onwards that examine literary texts in their interaction with other kinds of texts. The key insight of these approaches was that texts can be viewed from a historical angle, and that history for its part can also be viewed from a textual angle; literary scholars are not limited to the study of literary texts, sources and cultural signs, and a critical-historical study must consider the circulations and negotiations between literary and non-literary texts, and between past and present literary culture. Stephen Greenblatt was New Historicism's first notable proponent. Hardly had he coined the term, however, before he realized that it was not a question of some clearly definable theory or method, or a cohesive school of researchers. New Historicism stood for various types of practices – a point that Louis Montrose also emphasizes in his essays on the subject, which do not speak of one new historicism but of several. New Historicism does not give literary texts preferential treatment over other texts but is interested in circulations between texts and also stresses that the literary historian must include his or her own cultural context. New-historical reading is essayistic and anecdotal in its style of narration and often includes a whole host of varied and lesser known texts. *Danish literature from 1000 to 1900* and *Danish literature in the 20th and early 21st century* do not slavishly observe 'the doctrine' of New Historicism– such a doctrine does not actually exist anyway. But it is hoped that the present book will evoke that combination of scholarly reliability and an exciting form of communication that typifies New Historicism.

The narrative elements included in New Historical readings are of great importance in terms of giving the reader a better understanding of the historical dimension of literature. This line of thought regarding the relation between time and narrative can be linked to analyzes carried out by the French philosopher Paul Ricœur. Particularly relevant are the ideas and concepts of his major three-volume investigation *Temps et Récit* (1983-85). His thesis here is that the reader needs narrative to be able to gain an understanding of the past. Historical time, at first an abstraction, becomes human time when it is narrated. It is narratives that make time meaningful, since narratives are configured via a plot, i.e. a comprehensible whole that governs the sequence of events. According to Ricœur, the narrative is created by events to the extent that they are perceived in an order. And here one has to understand that a complex time-relatedness can be developed in the narrative. A progressive, linear chronology is only one option. The writing of history has, according to Ricœur, become too naive in its attitude towards chronology, because in its attempt to explain it has become blind to its connections with the narrative. To Ricœur, narrative is not something one 'adds' to historical events, which could otherwise be seen independently. It is only by acknowledging these events *within* narratives that we get closer to a lived understanding of previous, distant time, something that Ricœur refers to as history's third time.

If one accepts Ricœur's emphasis of narrative in human understanding of time and history, it stands to reason that literary history will be weakened if it abandons the narrative and becomes a series of oeuvre portraits, lifting works out of historical processes into eternal significance. It is Paul Ricœur's thesis that humans relate to two separate time dimensions: partly their own existential experience of time that binds together past, present and future in the now, and partly cosmic, irreversible time. So humans need the third time of the narrative in order to be able to gain an understanding of the more distant past. This way of thinking might seem to promote a return to the Romantic grand narratives of spirit, folk and nation. Ricœur, along with most postmodern philosophers, is critical of the notions of Friedrich Hegel and the Romantics regarding the sure progress of the spirit via national history and national art. Even so, Ricœur insists, one must use *some* narrative to formulate one's identity, and this is especially true with regard to culture and literature.

So it is a combination of New Historicism and Ricœur's narratology that forms the theoretical framework for *Danish literature from 1000 to 1900* and *Danish literature from the 20th to the 21st century*. The book's focus is on Danish-language literature, but it also considers phenomena beyond the boundaries of a narrow national-literary context. It will likewise discuss other studies of Danish literature and important arguments from this field of study. The work seeks to provide a picture of the literary culture and literary debate in which the various individual works and oeuvres participate. Danish contributions to literary periods such as the Middle Ages, the Renaissance, Classicism, Romanticism and modernism are thoroughly discussed in the various periods as is the inspiration gained from European and American literature.

The history of literature from 1000 to 1900 has often be divided into nine periods: antiquity, Middle Ages, Renaissance, Baroque, classicism, Rococo, neoclassicism, Romanticism and the modern breakthrough. Central international contributions to literary studies and extensive discussion on periodization is included in the presentation so that the readers may relate this periodization to the periodization of other national literatures. Notes provide access to influential recent research and approaches to the material.

The canonization of works and authors of Danish literature is a never-ending story, and in the last fifty years, new attention has been given to women writers. I have been one of the chief editors of *Nordic Women's Literature* (1993-2016) and, compared to the latest work on the history of Danish literature, the anthology, *A History of Danish literature* (1992), edited by Sven Hakon Rossel, more women writers are included both in the early periods and in the presentation of contemporary literature. Also, women authors are not described in a special chapter; their works are included in the overall presentation of periods.

In positing canonical works of Danish literature in the 20th and 21st centuries across various genres, this study often finds it necessary to rely on qualified guesswork. *Danish literature in the 20th and early 21st century* deals with periods where the canon has not yet been laid down, and a number of the works dealt with will perhaps be consigned to oblivion in the future. Now, however, they have at least the advantage of being accessible to readers with a knowledge of English, and it is hoped that through these chapters they will show the richness and diversity on offer in Danish literature. Danish writers are invited to give readings all over the world, and Denmark invests in good translations. *Danish literature in the 20th and early 21st century* follows up on this interest with its literary-historical narrative about the art of words in Danish and *Danish literature from 1000 to 1900* gives a new interpretation of the early periods of Danish literature, based on the ongoing discussions of literary studies.

I was concluding the work with *Danish literature in the 20th and early 21st century* when I became Principal Investigator of the research project Uses of literature (2016-2022), has Professor Rita Felski as the leading Niels Bohr-professor. The research project is funded by The Danish National Research Foundation. Rita Felki's Bruno Latour-influenced ideas on literature and literary history became a new source of inspiration to my understanding of literary history, and I realized that what I had been doing could be seen as a way of practicing some of Rita Felki's and Bruno Latour's ideas on literary actors and networks. My analysis and description of literary history form, in fact, a kind of network or 'work-net' of many actors, a network that is constantly being expanded and ramified, full of cross-references between various times and places. The authors, the readers, the publishers, the librarians, the communicators, the researchers, the institutions, the places and the books and manuscripts themselves are all actors in the literary worknet of different ages.

In *Reassembling the Social. An Introduction to Actor-Network Theory* (2005), Latour discusses how the concept of the work-net arises from the Actor-Network method, an approach to social theory which describes both things and human beings as actors in networks/worknets that are always in processes of change and transmission:

The ontology of Latour's actor-network-method is flat. The status of an actor is not defined with reference to hierarchy or depth; human beings may be classified as actors in the same network as things we think of as having far less agency. Action is always defined relationally, and concepts of translation and mediation are essential in describing how the actors exert influence, connect to one another, change one another and transform the worknet that contains them. The idea of 'translation' helps us to understand the relations between actors. When actors communicate or exert influence, their messages or actions are not simply transmitted, but always achieve their impact through mediation.

Latour is interested in empirical studies and descriptions and wants to avoid theoretical prejudices in the study of the actors and networks; he prefers a radical empiricism, and his actor-network-theory has been used to describe laboratory work processes, as well as both the research process and the public reception of work by Louis Pasteur.

In my analysis, I have tried to avoid the traditional 'boxes' of literary history and instead describe a flow and connection between authors, books and ages.

Inspired by Latour, Rita Felski suggests that humanities are about:

> practices of curating as well as criticism, about preserving, conserving, and caring for. Because they are conveyed and communicated to intellectual strangers, we should expect, and even welcome, translation, mistranslation, and transformation. And rather than embracing a perpetual ethos of deconstructing or dismantling – a persisting tendency in my own field of literary

> studies – we might think more about making, building, and connecting. Perhaps retooling our frameworks along these lines might help us make a stronger and more eloquent case for why the humanities matter (Felski, 2020, 244).

Danish literature from 1000 to 1900 and *Danish literature in the 20th and the early 21st century* are attempts to practice literary history in a retooling, composing and connecting way.

In *Limits of Critique*, Felski describes the problem of literary history as a set of 'boxes' or 'containers':

> Refusing to stay cooped up in their containers, texts barge energetically across space and time, hooking up with other cofactors in ways that are both predictable and puzzling. [...] The literary text is not a museum piece immured behind glass but a spirited and energetic participant in an exchange – one that may know as much as, or a great deal more than, the critic.
> (Felski 2015, 182)

I hope to present a networking and inviting literary history that does not turn literary texts into mute museum pieces. In our discussions on my volumes, Rita Felski has supported my practice, but still underlined that the readers and literary students who will use my volumes need to know about a more traditional periodization. I agree and I have included chronological overviews and notes on literary studies' discussion of histography of traditional periodization.

The illustrations are mainly photos of locations of Danish literature and I have chosen to use these photos to show that literary history is present all over Denmark and is part of our everyday life.

Anne-Marie Mai

From God's time to man's time

1000-1700

When does the history of Danish literature begin? What century or year is one to focus on? Which text is the first one? Who wrote it? Such questions seem completely proper and reasonable at first glance. Put this way, however, they are impossible to answer. The only result is a deluge of new questions: What is a beginning? What is Danish literature? And what is literary history? This deluge can be unnerving, but the questions are worth asking, since they contest the validity of concepts that we take for granted. And there is no easy way of getting round them. For that reason, I intend to discuss, in terms of method and theory, just how and on what basis it is possible today to write a contribution to the history of Danish literature.[1]

If one understands the history of literature to be concomitant with that of language itself, one could begin with the old runic inscriptions found within the area that made up Denmark when the kingdom was first unified.[2] Starting here, we are not dealing in any way with literature as we now understand it. The runic inscriptions belong to early history and prehistory, to an age when oral culture predominated, and the words and letters of the inscriptions do not immediately resemble present-day Danish. But there are nevertheless connections to be sought between these early texts and the Danish literature of later ages.

The runes use language in a way that writers and readers of later periods have found thought-provoking, surprising and inspiring. They still speak to the reader, whether they are magic formulae, constructions resembling verses and poems, or incomprehensible signs whose meaning no one has recovered.

The age of magic

Let us begin by looking at a very old ferrule inscription from Torsbjerg on the Angel peninsula in Southern Schleswig in present-day Germany: 'Ull's servant – not spare MariR (owlþuþewaR niwajemariR) – it says in

Ferrule from Torsbjerg, on display at Gottorp Castle

runic letters, according to the runologist Erik Moltke.[3] The ferrule, may possibly have belonged to a man by the name of owlþuþewaR.[4] One can also imagine that the person who has inscribed the runes has dedicated the sheath to the gods, so that the sword has become 'Ull's servant'.[5] Ull was an ancient deity of single combat and hunting, perhaps once a major god who was eventually pushed into the background by the god Odin.[6] 'Ull's servant' was thus a strong and appropriate epithet for a warrior. But who was it that Ull's servant was not to spare? The sheath says 'Mariz', and that can perhaps be understood as the name of the sword. If so, the inscription may mean that the warrior is not to spare his sword. But this interpretation is very uncertain – the runes can also be translated to mean: 'Ull's servant – the not badly famed', 'Ull's servant – the one who is not mocked' or 'Ull's servant – never spares the famous one', meaning that the god Ull never spares anyone from death.

The runic inscription on the sword sheath is from 200–250AD. It dates from the age that historians and literary historians have agreed to refer to as 'oldtiden' (ancient or prehistory), i.e. the times prior to the beginning of the Middle Ages, with the transitional period falling from

900AD to 1100AD. Archaeologists would call this age of warriors the Roman Iron Age (0–400AD) or Late Iron Age (150AD–375AD).[7]

The inscription on the sheath is written in older runes, the so-called Elder (Germanic) Futhark.[8] This futhark was probably used across the Germanic area from Alsace-Lorraine and England in the west to Poland in the east, and from Romania in the south to present-day Norway, Sweden, Denmark and Schleswig in the north, where the Primitive Norse language, which was one of several Germanic languages, was used.[9] The warrior's sword ended up in Torsbjerg bog as a spoils-of-war sacrifice.[10] The age was one of numerous conflicts between various clans and regional population groups. Denmark was not a unified kingdom, and there was no border, linguistically or politically, to the south.[11]

The warrior who owned the sword was perhaps a conquered enemy. He may have believed that the runes could protect him in battle and give him courage in swinging his sword. If it is the victor who has written the runes on the sword, he may have wished to emphasize that the sword is now going to serve the god Ull. No matter which interpretation we choose, the runes reflect the context of magical beliefs to which the gods, nature, the sword, the warrior himself all belong. The inscription expresses a sense of coherence in the world, which could be invoked via runes and sacrifices to such gods as Ull, Odin or Thor.[12]

Other runic inscriptions have the same magical function as the runes on the Torsbjerg ferrule. But runes were not exclusively a magical system of writing, even though the word rune can have had the meaning 'secret' and 'sign that produces sound'. Runes were also used as decorative marks, on a comb for example, or for short messages. The elder runes are only found on loose objects such as the Torsbjerg ferrule, and some of the older inscriptions may have been made by craftsmen who did not know what the runes signified. There are also many writing and spelling errors in the runic inscriptions, which makes interpretation difficult. Some of the runologists believe that the runes were inspired by the Latin alphabet of the Romans. The runic script, however, contained several quite independent signs, and there is much to suggest that it developed far away from the Roman writing environment. It could have originated in Denmark, but no one knows for sure. The origin of the runes is highly contested.

The elder runes, which are those most familiar to Danish posterity, often acted as a trademark or signature; those that appear on one of the Gallehus Golden horns from c. 400AD refer to of the person who was the horn's first owner. The golden horns were lost when they were melted down in connection with a robbery in 1802, but their story acquired great importance as a motif in one of the epoch-making poems of Danish National-Romanticism – Adam Oehlenschläger's poem 'The Golden Horns' from *Digte* (Poems, 1803), which is central to the canon of Danish literature.[13] Even though the horns no longer exist, drawings of them show that the smaller horn bore a runic inscription that can be translated as follows: 'I Lægast Holtingen made the horn'. There is still debate as to whether the translation should be 'made the horn' or 'had the horn made', and whether the surname/nickname Lægast gives himself should be interpreted as 'Lægast from Holt', Lægast, son of Holt', or perhaps 'Lægast from the forest'. There is also disagreement about the possibility that the name 'Lægast' means 'the stranger seeking shelter and protection'. The meaning of many of the figures and signs on the horn is still uncertain.[14]

As Adam Oehlenschläger (1779-1850) wrote in his poem, the golden horns 'disappeared for ever'. The Torsbjerg sword sheath can still be seen at the Gottorp Castle museum in the town of Schleswig, south of the Danish-German border. The sheath was found in 1859, and it re-appeared on the historical scene at a critical point in Danish history, only a few years before the disastrous war against Prussia in 1864. Denmark suffered a crushing defeat in this war, which led to part of North Schleswig, which present-day Denmark now calls Southern Jutland, being placed under Prussian rule until 1920. The Danish sense of national identity was marked for many years by the defeat of 1864.

The archaeologist Conrad Engelhardt, who conducted the excavations at the Torsbjerg and Nydam bog sites, was well aware that war was on its way, and he worked at high speed to save as many of the ancient archaeological specimens as possible from Torsbjerg and Nydam, and to ensure that 'relics of the fatherland', as he described them, could remain in Danish hands. He managed to send off 32 boxes before the Prussians arrived on the scene.

When peace was concluded in 1865, Prussia stipulated that the relics from Torsbjerg and Nydam were to be handed over. The authorities in Denmark and Prussia had no idea what had happened to the major finds. Engelhardt did not officially know either, but his assistant had found a hiding-place for them at a merchant's house in Korsør.[15] But it was impossible to keep the relics hidden for long, and someone eyed the chance of cashing in. The affair ended with the Prussian ministry of education paying a considerable sum to a shady informer, and Engelhardt's fantastic finds left Denmark. From 1864 onwards, Danish and German interests clashed, not least when it came to language and culture. Was Danish

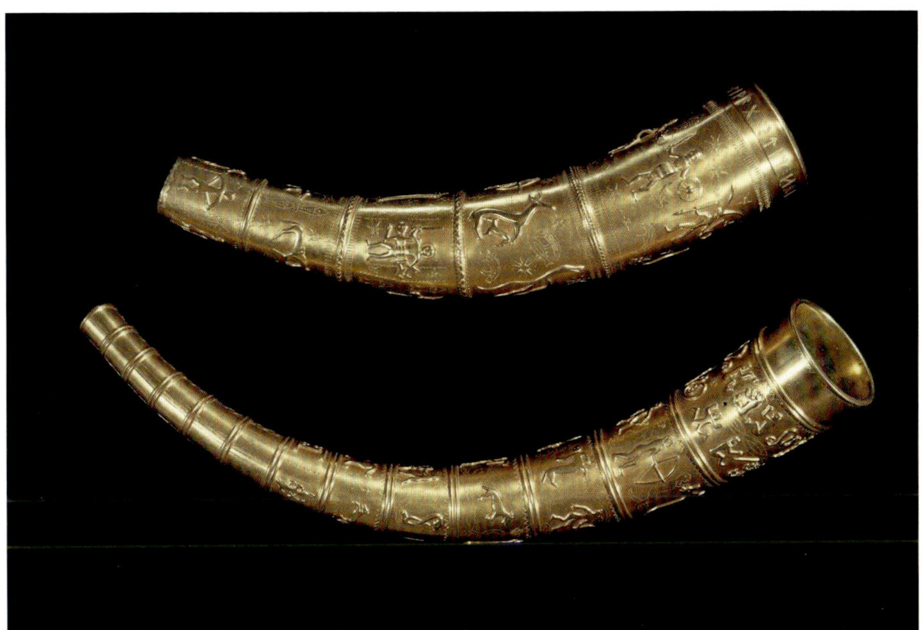

The Gallehus Golden horns, photo by Lennart Larsen

originally a dialect of German, or was Danish a Nordic language? Were the relics, including the ferrule with the runes, Danish or German 'relics of the fatherland'? These questions were of political and national importance, and political and national replies were part of a long cultural struggle that culminated in the referendum in 1920 concerning the national future of Schleswig.

Today, with the old cultural struggle between Danish and German replaced by European cooperation and shared efforts to solve the many challenges that face the European Union, the Schleswig area both north and south of the border is proving to be an incredibly interesting region, rich in common memories from the earliest times. It has become possible to provide a less one-sided and less nationally coloured history of the language and culture of the distant past than the one given after 1864 and, indeed, up to the end of the Second World War in 1945, when everything had to be either Danish or German and the national minorities were not protected.

The oldest runic language was neither German nor Danish: the runic language was, as mentioned, Primitive Norse – one of a number of Germanic languages. Primitive Norse later divided into the separate languages Danish, Norwegian and Swedish, and present-day philologists are very wary about making dogmatic conclusions: much work has continued the academic tradition begun by the philologist Peter Skautrup and his standard work *Det Danske Sprogs Historie* (The History of the Danish Language, 1944-70). Increasingly rigorous definitions ensure that no one is tempted to draw any hasty conclusions that either give the Danish language a more glorious and magnificent past than is justified, or erroneously reduce Danish to an inferior subspecies of German.

The runes were used in a culture that was predominantly oral. Communication was by word of mouth, as well as memorized poems and stories, and the written language was not used for preparing lengthy, informative texts – a situation which is hard to imagine in a culture like that of today, where electronic media can automatically convert spoken language into writing.[16]

The runes may perhaps have been constructed by knowledgeable Scandinavians who were capable of reading one or more of the written languages of the time. Instead of just absorbing Latin, they may have elected to construct a new set of signs, since they must have regarded themselves as being culturally independent and distinct from the Romans.[17] The runes were used to connect people, objects and the divine powers and to mark ownership and the order of succession. In Nordic folklore, the runes come directly from the gods. In a poem from the great Poetic Edda, *Hávamál*, the god Odin tells of how he hangs in the world-tree Yggdrasill, where he has sacrificed himself to himself. He thereby gets access to the wisdom of the underworld and is able to master the runes.[18]

Writing on stone

The inscriptions on the runic stones found everywhere in the area that is now Denmark use the Younger Futhark, which began to appear around the 7th century. The younger runes were a simplification of the Elder Futhark and were also used throughout the Nordic area, even though there was a further simplification of the runes in Norway and Sweden.

The written language in the Nordic area thus retained a common Primitive Norse character, though there were differences between the various areas as far as spoken language was concerned. The 13th century historian Saxo Grammaticus and the Icelandic chronicler Snorri Sturluson used the terms 'Danish voice' and 'Danish tongue' to describe a single language spoken in Denmark, Sweden and Norway. But as early as the 12th century, there are differences between the West Nordic Norse dialects and the East Nordic Danish and Swedish dialects of the Primitive Norse language, and philologists are beginning to use the term Old Danish about the language of that period.[19]

In the area that is now Denmark, the runic stones from the period c. 800–1050 (the time historians and archaeologists call the Viking Age) are famous, and they were raised to commemorate important deceased persons at grave sites as well as at bridges or roadsides – for example, at several points along the Jutland *Hærvejen* ('army road'), a system that actually consisted of many different roads, whose age is unknown. The runic stones mark the sites where people lived and the routes they travelled.[20]

Today, the stones are still part of the landscape, although not all of them are at their original locations, many having been moved to museums.[21] Here, one has the chance to see the stones lined up, protected against wind and weather and glossed with excellent explanations and translations of the runes. But wherever the runic stones still stand in the landscape, they continue to connect people, writing, place and time with each other. The inscriptions often refer to the past, the present and the future together. The longest runic inscription in Denmark, which comprises 210 runes, is an excellent example.

These runes are inscribed on the Glavendrup stone on Funen, which dates from the early 10th century. There is still some uncertainty about the meaning of the text. A possible translation is 'Ragnhild raised this stone after Alle, the 'gode' (sacrificial priest) of the Sølvs, the glorious 'thegn' (military leader) of the uia clan. Alle's sons made this monument in memory of their father and his wife of her husband; but Sote carved these runes in memory of his 'drot' (lord) – May Thor consecrate these runes – May anyone who damages this stone or removes it and places it as a monument to any other person be made a 'ræte'.'[22] The concluding words sound like a curse and point to a magical connection that the runes may be a part of, although the meaning of the word 'ræte' is unknown.[23] But when one reads the inscription today, one still feels one is being addressed as a reader and is obliged to honour the memory that Ragnhild, the sons, the rune-master Sote and the god Thor have all helped create. The Glavendrup runes have the elements which, often in different sequences, form what is known as a runic stone formula: 1) information about who has raised the stone (Ragnhild, who has taken care of this assignment, and the sons, who have taken care of the inscription); 2) praise of the deceased person (all of them were high-ranking military figures); 3) consecration of the stone to the gods (the runes are dedicated to Thor); 4) a wish for the dead person and the preservation of the stone

The Glavendrup stone

or a curse on anyone who disturbes the grave (the threat of becoming a 'ræte' if one damages the stone or dedicates it to any other person); 5) mention of the rune-master (Sote, who has inscribed runes to his lord).[24]

The Glavendrup stone is part of a ship tumulus, a grave construction that illustrates the voyage to the kingdom of the dead, and the gravesite was used as a sacrificial grove. The inscription thus links times and places in a characteristic way, since the runes not only bind together past, present and future but also point to the kingdom of the dead, to which the glorious Alle is travelling in his ship of stone. The runic stone, the grave site and the sacrificial grove are not a metaphor restricted to the imagination – they are parts of the magical whole: the voyage from the living to the dead. The person standing at the stone today takes part in that same long journey.

A stone book

Traces of another, even larger ship tumulus are found in Jelling. The smallest of the Jelling stones is Gorm the Old's stone raised for his queen, Thyra. In the latter half of the 10th century, Gorm's son, Harald Bluetooth, raised another, larger stone in memory of Gorm and Thyra on the middle axis of the ship setting. Harald Bluetooth's stone differs in several ways from other runic stones, not least because it relates that Harald has converted the Danes to Christianity. On the eastern side of the stone there is this inscription, with the translation provided by the museum in Jelling:

> Harald the king ordered
> *Haraltr kunukr bath kaurua*
>
> these runes commemorating Gorm, his father
> *kubl thausi aft kurm fathur sin*
>
> and Thyra his mother, that
> *auk aft thaurui muthur sina sa*
>
> Harald who conquered all of Denmark
> *haraltr ias sar uan tanmaurk*

On the northwestern side of the stone it says:

> and Norway
> *ala auk nuruiak*

And on the southern side of the stone:

and made the Danes Christian
auk tani karthi kristna[25]

Harald was admittedly not the first ruler to become Christian. Harald Klak had been baptised in 826AD in connection with an alliance between the Christian king of the Franks, Louis the Pious, but he was soon after driven out of Jutland, and his missionary Ansgar did not have much success in establishing churches in Ribe and Hedeby.

Things went slightly better for Harald Bluetooth, as regards both regal power and Christianity. His Jelling stone has been referred to as Denmark's certificate of baptism, because the stone bears witness to a victorious, powerful ruler of a unified country, it states that Christianity has been introduced and it uses the name Denmark – as does Gorm's stone as well. Historians tend to suggest, however, that the introduction of Christianity was perhaps more an ambition of Harald's than something realized unequivocally within his lifetime. Belief in Christ and the worship of Odin, Thor and the gods of the old world ran parallel for a long time, as can be seen from other runic inscriptions. Harald's baptism may have taken place after pressure from the German emperor Otto the Great, and it might well have been Harald's only chance to remain a king. At any rate, the baptism led the German emperor to view the Danish king as his vassal. Harald may not have shared Otto's view on the matter, but the peace allowed him to strengthen his hold and establish four ring fortresses, of which the most famous are Trelleborg and Fyrkat. Harald's stone tells us one other thing – that the name 'Denmark' was probably mostly associated with the lands east of the Great Belt (the strait Funen which separates and Zealand), lands like Zealand itself and present-day southern Sweden, which were now included in Harald's Jutland kingdom.

Significantly, the entire working of Harald's Jelling stone reflects craftsmanship that originates in various places throughout the European continent, as well as the British Isles and Ireland.[26] The runes are to be read horizontally from left to right like a Latin text, not vertically as, for example, the Glavendrup stone and many other runic stones. The large Jelling stone is simply a stone book with three written and illustrated pages: The reader is to begin with the eastern page, where Harald presents himself as the originator of the stone and tells of his parents and his achievements. One then continues along the northwestern page of the stone, where a lion-like animal is seen together with a serpent. The lion shows similarities

The Jelling stones

with decorations found in Irish manuscripts from the 9th and 10th centuries. The art historian Lise Gotfredsen interprets the two figures, the lion and the serpent, as pointing in worship towards the figure of Christ on the southern page of the stone. There is no implication – as many people have claimed – of there being a fight between the lion and the serpent. On the contrary: The lion is lifting his paw, while the serpent is bowing down to Christ, breaking the form in which the serpent is most often seen: a closed circle where it bites its own tail and is invincible.[27]

After having read about the king and seen the worshipping, magical animals, one continues to page three, experiencing Christ and hearing about the Danish nation. The actual figure of Christ radiates power and victory, as can be seen from his plaited hair and open eyes, among other things. Christ is surrounded by graphic signs of the trinity: Father, Son and Holy Spirit, and even though Christ is shown in his crucified position with outstretched arms, he is not hanging on any visible cross.

Repainting of the serpent and the lion on the large Jelling stone, on exhibition at Kongernes Jelling

Instead, he is nailed to the tree of life – the tree resembles the world tree of Nordic mythology that Odin hung on – which twines around him with an unbroken vine of acanthus leaves. The stone's impression is both powerful and subtle, and attempts have been made to imitate its style on other runic stones.

During the Second World War and the German occupation of Denmark 1940–45, Jelling became a national rallying point. To prevent the occupying forces from violating the mounds, the National Museum instigated comprehensive excavations in 1941 and 1942.[28] The Nazis in Germany (and their supporters in Denmark) could easily have become extremely interested in Jelling; after all, they misused many symbols from the Iron and Viking Ages in their racist propaganda against so-called non-Arian peoples. Hitler's dreaded SS corps, which was responsible for the concentration camps, used two runic S's, which was the ancient name for the sun, as their logo.

One of the most important sources of knowledge about King Harald's early Christian Denmark is the 11th century Hamburg church history of Archbishop Adam of Bremen. Adam writes enthusiastically about Harald, who allows himself to be converted. In keeping with the political correctness of the medieval period, Adam attributes Harald's success as a king to his newly acquired Christian faith.[29]

If one wishes to consider Harald Bluetooth's Jelling stone as Denmark's certificate of baptism, one must remember that it was also a renewed membership card for a Germanic-Roman cultural connection. The Jelling stone is a stone book; it has a communicative and informative function and does more than state personal power or ownership.[30] It can be interpreted as a marker of a long transition from an oral culture to one that uses writing to communicate across far greater distances than previously – indeed, all the way from distant Rome to the almost unknown Nordic region.

Denmark acquired its own position in the increasingly powerful Catholic network with the establishment of the archbishopric in Lund in 1103, under Eric I, called the Good. King Eric was lucky enough to have his wish realized at a time when the pope and the German emperor were at odds with each other, and the history of many succeeding centuries has to do with the relationship between these different kinds of rules, who were called the two swords - the sword of the church and the sword of the king. Things went best for king and church when they cooperated, as in the glorious age of the Valdemar kings between 1157 to 1241.

Initially, Christianity's main following was found among the upper echelons of society, the landowners, who could give gifts to monasteries and build churches. Many Romanesque village churches were built in the early medieval period (12th and 13th centuries) in a burst of energy that seems incomprehensible today. The churches were squires' churches, and their clergy introduced new forms of writing, studying and legislation.

The knowledge and the skills that the church possessed were of great value to the landowners, both when it came to legal matters and agriculture itself. The church also ensured contact with the European centres of learning and thereby with great discussions in theology and philosophy.

The Christian church brought with it a writing culture with a new language and a new alphabet. Latin was the international language of the church, and priests were educated in Latin either in Denmark itself or as students sent to the university of Paris, which was founded in the mid-12th century.

The introduction of Christianity marks the transition to the Middle Ages in Denmark, and the division between antiquity and the medieval period thus lies between 900AD and 1100AD. The beginning of the European Middle Ages is connected with the fall of the Roman Empire and is often dated to between 500AD and 700AD.[31]

Runes in verse

By about the year 1110, the West Nordic or Norse dialects in most of Norway, in Iceland and in the Faroe Islands had diverged from the East Nordic in Denmark, Sweden and some border areas of Norway. The Danish language had acquired its own characteristics. The term Old Danish is used for the language of this period. In this language's written form, the runic alphabet adapted to the Latin alphabet, and the runes remained in use until the year 1300. The runes were used as a legal language, as can be seen from a transcript of the Scanian Law from just before 1300, and they also appear in church contexts in connection with inscriptions on inventory and buildings. Gradually, however, the runes became a code language, whose magical significance became increasingly cultivated as the runes disappeared from everyday use. Present-day interest in magic and fortune-telling has led to a rediscovery of traditions such as rune-casting, where one takes auguries after casting pieces with runic characters written on them. The Internet has innumerable websites about practising runic magic.

In Norse, we know of orally recited heroic poems, stories and sagas from antiquity, written down in the 13th and 14th centuries. The runic inscriptions reveal, as mentioned, that Odin, Thor, Ull and Frey were also worshipped in the area known today as Denmark, but no poems about the gods have been recorded in Old Danish. Skjalds from Iceland, which was the capital of skaldic poetry, visited both Nordic and English courts, but a literature of antiquity in Old Danish has not been preserved.

The heroic and mythological poems written down in the Icelandic manuscript called the *Elder Edda (Codex Regius),* from 1270, are of West Nordic origin and in a West Nordic, Norse language. This same is true of the learned Icelandic historian Snorri Sturluson's textbook of the skaldic art from the 1220s, the so-called *Younger Edda,* in which Snorri contributed to a renaissance of skaldic art by showing examples of the old mastery. The Icelandic sagas represent a prose genre unique to Iceland, a completely original Icelandic contribution to heroic storytelling that stands alongside the legendary Greek poet Homer's *Iliad* and *Odyssey* from around 700BC.[32]

The writing down of Old Norse oral poetry is a Nordic branch of the first European Renaissance, i.e. the cultural movement that rediscovered and cultivated the epic and heroic oral modes of the past. This first Renaissance is an important but overlooked precursor to the subsequent Renaissance, which began in southern Europe in the 14th and 15th centuries. In this second, better-known Renaissance, it is the art of ancient Greece and Rome that are rediscovered and cultivated. But if one is to understand Renaissance as a pan-European term, one must include the early Nordic Renaissance and its rediscovery of the northern European past.[33]

The Old Danish language, however, does not play any real part in this early Nordic Renaissance – there is simply no recorded writing from antiquity, no extant saga literature. One can, however, consider the inscriptions on the runic stones in Denmark as literature from antiquity, and Denmark was also part of the oral culture to which the works eventually written down all refer.

The runic inscriptions, as we have seen, have their own concise form of language. They use patterns of alliteration, repetition and a particular sentence structure, all of which create an effect that was probably imagined more in terms of magic than of art. The rune carver used these effects highly consciously. Sometimes they may have been impossible to avoid – the Lægæst of the Gallehus Golden horns can hardly escape alliteration, since his name 'hlewagastir' and his surname 'holtijar' alliterate with the word 'horna'. But some of the inscriptions are clearly and intentionally composed in Norse metre, with characteristic word order, repetitions, alliterations and the use of accentuated syllables (the so-called stress system found in much Germanic poetry).[34]

For example, a Norse metre called *ljoðaháttr* (which is often thought to mean the metre of incantations) is used in the cursing line about the 'ræte' on the Glavendrup stone and on the so-called Ribe rune skull, an amulet from the period between 700AD and 800AD which consists of a piece of a skull inscribed with a magic text. The runologist Niels Åge Nielsen proposes the following translation: 'Ulvur and Odin and Højtyr are help for Bur against these (things): ache (pain) and dwarf sword.'[35] The translation does not convey any of the many alliterations, or the characteristic use of three final accented syllables: **wi**þr þæima **wær**ki auk **dwærg**unniu.[36] But the translation preserves one important stylistic characteristic: synonymic variation, or the use of several names for the same figure. Odin is referred to both as 'Ulvur' (wolf) and 'Højtyr' (the high god) and finally 'help for Bur'. The animal name for the god being invoked comes at the very beginning of the sentence, the inscription starting quite simply with the word 'Ulvur' (wolf). The language has been fashioned, put into alliterative verse to enable the magic to work, so that the man Bur could be rid of his pains and avoid meeting one of the dangerous dwarf swords. The belief was that a sword forged by dwarfs carried a curse and was bound to kill as soon as it was drawn from its sheath. There was good reason to ensure one had the help of Odin against such curses!

Another Norse metre is *fornyrðislag*, 'the metre of old words', and it also appears on runic stones in Denmark. In *fornyrðislag*, lines are joined together in couplets with the aid of alliteration and stressed syllables, and the metre is often used in sections of the runic inscription that describe the deceased, or as the concluding words. When the woman Sasgerd's husband Odinkar is described as 'den dyre og drottro' (valuable and faithful to his leader) on a runic stone in Skjern from around 1000AD, this metre is used:

þan ***dy****ra*
ok hin ***drott****in****fast****a*[37]

The most literary of the runic stones in the East Nordic area is the Swedish Rök stone from Östergötland, from the beginning of the 11th century. Here 'the metre of the old words' is used to dedicate a monument to the Ostrogothic king Theodoric the Great (d. 526AD). The enigmatic text is highly reminiscent of the heroic poetry written down in Iceland in the 13th century, and of English heroic poetry about the same Theodoric. The stone seems to be an experimental use of narrative expression.[38]

On a stone from Års from the period 750–1050AD, *fornyrðislag* is used in the conclusion of the runic formula:

***Sten** kwæþsk **hers**i*
stand**e **længi
***SaR Wal**toka*
***warþ**a **næf**ni*

The stone announces
that it will stand here a long time
It will name
Valtoki's cairn[39]

The stone speaks in verse and, so far, it would seem speak the truth. It has stood for a long time in Års, reminding people of Valtoki, and of Asser, who raised the stone. It has clearly not considered ceasing to announce the fact.

As their own network of the past, the runic stones and their inscriptions draw lines through present-day Denmark as well as lines outside of the country, to distant regions of England and Germany – indeed, even to Romania and Poland, where the runes were once known as well. Perhaps the runic stones do not always stand where they were originally placed. But they are still here, in the places where present-day Danes live. And it is thought-provoking that many of us live in places named after such ancient gods as Odin (e.g. Odense) or Thor (e.g. Torslunde). The gods also survive in some of the weekdays: Tyr in *tirsdag* (Tuesday), Odin in *onsdag* (Wednesday), Tor in *torsdag* (Thursday) and Frigg in *fredag* (Friday].

When one looks at the runic stones, one senses how words, places and times can become a totality and how old traces of verse and poetry can be discovered. One finds oneself at a point of intersection between past and present – a long way from the past and those who lived then, and at the same time very close.

The end of the world and the power of poetry

Even though no literature from antiquity exist in Old Danish, Denmark was part of the oral culture to which such literature as that written down in Iceland during the 13th century Nordic Renaissance refers. This is particularly demonstrated by the magnificent Latin work of the medieval historian Saxo Grammaticus *Gesta Danorum* (*The Danish History of Saxo Grammaticus*, 1905) from the early 13th century. Saxo (c. 1160 – after

1208) was the first Danish historian, and his *Gesta Danorum* is still a Danish classic. The book has been printed many times and is still the object of new interpretations by modern artists and historians. In *Gesta Danorum*, Saxo makes it clear that he has a collection of heroic poems at his disposal, translated by him for use in his history. The book includes lays about Ingald and Starkad, Hagbard and Signe, and Hrolf and his warriors, rewritten in Latin. A collection of such Eddic poems in Icelandic has, as mentioned, been preserved in the manuscript *The Elder Edda (Codex Regius)*, and poems about gods and heroes are also included in Snorri Sturluson's textbook on Eddic poetry, *The Younger Edda*. The two books are among the most important of the old manuscripts and are major sources of our knowledge about the literature, mythology and legends of the Viking Age. *The Elder Edda*, which comprises 45 pages of hide (one sheet is missing), is divided into two groups of poems, the first of which consists of ten poems about gods and the second of 19 poems about heroes. It is thought that the texts are transcriptions of poems handed down by word of mouth. At the beginning of the manuscript is the great poem *Völuspá*, which deals with the Norse gods and the Norse religion's picture of the world, cosmology and mythology.[40] The poem also appears in *The Younger Edda* and in the manuscript *Hauksbók*, which is an anthology from the early 14th century. There is no written connection between the three transcriptions of the poem, but they indicate that the poem had a fixed form by the time of the 13th century transmission.[41]

The *Völuspá* is for present-day readers an enigmatic but powerful text, and its narration of the creation of the earth, its destruction and possible rebirth has challenged and inspired large numbers of writers and researchers from later ages.[42] In a Danish-Norweigian context, Suzanne Brøgger, Thøger Larsen, Preben Meulengracht Sørensen and Gro Steinsland have all attempted to translate this difficult text. The *Völuspá* is thought to date from around the year 1000AD, i.e. from the transitional period between paganism and Christianity. Traces of the new religion can perhaps be found in the poem's vision of a strong deity who creates a new order after *ragnarök*, the destruction of the world.[43]

Most of the poem is spoken by the figure of the völva, who prophesises in the *fornyrðislag* metre (the metre of the old words). The völva is known from saga literature as a travelling shamanic seeress who, placed on a special high seat, speaks her prophecy to the assembled members of the household. Her knowledge and insight are ancient and greater than those of the mighty Odin. In the poem, it is precisely Odin who summons the völva and asks her to share of her knowledge:

I asked for hearing from all
hallowed seed,
greater and humbler
sons of Heimdallr.
You wish me, Sire of the Slain,
well to narrate
the world's old news,
such as I remember from remotest
times. [44]

The völva is to tell of the past and future to the sons of Heimdall (humanity), as well as to the family of the gods (the æsir) because Valfader (another name for Odin) has asked her.[45] There are many interpretations of the text that follows. One interpreter believes that the prophecy has to do with the conflict between an ancient, female, oral culture – represented by the völva – and a more recent, male, written culture, represented by Odin.[46] Others have regarded the text as an allegorical analysis of ideological conflicts in Icelandic society in the 13th century[47], but practically all scholars agree that it is hardly possible to arrive at any final, unequivocal conclusion.

One perhaps-essential fact about the text's cosmology is that good and evil come from a common source.[48] The good gods (æsir) and the evil giants (jǫtnar) are related to each other, while humanity stands midway between them. The balance between good and evil is, however, insecure, and in an attempt to find equilibrium, the gods create the dwarfs, who are named in a long list in the middle of the poem. But the war between good and evil breaks out even so, caused by a dispute concerning the woman Gullveig, who is said to have been burnt three times and come back to life afterwards each time. It is uncertain who Gullveig is – perhaps she represents the gods' desire for gold. After the conflict to do with Gullveig, war breaks out in a series of violent events that end in *ragnarök*:

Brothers will fight
and kill each other,
sisters' children
will defile kinship.
It is harsh in the world,
whoredom rife

– an axe age, a sword age
– shields are riven –
a wind age, a wolf age –
before the world goes headlong.
No man will have
mercy on another.[49]

It is possible to claim that the poem describes how agreements and words of praise hold together a world where good and evil are constantly in conflict, or are even indistinguishable - as in the figure of Loki, since he is both god and giant.[50]

One can add to this interpretation the poem's sharp underlining of varying degrees of insight: Odin knows a great deal about past and future, but the völva knows more than humanity, the dwarfs, the giants and the gods – even more than Odin himself. Indeed, Odin has to give her jewellery to get her to speak, and she describes how he tempts her in order to get hold of some of her knowledge:

Alone, she held séance out in the night,
when the old fellow came,
Æsir's son of Dread,
and looked into her eyes,
'What do you ask me?
Why do you try me?
I know it all, Óðinn,
where you lodged your eye:
[...][51]

The poem is driven by the recurring question 'Seek you wisdom still?' as the völva asks Odin how much he wishes to know. What she tells him is the story of Odin's own fall and destruction and the rebirth of the world under a different ruler. The völva is asked to speak her prophecies about Odin, but the prophecies turn out to be better for humanity than for Odin. A new world, 'Gimle' is waiting for humanity but not for the old gods:

A hall she sees standing,
brighter than the sun,
roofed with gold,
on Refuge from the Flames.

There shall the worthy
warrior bands dwell
and all their days of life
enjoy delight.[52]

The poem ends strikingly with the first signs of the approaching *ragnarök*, visible in the sky in the form of a gleaming dragon, while the völva herself sinks back into the earth from which she has come. The sight of the dragon is both horrible and enigmatic:

There comes the shadowy
dragon flying,
glittering serpent, up
from the Dark of the Moon Hills.
He carries in his pinions
– he flies over the field –
Malice, Striker, corpes.
Now she will sink.[53]

The dragon can be seen as an image of the poet himself, a kind of self-portrait that shows the poet weighed down by his frightful visions and experiences of the past. And yet the poet flies high like the dragon: his poetry reaches the ears of Odin himself, who is the god of poetry.[54]

The *Völuspá* does more than predict the destruction of the gods and the world; it is also a prophecy about the might and power of Norse wordsmiths. The strength of the Norse tradition is shown by the fact that it was still important after the transition to Christianity, for the old metres were bound us in new, Christian poems. This applies, for example in Einar Skúlason's song of praise *Geisli (Ray)*, which was spoken in the new cathedral in Nidaros in 1153 in honour of Olav the Holy, king of Norway, who was canonized in 1031. In this long poem, Christian imagery is mixed with pagan kennings, i.e poem metaphors, such as the depiction of Olav as the ray from God and as the one who gives Odin's raven Hugin blood to drink from fallen warriors.[55]

The new media of the Middle Ages

While people of Danish antiquity (0-1100AD) wrote magical words on stones, swords and amulets, the art of writing acquired completely new media in the medieval period. This period stretches from about the year

1100 to about the year of the Danish Reformation in 1536, when the Catholic Church and its monasteries were dissolved and Martin Luther's reformed Christianity introduced.

Recent research into medieval history, culture and art emphasizes the fact that the Middle Ages were not dark, barbaric or stagnant, as historical clichés and the expression 'The Dark Ages' imply.[56] On the contrary, the long period was characterized by cultural exchange and interaction between many environments around Europe. People studied the cultural heritage of previous eras and developed new ideas. The medieval period can be seen as an extremely dynamic period, and the Italian Renaissance in the 15th century can be conceived as the last of a series of movements of medieval innovation. It is during the Middle Ages that Denmark becomes integrated into a European cultural system, in terms of a writing culture, learning and art. Financially, too, Denmark finds a place in Europe, exporting agricultural goods to the more densely populated areas of the continent.[57]

During the medieval period, Denmark was a Catholic, European country,[58] and the first new medium was the manuscript on parchment. With the manuscripts came new types of writing, new literary genres. The art of writing on papyrus or parchment also has a very long pre-history in European cultural circles. Here, the history of the manuscripts goes all the way back to the texts of ancient Egypt from the year 2500BC and also includes the sacred writings of the Phoenicians and Jews, as well as the texts of Greek Antiquity where it is likely that people began to write down poems in the 7th century BC.

In Denmark, manuscripts started to be used relatively late, around 1000AD, in the transitional period between antiquity and the Middle Ages, when the Christian faith was gaining a footing and the Catholic church established its own institutions in the country. Two early manuscripts from the area that was then part of Denmark are Canute the Holy's deed of a gift to the cathedral of Lund from 1085, and the Scanian *Dalbybog* (The Dalby Gospel Book) a collection of gospels from c. 1060. The *Dalbybog* was used in church services and has decorations that are inspired by Irish and Anglo-Saxon manuscripts from localities frequented by the Vikings.

Later in the medieval period, another medium made its appearance: the book printed on paper. The German book-printer Johannes Gutenberg's bible from c. 1454 is the oldest preserved printed book in Europe. The art of book-printing came to Denmark in 1482 when the bishop of Odense commissioned a German book-printer to print the diocese's breviarium, i.e. church prayer book. The first printed book in Danish is the rhyming history of Denmark *Den danske Rimkrønike* (The Danish Chronicle in Verse and Rhyme)[59] which was printed in 1495 by the Dutchman Gotfred of Ghemen, who established the first printing works in Copenhagen.

The art of writing

Parchment was made out of animal hides from calves, sheep or goats that were tanned, bleached and calendered with pumice stone and rubbed with chalk. In addition, the parchment – depending on its size – was folded into various page sizes. Present-day printers still use the old terms for page sizes from the time of parchment: folio (or foolscap) (hide folded once), quarto (folded twice) and octavo (folded three times). But before the writer could begin using the parchment and painstakingly print his letters, he had to add horizontal and vertical lines to guide him, and also cut a considerable supply of quills and make an ink mixture that would ensure that the writing would remain on the parchment. A scraping knife could be used to erase if one made a mistake. The art of ink-making was refined to perfection in the Middle Ages – as opposed to later periods. Many of the books now printed will hardly last the century. The quality of the printing ink is too poor – it simply disintegrates. The fine craftsmanship of the manuscript period was, on the other hand, designed to last virtually to the end of time, which, as far as the church was concerned, was the Day of Judgment when Christ would come again and judge every single person, both the living and the dead.

The manuscripts were produced at so-called *scriptoria*, writing workshops, which were linked, *inter alia*, to the Cistercian monasteries. The Cistercian monks had arrived in Denmark in 1144 under Archbishop Eskild, and they founded the monastery at Herrevad in Scania. More monasteries were established during the 12th century at Sorø and Esrum on Zealand, at Løgum, Vitskøl and Øm in Jutland, at Holme on Funen and at Ryd in Schleswig, with nunneries being established in Slangerup and Roskilde. More than 1000 Cistercian monasteries and nunneries were established across Europe.

The Cistercian monasteries were all to be equipped with an *armarium*, i.e. a library of religious writings in Latin.[60] A list of written material held at the Cistercian monastery of Øm states that, in 1554, the abbey had 346 books and manuscripts in its armarium. Many of them were, as it happened, Protestant writings. The pragmatic, foreseeing abbot of Øm, Peder Sørensen, tried actively to follow the stipulations laid down by the

Ruins of Øm Abbey

University of Copenhagen concerning the conversion of the monasteries into Protestant centres of learning. The last abbot of Øm, Jens, ended up as a rector in Lyngby, probably dying in 1579.

Archaeological finds at Øm seem to indicate that the monks in their writing workshop worked zealously at transcribing books and repairing manuscripts. At the end of the 13th century, they even wrote a chronicle about the history of the Abbey.[61]

Apart from manuscripts and the monastery's deeds of gift, the monastery libraries also housed transcriptions of statute books. It may have been monks from the Cistercian monastery at Sorø – signs point to a brother by the name of Niels – who in the latter half of the 15th century produced the manuscript that became the printed book *Den danske Rimkrønike* (The Danish Chronicle in Verse and Rhyme), a history of Danish kings.

Opinions vary about how the rhymed chronicle came into existence. Was it written by one or more monks? And what role is played by Niels, who is mentioned as the author of a Low German translation? The rhymed chronicle and the discussion of its exciting history lead us into both the old manuscript culture and into the new art of book-printing.[62]

Scribes and readers

The readers and writers of the early Middle Ages were, then, to be found in the monasteries and at the schools of the new cathedrals, where boys who were destined to serve the church learned to read and write with the aid of wax tablets. Parchment was far too expensive for daily use by schoolboys, and paper did not become widespread until the 14th century. The language of the manuscripts was normally Latin, but the Danish language was also used, and there are manuscripts with both runic and Latin letters. The runes were adapted to the Latin alphabet and beautifully drawn in texts such as the *Codex Runicus*, a parchment book of 101 pages from c. 1300, which includes the Scanian Law, among other things. By the time *Codex Runicus* was written, Latin letters had replaced runic ones in ordinary use, and the use of runes in the manuscript could well be an attempt to idealize the writing of earlier ages, to lend the book a certain gravity and patina. It could even be a rejoinder to the dominance of the new Latin letters.

It certainly seems that the writer wanted to underscore the importance and power of the runes when, on the last page, he chose to insert a small piece of musical notation and text: *'drømde mik en drøm i nat um silki ok ærlik pæl'* (I dreamt a dream last night of silk and fine brocade)[63] it says at the bottom of the parchment. The music notation is the oldest surviving music for a secular text anywhere in northern Europe, and the snippet of text and tune could well be a quotation from a ballad known and loved at the time. The writer may have thought that the miniature dream narrative was a fitting conclusion to the beautiful runic manuscript with statutory provisions and lists of kings.

Until 1200, the Latin letters used were the Carolingian minuscule, named after the emperor Charlemagne (d. 814AD), whose court left an indelible mark on European learning, church art and manuscripts. The minuscule had clearly drawn, rounded letters that even today are easy to read, and the script was used everywhere in Charlemagne's extensive Frankish empire. It was replaced by Gothic script, the so-called blackletter script, which has many broken edges and sharp angles, and which was later used in printed books and also in handwriting, right up until the early 20th century. The pointed Gothic letters gained ground at the same time as the pointed arches of Gothic church architecture started to be used in Denmark.

The manuscript was an extremely useful medium for the church and the monarchy, and it was used to consolidate both the Crown and the Church and thereby ensure the monarchs in Denmark an independent

The entrance to Sorø Academy with the so-called Saxo Cell where Saxo is said to have worked on *Gesta Danorum*, a piece of information that has not been documented

position in the Catholic world. Manuscripts could contain the Christian gospels, prayers, sermons and religious writings. They could bear witness to holy men and women and tell stories from distant times and places.

They could be used to commit old, orally transmitted laws into writing and to issue deeds of gift to churches and monasteries, with fixed stipulations that would apply long into the future.

There could be several originals for a manuscript. Saxo Grammaticus, for example, went over his history of Denmark in a number of transcripts before a finished version could be passed on for further transcriptions. Of the original of this work, written at the beginning of the 13th century, only a fragment of four pages has survived. Here, one can see Saxo's extensive corrections of the section of the narrative that deals with the Danish king Skjold.

The texts of the manuscripts are thus an exclusive functional literature, where the written word serves the cause of the church or the monarch. But when one looks at the old manuscripts, one cannot avoid noticing how the use of language also reflects the joy the scribe felt in being the person to tell story about a saint or a king. Few people at this time mastered the art of writing. But those capable of producing manuscripts seem to have put great enthusiasm and energy into their work. The words and the script were used with care and a sense of impact, things which are also evident when transcripts were made or when various scripts were compared for a new book. *Øm Klosters Krønike (*The chronicle of Øm Abbey), begun in 1207, starts with the monks' declared and fervent wish that posterity should learn of the beginnings of the abbey, and the words of the manuscript are directly addressed to the reader.

For medieval people, the word was something fundamental. It came from God, as described in St. John's Gospel: 'In the beginning was the Word, and the Word was with God, and the Word was God.' (John I, v.1). The word, in speech or in writing, is full of spiritual power, and anyone using the word in writing or in speech must take care that their use is pleasing to God.[64] Loose speech could quickly have fatal consequences, and the same was certainly true of ill-considered writing. Neither God nor king, or church for that matter, were known for being slow in meting out punishment!

The oral literature that circulated in the Middle Ages outside the monasteries and churches is only known from later transcriptions. In the 19th century in particular, folktales and ballads were collected that may have existed in the Middle Ages. But scholars disagree as to how far back in time these ballads were actually present in Denmark.[65]

Access to knowledge was restricted in the medieval period, and it was even difficult to get permission to write. Yet, one can sometimes sense the joy felt by the medieval person when able to use his or her skill.

In Tornby Church in Vendsyssel, a man by the name of Torsten Brede scratched a small inscription into the still wet, plastered wall while working on the interior of the church around the year 1200. Two highly differing interpretations of the inscription exist. The runologist Erik Moltke has suggested the following: 'Torsten Bre... wrote these runes during the days of Whitsun... He was extremely glad about the morning notes (singing) there.'[66] In this reading, Torsten took pleasure in the church service and the beautiful singing. Another interpretation comes from the runologist Lis Jacobsen and is as follows: 'Torstæin Brædi(?) wrote these Runes during the days of Whitsun... ...much pleasure with Johanne in the morning there.'[67] Here, Torsten was happy about a love tryst he had shared with a woman named Johanne! If this interpretation is right, Torsten was transgressing against all the limits of the church by using the runes to express his licentious meeting. Even the first interpretation, in which Torsten expresses only his enjoyment of church music, would be a bold piece of medieval graffiti.

A precious work

Medieval Denmark was home to two major works, both of them among the most important in Europe. These are Archbishop Anders Sunesen's *Hexaëmeron*, which dates from between 1196 and 1206 and was perhaps only completed after Sunesen returned in 1223,[68] and Saxo Grammaticus' history of Denmark *Gesta Danorum*, from the beginning of the 13th century. There is a very direct connection between these two Latin works, since Saxo dedicates *Gesta Danorum* to Sunesen, particularly in memory of *Hexaëmeron*, which Saxo quite simply refers to as Sunesen's precious work. Saxo and Sunesen respectively master the two most important genres of the time: the historical prose narrative and the large poem about The Creation in verse. Saxo was well known to posterity, and his work was printed as early as 1514. Sunesen's work, on the other hand, remained unprinted until the 19th century, and its printing even then owed a great deal to chance. While Saxo's writing of history was inspiring for the Renaissance historians who followed him, Sunesen's work was connected to a specifically Catholic culture of learning and was therefore of less interest to men of the Reformation.

Anders Sunesen (not later than 1170 – not later than 1228) became archbishop of Lund in 1201, and in Danish national mythology his name is linked to the story that the Danish flag, Dannebrog, fell from heaven during the battle at Lundanis in Estonia in 1219. Anders Sunesen joined

King Valdemar II's crusade to Estonia in properly 2019. The later legend tells that the archbishop was kneeling with his arms raised towards heaven during the battle; but when he lost his strength and had to lower his arms the Danish army had to withdraw. The priests thereforce supported Sunesen, and suddenly Dannebrog fell from heaven and King Valdemar and his men won the battle.

Anders Sunesen's *Hexaëmeron*, an interpretation of the account of the six days of Creation, consists of 8,040 hexameter lines in twelve songs or books. The first three books deal with the six days of Creation. The fourth book interprets the Creation and the Fall allegorically, while the three following books depict man's guilt and sin. The eighth and ninth books analyze the question of free will and original sin, while books ten to twelve describe the passion, death and resurrection of Christ, and the final Day of Judgment.

The hexameron is an ancient, learned genre, dating back to the Jewish philosopher Philo of Alexandria. In the 1st century AD, Philo commented on the story of Creation in Genesis and attempted to link Jewish belief with Greek philosophy. Another important precedent was the *Confessions* of the Church Father St. Augustine, which also offer a substantial account of the Creation plays. Such interpretations formed a practice which stretched from late Antiquity and into the Middle Ages, taking shape in sermons and theological analyzes from St. Augustine to Peter Lombard. But with Sunesen's poem of the Creation, the hexameron theme gains real poetic form for the first time. Sunesen's highly original contribution is his use of the classical epic. Using epic, he lends the vast material a poetic genre that gathers the complex theological teaching into a single narrative.

Like the classical epic, Sunesen's text has its heroes – first and foremost, God and Christ. But man, who is at the centre of Creation, also belongs among the heroes, since despite the Fall, man can be redeemed by Christ and gain God's everlasting kindgom where the blessed souls will have everything they desire. *Hexaëmeron* is a book about the eternal purpose and ultimate goal of mankind. Sunesen's work is thus also a significant work of medieval humanism, which praises man as a fantastic creation who, despite his fall, is the only creature that can walk upright and enlighten himself by fixing his gaze on God.[69]

While the cosmology of the völva describes a balance between good and evil that cannot be maintained, Sunesen's cosmology is based on the idea of a conscious breach of order: The fallen angel Lucifer and later Eve both consciously break with God's plan. This breach is conceived

Motif from the account of Creation with sea-folk, Gjerrild Church, made at the Brarup workshop around 1500

as originating in a desire to become like God, a desire made possible by free will, felt first by Lucifer and then by Eve. About Lucifer the text says: 'bursting with pride at many natural merits (...) he dared to wish to make himself His equal.' Of Eve, Sunesen writes that 'seemingly desiring to become as God, she lent her ear to the words of promise'.[70] The völva and Sunesen seem to share the idea that it is pride and a desire for power that cause the world to totter and lead to damnation or ragnarök.

While the völva proudly displays her poetic gifts and links the gift of prophecy with verse, Sunesen conducts a lengthy discussion of the extent to which he can even allow himself to make use of poetry. For this art is suspect – it may tempt its readers with useless talk and empty lies.

As Sunesen puts it, is it the enticing song of the sirens what he hears in the poetry of Antiquity, though he counters that, when the art of writing verse is combined with Holy Scripture, poetry also reveals its more meaningful side. What actually comes across is, of course, that the art of poetry is extremely useful and something Sunesen loves using; he was sure to find a way of making it completely legitimate. Holy Scripture, Sunesen insists, could indeed be transformed into 'well-sounding verse' and 'sweetness' that would seduce people to both teaching and salvation.[71] Furthermore, one actually sees God himself best when one sees him as an artist of love: 'Let us regard God in his art, in the fruits of his love/Be warmed and rejoice over the fire that his love ignites.'[72]

Sunesen's masterpiece was the first in a renewed European tradition of hexameron poetry, from the Italian Torquato Tasso to the French Du Bartas, the Danish Anders Arrebo and the English John Milton. When Sunesen concluded his work with the words: 'The work is complete! I have attained my goal with the book I have written,'[73] he had opened up a new genre for writing in Europe.

A major work from Denmark

While Sunesen's work was part of medieval church culture, Saxo Grammaticus' Latin chronicle of Denmark was a contribution to the life of the court. *Gesta Danorum* was written with the aim of showing that the Danes and their king could bear comparison with other civilized nations – even with the Romans themselves. Oral and written language, myths, tales and war reports blend colourfully in this work, and Saxo's heroes have all the knightly virtues and courage.

Saxo was secretary to Archbishop Absalon of Lund. Recognized as the Church's most proficient writer, he was commissioned by Absalon to give monarchs a written record of all their feats. Although the work is in Latin, it makes generous use of orally transmitted tales and ballades, also known from the Icelandic tradition. Saxo acknowledges the oral tradition, speaking of the visits paid to the court by various bards.

The stated aim of Saxo's chronicle is to provide the Danes with an entertaining and true history. According to Saxo, Absolon found it unacceptable that the Danes did not have a historical account that could bring praise to the memory of their fathers at a time when other civilized nations were getting their own such accounts written down. In the introduction to his huge work, Saxo writes:

> Because other nations are in the habit of vaunting the fame of their achievements, and joy in recollecting their ancestors, Absalon, Archbishop of Denmark, had always been fired with a passionate zeal to glorify our fatherland. He would not allow it to go without some noble documents of this kind and, since everyone else refused the task, the labour of compiling a history of the Danes was thrown upon me, the least of his retinue, his powerful insistence forced my weak intellect to embark on a project too huge for my abilities.[74]

Modesty was essential for a scholar in the 13th century, but Saxo was perfectly well aware that the work would show all his talents as a historian and storyteller.

As in other chronicles from the period, various forms of text and narrative intertwine in *Gesta Danorum*. In particular, an oral mode of narration forms a layer beneath the rhetorically deliberate Latin, which makes elaborate use of 24 different metres. Saxo even thematizes the relationship between oral and written language, contrasting a concept of 'speech' with a concept of 'reliable written history'. Research has pointed out the linguistic shifts in the work,[75] and its didactic structure: the first eight books present examples worthy of imitation or intended to deter, while the last eight books show how the examples can be put into practice.[76] The chronological structure is heavily inscribed with moral teaching, and the history is in actual fact a catalogue of morals.

This does not, however, prevent Saxo from treating grim situations with grotesque, carnival-like humour. This humour occurs, for example, in the dramatic story of Prince Amleth, whose uncle Fengi has murdered Amleth's father, the king. Fengi is suspicious of Amleth, who pretends to be mad, and he sends spies out after him, one of whom Amleth manages to murder, cut into small pieces and feed to some pigs. Saxo relates:

> Fengi returned to discover that his spy was nowhere to be found, not even by unremitting investigation, nor had anyone caught a glimpse of him. For the sake of a joke Amleth too was asked whether he had detected any trace of him; he replied that the man had gone into the drain, tumbled down to the bottom and, buried under a heap of sewage, had been devoured by the pigs which frequented the place. This story, though it revealed the truth, seemed crazy to his audience and caused merriments.[77]

One of Saxo's most important techniques as a storyteller is his ability to switch between concretely narrated situations, in-depth analysis of characters' motives and grand overviews of plot. There is always a human aspect in the story – an impulse of some kind, a personal trait or some wickedness that motivates actions and events. Everything fits into a comprehensive moral system and the norms of the Latin scholarly culture, and the story is definitely not the expression of a modern, individual-psychological analysis. But the interest in the human is indisputable.

Saxo moves incredibly skilfully between several sequences of events, and the time indications 'in the meantime', 'meanwhile' and 'at the same time' are used frequently to bind the threads of action together. Saxo switches between focused and panoramic narration with inserted anecdotes and moral points, as when the Wendish Bugislav passes out drunk under a table at a feast with Absalon and his men and is afterwards laid in a tent surrounded by armed Danes: 'For Danes have always treated their guests with great care and guarded them as if they were their own. This gesture placed Bugislav in so great a debt to Absalon that he began to work for a tone of reconciliation between the Wends and the Danes,' it says.[78]

Many paths cross in Saxo, and quotations from heroic poems and references to Norse mythology show that it belongs to a Nordic cultural context.[79] The story of paganism's replacement by Christianity is, for Saxo, mainly a matter of the old gods losing their power and no longer being able to help the Danish kings. In the eighth book, when the warrior Thorkil Adelfar visits Loki at the command of King Gorm to find out if the soul is immortal and what will happen when the king dies, he finds a stinking, powerless Loki chained inside his cave.[80] Now, the poem concludes, it is time to seek help from a stronger deity.

Manuscripts in Latin and Danish

Sunesen's work is preserved in a manuscript from the end of the 13th century, but only a fragment of Saxos's original manuscript has survived the passing of years. The growth of new media – the manuscript and later the printed book – results in many different types of text: legal documents, year books, obituaries, prayer books deeds of gift, letters, collections of gospels, historical books, and saints' lives were all found throughout Europe in the Early Middle Ages. The Church Father Hieronymus translated the Bible into Latin at the end of the 4th century; the French bishop Gregory of Tours wrote *History of the Franks* at the end of the 6th century; in Rome the theologians wrote dissertations in the 6th century; in Byzantium legends of saints and histories of emperors appeared in the 5th–6th centuries; in the 8th century, bible transcriptions were made in Ireland and church history was recorded in English. Now the genres of the manuscripts came to Denmark as well. Most of what resulted was not literary art in the present-day sense. But the people of the medieval period cultivated in their manuscripts a finely formed use of language and storytelling, and there was certainly artfulness in the choice of words and the creation of narratives. Manuscripts are written in both Latin and medieval Danish. It is difficult to speak of Danish literature with regard to texts not written in Danish, but the Latin manuscripts were part of a Danish cultural context. They were used in Denmark, and they often deal with Danish history or chronicle Danish-born saints. The Danish language was soon adopted in law texts and royal letters, and this development corresponded exactly with what took place in other European countries. The titles and lands of the Danish king were not a modern nation state, but a federation of large and small areas under one leader, each with its own laws and policies. Present-day historians believe, however, that as in other European countries at the end of the Middle Ages, i.e. in the 15th and 16th centuries, a feeling of national identity began to emerge. In the literature, both the approach to history and the choice of language itself reveal that people were beginning to see the kingdom as a single unit.[81]

The incredibly enterprising and far-sighted canon Christiern Pedersen (1480–1554), who was a member of the diocese of Lund, shared this early national sensibility, and published the first printed version (editio princeps) of Saxo's *Gesta Danorum* in Paris 1514. This marvellous edition made Saxo's Danish history famous to the learned European public.

Although the language of faith and learning was Latin, the Catholic Church also made use of Danish. When preaching took place in the street outside of church services, it took place in Danish, and it was also possible to preach in Danish inside the church when the common people were present. The Latin sermons preserved in manuscripts may very well have been given in Danish, even though they were written down in Latin, the international language of the church. Priests used Latin so that the sermons could be used by other clergymen, irrespective of their mother tongue and origins.

Just short of twenty years before the Reformation, c. 1515/1518, Christiern Pedersen published a collection of gospel texts, textual elucidations and sermons in Danish. He called this collection *Jærtegnspostillen*, a name referring to the fact that the book indicates divine omens (jærtegn) for each day, taken from sources such as the stories of the saints. Pedersen emphasizes in the preface that he wishes to address those who do not understand Latin and perhaps seldom hear a sermon. There were many, strict rules as to how a sermon was to be constructed, but the genre apparently permitted the inclusion of various shorter texts: stories with moral messages, tales and adventures, animal fables, maxims and popular sayings. The composite effect requires listeners to follow a narrative and form ideas and images in their own consciousness. In one of his sermons from the mid-15th century, Peder Madsen, a priest from Ribe, tells of an Indian fish that came close to the shore in the morning and, when the dew of the sky and the heat of the sun come, it conceives and gives birth to a precious stone. The story sounds almost like a surrealist poem from the 20th century, but it is medieval theology pure and simple. Madsen explains how the story of the Indian fish represents man (the fish) in search of the Virgin Mary (the shore). Aided by the mercy of the Holy Spirit (the dew) and God's love (the heat of the sun), the individual conceives and gives birth to a pious soul (the precious stone).[82]

God's time and place

The art of words finds its place in churches and monasteries alongside other forms of art - architecture, visual art and music - and is part of church ceremony. The purpose of the various types of art is to guide the human soul onto the right path, and there can be no doubt where that path ought to lead – directly home to God. Medieval art has European, Middle Eastern and Jewish sources. Scholars were familiar with ideas from Greek Antiquity and Rome concerning beauty – that it had something to do with proportion, symmetry and light. The transmission of such ideas from Antiquity depended on, among other sources, an anonymous Syrian philosopher from the 5th and 6th centuries. The collection of writings by Dionysius the Areopagite, known as *Pseudo-Dionysius* of *Pseudo-Areopagite*, perhaps because the writer was not the person some believed, bases itself on the ideas of Plato and Plotinus. Plato conceived beauty in art as being a shadow of the pure, ideal form of beauty. When we experience beauty in art by means of our senses, it is because art attempts to get hold of the very being, the inner or spiritual beauty, of the thing depicted. By attempting to represent this inner quality of things, art acquires part of the idea of beauty (a Form-copy of the Beautiful). But the concept of beauty itself is beyond the grasp or experience of man. Plato opposed the use of illusion in art, arguing that the attempt at realism creates a false impression that one is giving a true picture of the world, whereas a purified, abstract formal language would point to the world of ideas.[83]

Unicorn, Gudme Church, made at the Clog Painter's Workshop and dated 1488

One of Plato's successors, the philosopher Plotinus, believed that the world is held together by a single spiritual principle that constantly emits its rays in ever higher forms. One could experience this singular principle in the form of light, which gives the world form. The related writings of *Pseudo-Dionysius* or *Pseudo-Areopagite* about light and the spiritual connection were later passed on by the philosopher Abbot Suger of St. Denis, who was a scholar in the Frankish Empire. Charlemagne's successor, Louis the Pious, had been given the writings as a gift by the Byzantine emperor and had them translated into Latin in 835AD. Abbot Suger believed that by meditating on the nature of light it was possible to come into contact with God. His ideas about light came to be very important for Gothic church architecture in the 13th century. But medieval art also drew on the Old Testament idea that beauty is found in nature, in the whole of God's creation. Nature, which God has created, is a symbol of His existence, and art makes it possible to sense invisible beauty behind the visible. Sensory experiences of colour, taste, smell and sound, as in *The Song of Solomon*, the love poem of the Bible, acquired great importance in the Middle Ages. The Jewish cultural tradition's joy in materials and the physical world that God has created is continued here.[84] 'I am come into my garden, my sister, my spouse: I have gathered my myrrh with my spice; I have eaten my honeycomb with my honey; I have drunk my wine with my milk: eat, O friends; drink, yea, drink abundantly, O beloved.' This is what is said in *The Song of Solomon* say by the sensual imagery of love and of the union between man and woman.[85]

Medieval art and literature aimed to enable the individual to experience the meaning of God. The church or monastery were to use the dimensions of time and space in such a way that man could sense God's nearness. Emphasis was placed on displaying the beauty of creation through the proportion and through light, clarity and harmony. Abbot Suger regarded sensory experiences in the sacred space of the church as a way of sensing God, whereas the Cistercian Bernard of Clairvaux (1090–1153) believed that one should turn away from sensory experience and seek to enter into a world that was purely spiritual.[86]

In Danish churches, the use of images was influenced by the view of art held in the Carolingian empire. There, craftsmen and philosophers regarded images as pedagogically useful, not least for the common people, who were unable to read or write. Images were not thought of as being divine in themselves, but it was believed that they created a connection between God and humanity. It was important, however, to ensure that the image could not be confused with God himself. Images were not to resemble the things depicted too closely and were to work in combination with words and texts from the Bible. The Carolingians were highly interested in writing. They stressed that holy writ was God's own words, and therefore had to have a special significance and spiritual power. When the church murals referred to particular places in the Old and New Testaments, image and word had an edifying effect, and art served the good cause. Picture bibles were used towards this same goal. *Biblia Pauperum* (Poor Man's Bible) was one of the picture bibles that began to appear as a block print in the 15th century. Despite the name, this beautiful and expensive book was definitely not for poor people. The work consists of Latin bible passages, elucidations and illustrations, with each page being composed of three layers of texts and images, and the work was probably used mainly by lower-ranking clergymen. The pictures served as a model for other art forms in their mediation of biblical stories.

The illustrations in the picture bibles were organized around the idea that events from the Old Testament always predict events in the New Testament, and that the pictures should refrain from resembling any outer reality. In church art, as well, steps were taken to prevent religious pictures from resembling reality too closely, by avoiding illusion and by working with a so-called omni-perspectivism where one folded several worlds and several stories into the same picture. An inverse perspective was also used, where the most important figures were larger no matter whether they were seen up close or at great distance. Some church art sought to make the onlooker feel that the picture looking at him or her was, and thereby calling the individual to work for his or her salvation.[87]

Just as word, image and architecture combined to further the pious aim of showing the soul its way home to God,[88] so the participation of the congregation in processions during church festivals also served this purpose. One of the forms of expression in church services was the liturgical enactment of Christ's Passion and of the acts of the saints. In Denmark, certain 16th century versions of individual plays about saints have been preserved: *Dorotheæ Komedie* and *Ludus de Sancto Kanuto Duce* (The play concerning the holy duke Knud). The latter deals with Knud Lavard, who was canonized in 1170. The versions of the plays that have survived are from a period when the cathedral schools had taken over their performance and introduced moralizing comedies and coarse-grained Lent plays.[89]

The piety of the Middle Ages went hand in hand with horseplay, not only in connection with the beginning of Lent but also in noisy fun directed at the mass, the clergy, saints and the Virgin Mary herself. Many scholars have thought that this kind of satire was a carefully calculated reversal of the everyday order. A few times a year, people were simply allowed to turn the order of the church upside-down and disregard all its prohibitions. Others see the 'Mass of Asses' and the recurrent poking fun at the saints as part of everyday life and a way in which one could become familiar with the holy throughout the year. There was simply nothing in this world that did not have something to do with God – not even the most coarse and vulgar laughter at the saints.[90]

It can be difficult to understand the medieval mind-set and understand its motives. A great deal has been lost, and much research still remains to be done.

The churches from the 12th and 13th centuries are, however, still standing, although often characterized by later additions, changes, demolitions, overpainting of images or heavy-handed restorations. The many Romanesque and Gothic murals were virtually all painted over around 1700. Most of the monasteries have been demolished, though a few are preserved as ruins. But if one is to get an impression of what the art of words in this period means, what literature was in the medieval period, one must enter the churches and monasteries and try and track down the context in which so much of this literature belonged: God's time and God's place.

A world of signs

Bernard of Clairvaux and the Cistercians opposed the Romanesque church art of the 12th century with its murals and many ornaments. They felt that emotions should be roused and God made present by referring to God's beautiful order in proportion and light, not by adorning the interiors with images and decorations. For the monks were not to be distracted too much by the material and the sensual.

Romanesque church art, on the other hand, deliberately used images to teach and instruct the congregation. Instead of the Cistercians' strict simplicity, the Romanesque style fills the walls and interiors with pictorial material that will appeal to the great majority of the population who were unable to read or write. Romanesque church art was carried out by both visiting and local craftsmen and displays English, German, French, Spanish and even Byzantine characteristics. In general, visual art, literature, architecture and music in Denmark during this period are all variations on forms and themes known across Europe, and inside the churches the various art forms work together. If one is interested in Danish literature, one therefore has to look at the architectural, ritual and artistic context in which the literature functions. The church interior is to be conceived as an image of the new Jerusalem, God's own kingdom, and its whole organization is to bear witness to the relation between God and man. Entering the church, one gets a foretaste of heaven. The chancel with the high altar – sometimes a gleaming golden altar – is placed at the east end,[91] for in the east lay the earthly Paradise and Jerusalem, and the sun rising in the east is a daily reminder of Christ's resurrection. Only during special church festivals is the congregation allowed to move in procession from the nave of the church through the triumphal arch into the chancel and apse, the vault of which was an image of heaven.[92]

During the mass, the priest read aloud, mostly with his back to the congregation and his face turned towards the altar – symbolically towards God. Man's turning to God is answered by God's gifts to mankind: the communion with Christ's body and blood, which was shared out by the priest. The congregation was, however, precluded early on from drinking the altar wine. It had to make do with the bread that had transubstantiated into the body of Christ. The church greatly feared that people could misuse communion wine and bread for sorcery and witchcraft. It was thought that witches would accept the bread but not eat it, instead saving it for the devil, which could of course have the most frightful consequences.

The walls of the church itself were used to tell powerfull and edifying stories, about God, the Day of Judgment, the splendour of heaven and of pious, worshipful persons. Stories appear on ashlar stones, portals, columns, altars, reliquaries, fonts and on coloured sections of the plastered walls. The ruling God is often depicted in the chancel, while the wall with the triumphal arch has motifs of humans seeking God as well as the three wise men worshipping the infant Jesus.

The Romanesque church shows us a world full of signs and marvellous creatures. One often finds devils sticking out their tongues, angels worshipping Jesus, symbolic animals and threatening beasts swallowing people, and faces staring out from stones and columns, as well as Jesus hanging on the cross, serene, fine and strong as a king. The images sometimes form long narrative sequences from the Bible, and their effect is combined with that of the sermons, preached to the congregation in Danish. Woven into the sermons were stories, examples, sayings, fables and cautionary tales.

Medieval theologians believed that holy writ always had a literal meaning and a spiritual meaning – and eventually it was argued that the text had four meanings. The so-called quadriga or allegoresis deduces the four meanings from sacred writings, and it is an effective method to create cohesion and order in biblical interpretation.[93] The four different readings were these: 1) The literal reading, where one concentrated on understanding what the text actually relates, e.g. that Adam and Eve are banished from Paradise because they have sinned against God. 2) The allegorical meaning, which concentrates on showing how the meanings refer to Christ and his church. Here, one demonstrates how the events of the Old Testament prefigure or anticipate events in the New Testament, e.g. the story of how God commands Abraham to sacrifice his son Isaac prefigures Christ's crucifixion. Jesus' death on the cross in turn anticipates the death of saints and martyrs. 3) The moral reading of the text, where emphasis is placed on extracting a moral lesson from which the soul can learn. The story of Adam and Eve underlines, for example, that we humans find it hard not to sin, but that we must strive to avoid sinning. 4) The anagogic reading, where one shows how narrated events point to the higher, spiritual truths behind visible forms. For example, Jesus' parttaking in the wedding in Cana is taken as an image of the fact that Jesus gives humanity expectations of a repetition of the original

Small devils, Egtved Church, 1450-1500

marriage between God and humanity in Paradise, where humanity is once again united with God and filled by his love.

The Middle Ages often used Jerusalem as a metaphorical explanation. Jerusalem is 1) an actual city, 2) an image of the soul, 3) an image of the battling church, and 4) an image of the victorious church – the new Jerusalem.[94]

The Middle Ages loved interpretation, and medieval readers and commentators were diligent in enumerating every possible meaning in texts and signs. They looked for specific parts of what they saw as the totality that is God's order. Everything did not always fit, but that was of lesser importance, as long as one had found a similarity or was able to see the individual phenomenon as part of a greater whole. In this universe, mankind is never alone – empty space simply does not exist. The physical world is always brim-full of signs and creatures, each with a meaning to be interpreted. A guardian angel or devil is always standing beside one. By the death-bed of a person there is usually a host of thousands of devils waiting to try and catch the soul when it leaves the body. The signs and animals that fill the world all connect us to meanings beyond themselves, and if one is unable to make out these many meanings, one can consult the many encyclopaedias and lexical poems that identify the significance of animals or plants and what position each one has in God's beautiful order.[95]

The in-between time

A very definite conception of time characterizes church interiors and the use of writing and words within them. Both the living and the souls of the dead find themselves in an in-between time – the time between the incarnation, i.e. Christ's birth, and Christ's second coming. The world began when it was created by God. The Fall of Adam and Eve disturbed God's order, but humanity was given a chance to escape from original sin and avoid certain perdition when Christ died on the cross. When Christ had judged all the living and the dead, God's order could be re-established. It was this chronology that governed the conception of time. An individual's goal in life was the salvation of his/her soul and to help one's dear departed to escape from purgatory through prayer or the holding of requiem masses. Purgatory, by the way, is closed at weekends, so during that time the living take comfort in the knowledge that the dead were not being tormented. One had to be zealous in one's play, to prevent the devils from working all the harder on Monday morning.

The Middle Ages sees man in three dimensions: body, soul and mind, with the mind finding expression in the will and the intellect. Plato's idea of the connection between will and mind deeply influenced the medieval perception of human psychology. When man of his own free will chooses to believe and act in a loving way, he is using his intellect sensibly and thereby cultivating his mind and his chance of eternal salvation.

God blesses all kinds of animals, Vester Broby Church, 1380-1400

Intellect and reason are man's highest qualities, and when one uses reason, one is actually outside the Devil's reach. Even pagans, according to this way of thinking, are equipped with reason and are thus able to live in accordance with God's order - heathens have Mosaic Law inscribed in their hearts. The Middle Ages was not a period of obscurantism. Medieval people venerated reason, and it is quite characteristic that the period ends with the development of a huge theological-philosophical system – the so-called scholasticism. This is a large-scale canon of learning, which made use of the logic of the Greek philosopher Aristotle in order to argue in favour of the truth of the Catholic faith. One still has to be a very sharp thinker to be able to follow the needle-sharp logic of scholasticism.

In a medieval way of thinking, it was only rational to ensures that newborn children were baptized – otherwise they would have to wait in limbo for Christ's second coming, that special forecourt of Hell for un-

Face painted around a hole in the wall, Gudme church, the work of the Clog Painter's Workshop, dated 1488

baptized children. Similarly, when one imagines time on the divine scale, it is quite reasonable to treat the differences between people of the past and of the present as insignificant. As the Church Father St. Augustine (354–430AD) emphasizes, God rules over all ages. The past, like the present, is only part of the in-between time, during which both the living and the dead wait for Christ's second coming and the Day of Judgment.

In the 21st century, we think of ourselves as living in a specific present. We often imagine time as a line moving progressively forwards and feel that it is impossible to turn back the clock and return to the past. We say that we have 'lost' our departed friends and relations. People in the Middle Ages, on the other hand, experienced life as an interlude and separations as temporary. One was in contact with the dead through prayers and requiems, and the dead were thus still part of the community. So it was not important to know when a great saint lived, for the saints were still present in the stories of their miracles that could help people here and now. When murals depict Old Testament figures like Abraham and Isaac dressed in medieval clothing, this is because these figures were viewed as contemporaries, inhabiting the same in-between time before the Day of Judgment. The really epoch-making events in God's great calendar can be heard about in the readings from the holy texts and seen depicted everywhere inside the church, whose monumentality and might remind one of God's power over time.

The medieval conception of time is also evident in the way in which texts were used in churches. The saints could be invoked and addressed in prayers and celebrated in masses and through the repeated reading out of their lives. The famous collection of hagiographies, *Legenda Aurea* (The Golden Legend) by the Italian archbishop Jacobus de Voragine (1230 – 1298), dated from the late 13th century was frequently used of in Denmark.

A number of Danish saints with their own hagiographies were gradually included in the international company of saints, and the best-known were venerated everywhere in Catholic countries. Alongside the official and recognized saints such as King Knud, who was canonized in 1101, there were many local saints such as Merthe of Sorø and Martha of Karise.[96] They did not get official biographies, but oral legends and stories made their lives well-known. The legend of the good, generous Martha from Karise relates that, when she died, the monks put down her coffin for a moment in order to rest when bearing her to her grave, and on this spot a healing spring appeared. Stories about local saints were an important part of local belief, while the church bureaucracy sometimes saw the lives of the saints as a kind of religious asset that could be sold off. People could buy pardons for their sins by paying the church, because the church could offer the intercession of the saints.

Marvellous minds and razor-sharp logic

The Gothic style started to appear alongside the Romanesque in Denmark as early as the late 13th century. Gothic art reflects a powerful spiritual striving. In Gothic architecture, flying vaults replace the rounded ceiling of the nave in Romanesque churches, and the many new surfaces are filled in the 14th to 16th centuries with murals and a great diversity of pictorial material. Everything in this universe strives upwards, and light falls in through metre-high panes as an expression of God's own presence. In this light, sculptures stand out as independent figures in church interiors. They are slender and attractive, intended to represent striving souls rather than the bodies of living people. The Virgin Mary is supernaturally beautiful and mild, and the fine Virgin Mary ballads that are widespread throughout Europe, and certainly present in Denmark, correspond to the

The Virgin Mary as Queen of Heaven, Ørbæk Church, part of the altarpiece from c. 1500

strikingly beautiful sculptures of her. One of the Danish-language Mary ballads, preserved in a manuscript from the mid-15th century, says of her: 'Your eyes burn like two rubies,/your face has the clearest gleam/beside the noble crimson.'[97] The manuscripts of the period are beautifully fashioned, with gilt and gleaming gold, blue and red colours. Here, too, artistic media are combined to bring out the spiritual reality.

Researchers have attempted to draw parallels between Gothic architecture and scholasticism's construction of a logical argument, the so-called *quaestio*. The scholastics divided their presentations into a very strict system, which emphasized that the totality of the presentation consisted of main sections, subsections and sub-subsections. It had to be possible in order to follow and understand the entire process of thought and all the logical conclusions, to follow all the elements and parts and their composition. The precise order and division of the main sections, subsections and sub-subsections is also present in Gothic architecture, both in the ground plan of the church with its main nave and side aisles and in the decoration of the building, where an enormous system of individual elements are placed in a precise order and connection with each other. Perhaps there are parallels between the sequence of the *quaestio* and the use of architectural elements in church buildings? One can, for example, see how the pointed Gothic arches seek to inscribe the older rounded arches and circular forms and outdo them on the large western facades of the cathedrals. The builders thereby conduct a discussion on their facade with stylistic and formal elements, trying to make a conclusive case for the superiority of the Gothic pointed arches.[98]

The *quaestio* gave shape to scholastic discussion. First, the scholastics asked a question. The most famous of the scholastics, the Italian theologian Thomas Aquinas, asks in a famous *quaestio* if it is necessary to have other sciences than philosophy. At the time, that was – to put it mildly – a dangerous question, one that seemed to threaten the abolition of both God and theology! This was not its purpose for Thomas Aquinas. He believed that both faith and knowledge originated with God. When he questioned the necessity of sciences other than philosophy, he first presented – in accordance with the rules of scholasticism – arguments from two authorities for the hypothesis: The first argument was that philosophy dealt with everything related to human reason, and science has to do with reason. The second argument was that philosophy deals with everything that exists, and thus also with God. After the first two strong arguments, Aquinas advanced a contrary argument, which he took from a different authority, in this instance Paul the Apostle. Based on Paul it is possible to assert that it is necessary to have other sciences than philosophy, since Holy Scripture is not a result of human intellectual effort, but is inspired by God. The *quaestio* concludes with a *responsio* (I answer), where Aquinas tests the arguments logically one after the other and then concludes the discussion. He ends by saying that it is necessary to have other sciences than philosophy, because the things that are beyond reason cannot be examined by reason. It is also necessary to have other sciences than philosophy because one can gain the same knowledge in different ways from various sciences. It is possible both via astronomy and physics to show that the earth is round. In the same way, philosophy and theology can both be used to understand the divine. Aquinas manages to give both philosophy and theology a legitimate place, and thereby creates room for a mode of thought that was not rigidly controlled by an ecclesiastical authority.

A Danish student who also learnt to master the *quaestio* was Boethius de Dacia (Bo from Denmark), who studied in Paris and later also came to teach at the University of Paris around 1270. Boethius is accredited with various scholarly writings, including a controversial piece on *De aeternitate mundi* (The Eternity of the World), where he asks whether what God has created has always existed, or whether it came into existence as something new.[99] It sounds like a highly abstract discussion; it was one of the most dangerous subjects to discuss in the 13th century. For it indicated the many problems there were in connecting Christianity with the thinking of Aristotle, which the scholars of the church and Thomas Aquinas were attempting to do. If – as Aristotle had it – the universe is without any beginning or end, one could find oneself at odds with the Old Testament story that God had created the world in six days. On the basis of the biblical account of the Creation, the world must have been created at a certain point in time. In his *quaestio*, Bo concludes that there does not have to be any conflict between philosophy and religion. Belief is belief – it cannot and does not need to be proved. So Bo rejects neither belief nor thought, but he does insist that a philosopher has both the right and the duty to discuss everything that can be dealt with using rational arguments. This point of view was condemned in 1277 by the Bishop of Paris, who regarded it as a threat to the church's monopoly on truth.

When it came to the presentation of the human situation in earthly life, the Gothic world-view placed emphasis on spiritual dynamics and depicted the human spirit as always on the move: either just cast into hell, where the most frightful punishment awaited him, or allowed into heaven to eternal bliss. Man was lost, unless of his own free will he turned to God as the saints had done. The insistence on the reality of death and perdition that we see in church murals was driven in part by the ravages of the plague in 14th century Denmark. There were also political tur-

Christ as the Man of Sorrows, Klosterkirken, Mariager, c. 1500

moils, and the kingdom almost disintegrated in the first half of the 14th-century and was not re-united until the reign of Valdemar IV (1340-75). When Valdemar the Conqueror had written in the Jutland Law of 1241 that 'with law shall land/nation be built', there was almost no nation left on which to build it.

Alongside the beautiful saints of the church murals there were hair-raising and frightening depictures of Christ's passion. The figure on the cross is more cadaverous than any corpse, blood gushes out of innumerable wounds, the crown of thorns weighs down his tormented head, his eyes are often closed and the face of Christ is twisted in pain, fixed and deathlike. Once again, one sees how the aim of Gothic art is to grasp an essence – in this case, pain and suffering itself. We have to understand that what God's son is bearing is the totality of human misery. The Man of Sorrows is the term used for both the carved figures of Christ and the bleeding painted, Christ in Gothic art. We are far removed from the Vikings' triumphant Christ, the spiritual king of Romanesque art. Christ is linked to something essentially human: suffering. He appears as an increasingly human figure as Gothic art develops.

The efforts to hold on to the spiritual essential can also be seen in the stories of martyrdom and the recorded visions of holy women and men, which detail the torments of hell and the experience of Christ's passion. The martyrs are often proof against wounds. It takes almost inhuman powers to rob a martyr of his or her life, and the saints can be subjected to every conceivable method of killing or torturing without dying or giving in to their tormentors.

In the revelations of the holy Birgitta of Vadstena (1303-73), one finds both wild and terrifying scenes of Christ's passion and incredibly beautiful images of the Virgin Mary, especially in the vision when the Virgin gives birth to Jesus: 'With hands uplifted and her gaze fixed on heaven, she stood as if in contemplation and ecstasy, intoxicated by divine loveliness. While sunk in prayer in such a way, I saw the child move in her body and immediately, yes, in a moment, she gave birth to her son (...) so swift and instantaneous was this birth that I could not observe or distinguish how and with what part of the body the virgin gave birth,'[100] Birgitta relates.

Birgitta was a Swedish noblewoman who was canonized in 1391, and two abbeys were established for her in Denmark: in Maribo in 1418 and in Mariager in 1446. Her order was the last one to come to Denmark. Her visions, which were written down by priests, are a literary pinnacle.

The curious realism in Birgitta's revelations and in all of Gothic art and literature is not an attempt to depict or represent an outer reality. The goal is always to capture a spiritual essence, the inner reality of pain, suffering and the vision of the heavenly. The recorded visions and stories of saints have therefore more to do with God than with humanity. The stories in these texts could just as well take place today as in the past. Time remains at God's command, and the art of writing is strongly linked to God's place: the church and the monastery.

In Denmark, a step towards making man the main character in literary works occurs in a biography of Gunner, Bishop of Viborg, who had formerly been abbot at Øm. The so-called *vita* of Gunner starts at Øm Abbey in the mid 1260s, and it is clear that the story of Gunner's life is to serve as a moral example for the monks. The narrator chooses to focus on Gunner as a human being. The bishop does not perform miracles but good human deeds.[101]

Royal time

One of the important texts in medieval theology was the *Song of Songs* (The Song of Solomon) in the Old Testament, which was written down between 500 and 100BC. Here, one finds an impassioned love poem about the beautiful girl Sulamith, who is worshipped and loved by King Solomon. The *Song of Songs* has the form of antiphonal songs exchanged between the lovers, with the intense eroticism of these songs serving as a metaphorical image of the relation between God and Israel. Christianity turned the love portrayals into an image of the relation between Christ and the soul. In many of the theological writings of the Middle Ages, we thus find the relationship between Christ and the worshipper described in the language of love longings and love meetings.

The *Song of Songs* had its secular counterpart in the troubadour poetry of medieval France, the German minnesang, and the Italian canzone and sonnets. The songs of the Middle Ages about the strikingly beautiful Virgin Mary also overlap with troubadour poetry, and portrayals from the hagiographies of the church and the monasteries inspire heroic secular poems about the bravery and virtue of knights.

The itinerant singers and knights of the 13th century unfold a seductive, erotic scenery and allow a complex interaction of amorous devotion to alternate with mythical-religious portrayals. This love poetry, along with heroic poetry, belongs to the fine European courts and their cultures of chivalry. Here, a circle of knights worship highly gifted and very beautiful women – often unattainable married women. The knights wear the ladies' colours at their tournaments and praise their beauty in poetry and song, according to a fixed, elaborate pattern. Love is courtly, which means that brilliant, refined praise and flirtation is more important than erotic conquest and physical union. One of the most famous works of courtly culture is the 13th century French poem *Le Roman de la Rose* (The Romance of the Rose), about a knight's hazardous path to a meeting with the loveliest of roses, i.e. a union with the most beautiful woman.

Other poems and tales praise and idealize the knights themselves. Courtly culture spreads throughout Europe in the 12th and 13th centuries and becomes part of an early Renaissance in which writing and oral material is rediscovered in the popular idiom and mixed with material from Antiquity, love poetry and mythology from the East, and whatever else happened to be available and relevant. The leading European courts were interested in all cultural material and not afraid to mix sources of inspiration with good stories.[102]

In northern Europe, the strongest contribution to this early Renaissance comes in Iceland, where the historian Snorri Sturleson (1179-1241) writes down the Old Norse heroic poems, and at the Norwegian court. But examples of courtly culture in poems and ballads from Denmark during the same period have not been preserved.

We do find courtly scenes in church murals, which portray knights and damsels, especially in the 14th-16th centuries. We can also see how heroic poetry gains influence in the narration of saints' lives, in examples like the legend of St. George's battle with the dragon. The legend of St. George has been handed down in *Legenda Aurea* (The Golden Legend).

One very widespread French verse narrative was the courtly romance *Yvain ou Le Chevalier au Lion* (Yvain, the Knight of the Lion), which is based on Celtic legendary material about King Arthur and his knights. The verse narrative was translated into Danish at the end of the 15th century, but it was sure to have been familiar to people of high rank in Denmark earlier than that, having been translated into Norse as early as the 13th century. On Romanesque murals from this period, we find scenes of knights in battle or on their way to crusades against heathens, such as King Valdemar and Bishop Absalon, who defeated the Wends in Arkona in 1169. The crusades, which lasted from the 1090s to the 1220s, had the Holy Land as their particular goal, the expressed intention being the liberation of the birthplace and grave of Jesus from the rule of Jews, Turks or Arabs. The mythology of the crusades gave great prominence to the grail, i.e. the lost chalice used by Christ at the Last Supper and later used to catch his blood when he hung on the cross. At the end of the 12th century, the most important narrator of knightly romances, the Frenchman Chrétien de Troyes, made the first link between King Arthur and the tale of the grail – and some of the grail-focused church murals in Denmark may have had the knights of King Arthur in mind. The

The Nine Good Heroes, Arthur, Charlemagne, Godfred of Bouillon, Joshua, David, Judas Maccabæus, Hector, Alexander the Great and Julius Cæsar. The church of Dronninglund, 1520. The painting shows Hector and David

name Arthur appears along with the name Alexander on a mural in The Church of Dronninglund in the north of Jutland from the early 16th century. The mural is part of a unique frieze with nine knights: three

Jewish (Joshua, David and Judas Maccabæus), three Roman-Greek (Hector of Troja, Alexander the Great and Caesar) and three Christian (King Arthur, Charlemagne, the crusader Godfred of Boulluion), all of whom represent good, knightly virtues

The clearest instances of courtly poetry and culture are, however, not found in Denmark until the 16th and 17th centuries, when scholars and nobles began to collect and write down the oral ballads as part of the project of the Renaissance.[103] The oldest ballad-book written on Danish soil, the so-called *Hjertebog* (Heart-Book) from the 1550s, was written down by nobles at the court of the Danish King Frederik II. The first printed collection of ballads, *Hundredevisebogen* (The Hundred Ballad Book), was published by the historian Anders Sørensen Vedel (1542-1616) in 1591. Vedel's collection was Scandinavia's first and biggest printed collection of ballads, and his intention was to use the ballad-book in connection with his great task of writing a new history of Denmark. Strongly encouraged by Frederik II's ballad-interested wife, Queen Sophie, and her lady-in-waiting Beate Bille – mother of the world-famous astronomer and astrologer Tycho Brahe – Vedel completed and printed his collection in 1591, and in the manor houses around Denmark an increasing interest in collecting ballad manuscripts became the fashion. Vedel was particularly interested in connecting the ballads with royal national history and with Christian morality. He also pointed out that the ballads demonstrated that the ancient Danish poets could rival the Greek and Latin ones. In his opinion, the ballads were a professional literature which proved that the nation and the royal house had a long, glorious history and an artistic tradition that could stand comparison with those of other nations. Noblewomen such as Anne Krabbe (1552–1618) were inspired by Vedel's book and started collecting ballads to show the glory and dramatic history of the old noble families and their cultural and mental abilities. These noblewomen compiled a number of important collections of ballad manuscripts for subsequent generations,[104] and histories of Danish literature have placed much emphasis on Denmark's old folk songs, which are rightly considered to be a true historical gem.

One of the often sung and re-interpreted ballads is 'Ebbe Skammelsøn' (Ebbe, Son of Skammel) which describes the fate of Ebbe whose fiancé, Lucelille, is cheated by Ebbe's brother, Peder, to believe that Ebbe has died while he served at the king's court. Lucelille marries Peder, and when Ebbe returns to his home on their wedding night, his takes he revenge:

Anne Krabbe's portrait in Ørsted Church. She decorated the church in 1607

That evening late when dew did fall
and all had drunk and fed,
the time came for the fair young bride
to seek her wedding bed.

They all led the fair young bride
to where her bed was made:
before went Ebbe Skammelsøn,
his torch did light the way.

Along the gallery he led
the bride, though he was loath:
"And do you happen to recall
To me you did plight your troth?'

"All I ever pledged to you,
Has Peder now, your brother;
all the days I yet may live
I'll be to you as a mother.'

Then answered Ebbe Skammelsøn,
the tears ran down his cheek:
"It was as wife I you would wed,
and I no mother seek.

Hark you, Maid Lucelille,
With me now flee the land!
my brother Peder I will slay
and that hard fate withstand!'

"If brother Peder you do slay,
I'm lost to you for ever;
Then you must grieve yourself to death
as a bird astray must shiver.'

It was Ebbe Skammelsøn,
sword from sheath did draw;
it was Lucelille
he cut down to the floor.

His bloody sword he then did hide
beneath his purple coat;
he entered the stone chamber
that Peder, his brother, was in.

"Hark you, Peder Skammelsøn
the time too fast has fled!
A full hour by the clock has passed
since the bride went to her bed.

Hark you, Peder Skammelsøn
all does you avail!
The bride sits in the bridal bed,
and waits for you so pale.'

"Hark you, Ebbe Skammelsøn,
dear brother by my side;
I promise you this selfsame night
to sleep with my fair bride!'

It was Ebbe Skammelsøn,
sword from sheath did draw;
It was Peder Skammelsøn
he cut down to the floor.

His father parted with his left foot,
his mother her right hand;
So outlawed must Ebbe Skammelsøn
steer clear now of this land:
So outlawed must Ebbe Skammelsøn
tread tracks far from home.[105]

The courtly tradition of ballads shows its influence in Denmark as late as 1723, when the Odense gentlewoman Anne Margrethe Lasson published her Danish-language romance *Den beklædte sandhed* (The clothed truth). Anne Margrethe Lasson mixes both courtly and pastoral writing in her 'little novel', which also happens to be the key text about a celebrated royal marriage.

Courtly culture also colours the language of orally handed-down bal-

The Nine Good Heroes in the church of Dronninglund, 1520. The painting shows Charlemagne and Judas Maccabæus

lads in the autobiographies and letters of the common people far into the 19th century. This originally French legacy emerges in surprising places, such as the criminal Ole Kollerød's own account of his life story.

Kollerød uses the set expressions of courtly language when he describes his world, having become familiar with the values of courtly culture from the broadsheets and ballads that were in circulation in the 18th century.[106] The Romantic tendency in 19th century literature, from national Romanticism at the beginning of the century to symbolism at the end of it, also draws motifs from courtly literature and the Renaissance, as found in plays, historical novels and poetry.

Man's time and place

The churches bear witness to the shifts between various periods, especially the transition from the Middle Ages into the Renaissance. In many Danish churches, one can see this contrast by comparing the font with the pulpit. Many extremely old baptismal fonts from the time the churches were first built in the 12th and 13th centuries have been preserved. Their decorations were easy to erase, and a given font may have spent long periods after the Reformation serving as a flower bowl at a manor house before being returned to its place in the church. Holy-water fonts, however, almost never returned to the churches, but ended up as feeding troughs. They belonged completely to the Catholic age. The pulpits are of more recent dates. In the Catholic period, the priest read from lecterns in the chancel, and only a few of these have survived. Most of the Danish pulpits date from the Renaissance, i.e. the period which began just prior to the Reformation and lasted up until the end of the 17th century. With the Reformation, the Danish-language sermon became an important part of the church service, and the oldest known wooden pulpit bears the year of the Reformation itself: 1536.

The Lutheran movement came to Denmark via Holstein and Schleswig and gained supporters in Jutland, Funen and the southern part of what is now Sweden. Protected by the king, evangelical preachers spread the Lutheran doctrine. These years, the 1530s, were turbulent ones in the history of Denmark. The country was in a state of civil war. Two kings, Christian II, who was deposed by the National Council, and Christian III, whom the nobility supported, claimed the throne, both with the help of German mercenaries. In Funen and Jutland, meanwhile, peasants rebelled against the nobility.

Upon gaining a victory, Christian III immediately implemented the Reformation, dismissing the Catholic bishops and confiscating church property. The new king quickly inaugurated the first seven Lutheran bishops, among them Peder Palladius (1503-1560). Palladius and the learned reformer Hans Tausen (1494-1561) became the driving forces in the building of Denmark's new Evangelical Lutheran Church.

The Reformation changed the interior of the church. The tokens and symbols of Catholic mysticism were removed. The rostrum or reading area became more prominent and was adorned with carvings and a useful canopy. Carvings on rostra often tell stories of the four evangelists: Mark, Luke, John and Matthew. The evangelists are portrayed as responsible figures, clad in robes from Antiquity and accompanied by the gospels they have written. Columns and temple arches often form a space around texts and scenes, and the canopy lets holy, beautiful ornaments hover above the head of the clergyman, the father of his congregation, who reads and explains the gospels. Everything is done to illustrate the connection between man and Holy Scripture. Important maxims and biblical quotations are included on the pulpit, and the congregation is placed in pews as listeners to the clergyman's elucidation of the biblical texts. The Renaissance altarpieces also show how the word and writing have moved centre-stage. These so-called catechism altarpieces simply replace the imagery of previous periods with written text. The passages seem to speak from their separate places of inscription as eternally valid statements. The popular church art of the medieval period gives way to an art that stages the act of reading, and pays homage to study, erudition and personal economy.

The ornamentation often remains rich in detail, but new emphasis is placed on symmetry and harmony. Sometimes the marble of Antiquity is imitated in finely painted marble fields – on pulpits for example. The marbling is to be indistinguishable from marble, yet allow people to see that the imitation has been crafted by a master. Another item of craftsmanship is the new collections of hymns, which assemble and print older church music translated into Danish. Hans Thomissøn's Reformation hymn book is such an item. It appeared in 1569 and created something of a standard order among the myriad Reformation hymns and translations.[107]

After the Reformation, people take many liberties in the space that was previously God's and God's alone. The old altars to the saints were pulled down or converted into sepulchral chapels for the noble or the wealthy. The young scholarly humanists and standard-bearers of the Reformation viewed the recent past with scepticism, and the expression 'Middle Ages' was a derogatory term which these new thinkers used about the past. The previous centuries were regarded as a boring, callous interlude between Antiquity and the rebirth of Antiquity, its Renaissance. The rupture with the past could hardly be formulated more starkly.

The people of the Middle Ages were actually extremely interested in the art, literature and thought of Antiquity and had seen these traditions as the basis of their own efforts. Medieval culture was just as interested in renewal and just as artistically and culturally inquisitive. Even so, the new age felt a need to establish its own culture and to define itself in opposition to the old one. The Italian poet Petrarch referred to the past as being 'dark' as early as the mid-14th century, while the northern Italian princes and courtiers of the 15th century felt they were living in a new, great, golden era. The thinkers of the Renaissance believed in the perfectibility of the human being, the necessity of developing many different skills and talents, and of being self-aware and actively creative. The famous astronomer Tycho Brahe's (1546–1601) portrait of himself in the poem 'In Urania elegia autoris' ('Elegy on Urania by the author', 1573) shows him as a true figure of the Renaissance, with all the qualities of a modern, ambitious scientist:

> [...]
> Admittedly, as a child of the Brahe family, I bear a fine aristocratic name, and admittedly, through my mother I have in the ancient Bille family one that makes me a great noble, but all of this has no effect on me! For it is not something I myself have created – my family history and my ancestors I do not call mine.
> No, my mind is bent on great deeds, where the aim of my labour is higher.
> In elevated subjects there is worth and greater honour – low subjects often attract weak minds.
> It pleases me to rise with my mind to the dwelling of the god of thunder and observe the high signs of the firmament.
> It pleases me to see the gleaming diversity of the heavens, God's wonderful creation.
> That is a task for man – that is the divine urge that makes us the equals of the gods.
> For the one who delights in allowing his soul to fly among the peaks of heaven and with his intellect to draw near to the stars, his striving does not liken that of men but of gods – he possesses something that can raise his mind from the earth.[108]

The historical and art-historical concept of 'the Renaissance' has no more basis in the realities of the period than ideas of the Middle Ages do.

The idea of a Renaissance period was advanced in the mid-9th century, when French and German cultural history started to assert the birth of a 'modern' world in the 15th and 16th centuries, as new ideas within art and thought spread from Italy to the rest of Europe.[109] The concept of the Renaissance was quickly expanded, and the new departures in visual art in the Netherlands, which coincided with the Italian Renaissance, were labelled a special Dutch Renaissance. The German and Nordic Lutheran Reformation was also inscribed into the Renaissance. In the writing of Danish literary history, there is a tradition of using the term 'Renaissance' in connection with the Reformation of 1536 and uptil to the introduction of the absolute monarchy in 1660.[110] In this usage, the Renaissance often stretches from the Danish Reformation hymns and Latin poetry of the 16th century to the historical studies, autobiographies and translation works of 17th century, such as the 1658 translation of Seneca by the noblewoman Birgitte Thott, and *Memoirs* of the princess Leonora Christina Ulfeldt from the end of the 17th century.

Realizing one's humanity

The Renaissance sees the artist as a man of genius, a being sometimes even comparable to God. The artist partakes in the divine power of creation that flows through the entire universe and holds it together. In visual art, light is no longer exclusively connected with God but also with living nature, which humans can study, collect and write about.

As it happened, Renaissance ideals of beauty departed further from those of Antiquity than medieval art had done. Renaissance artists cultivated sensual beauty in mythological art and also created illusions through the use of linear perspective which gather all the lines of the picture into a vanishing point. Linear perspectives emphasize the individual human angle of perception, and the psychological quality of Renaissance portraiture finds literary parallel in autobiographies, commemorative poems, the art of letter-writing and essays, where in a great subject is individual humanity. The French philosopher Michel de Montaigne (1533–92) set himself the aim of writing an honest, candid book about himself as a human being:

> [...] I want to be seen here in my simple, natural, ordinary fashion, without straining or artifice. My defects will here be read to the life, and also my natural form, as far as respect for the public has allowed.[111]

This was part of the preface to Montaigne's famous *Essais* (Essays 1580). In this work, the effort of self-portraiture encourages people to examine their own feelings, to study themselves, think about their experiences, and renounce their pride and prejudices. According to Montaigne, man is to use his own powers of judgment and accept his possibilities and limitations in a changing world. While the thinking of the Middle Ages focuses on the fixed nature and constancy of things, Renaissance thought relates to a world that is changing and in motion.

Art is now on its way to acquiring its own independent meaning – it is no longer exclusively bound to a divine truth. In Artistotle, art was most significant as a cleansing experience for both body and mind, and in the Renaissance it becomes a sign of humanism and human values. The church is no longer the only important institution of art; also notable are the court and the manor house. The prince of rank surrounded himself with artists and scientists, and he himself engaged in writing and music. King Christian IV invited both visual artists and musicians by the score to his court. In the Renaissance, music became a demanding professional craft, and its performance was a ceremonial enhancement of the king's status and served to entertain him and his court. The life-like, illusionary pictorial art of the Renaissance was to have great importance for posterity, becoming practically synonymous with real, good art right up until our own age. The emphasis on the merits of Renaissance art by posterity led many to see medieval art as less developed and rather inept, while modern, abstract art was seen as a falling-off when compared with the techniques of the Renaissance.

The Renaissance church interior pays tribute to aristocrats and the wealthy, who donate to the church, write history books or pursue science, and are thereby seen as good examples worthy of being followed. Painted or carved epitaphs, i.e. commemorative/sepulchral tablets for clergymen, citizens and persons of rank gain ground along with the new altarpieces. The Renaissance rejected the idea that images could be magical, as well as the entire system of saints. Some religious permutations of the Renaissance were given to iconoclasm, or the prohibition of the use of images, and some of the old pictures and church murals were destroyed. Church murals continued, however, to be painted, but while image and text had in the Middle Ages formed a whole, they were now separated from each other, the text being placed in fields alongside the pictures.

One very striking effect of the Reformation was that a number of churches and monasteries were demolished, after which the materials were re-used to build manor houses. When the powerful member of the National Council (Rigsrådet) Jørgen Rosenkrantz built his Jutland home Rosenholm in the 1560s, he made use, with scant respect, of materials from some of the fifteen churches that were closed down in the county

Canopy over the pulpit, Egtved Church, 1608

of Randers. Jørgen Rosenkrantz was reputed to have been an extremely devout man, but to him, the old church stones were not in themselves connected to anything sacred. God did not dwell in stones, or in the church portals he so eagerly re-used. Shortly after the Reformation, Rosenkrantz had been to Wittemberg and heard the 'formidably learned men' – Luther and his colleague Melanchthon – lecture, and from then onward he was a soldier of the Reformation.

The most important new items in Danish churches in the Renaissance were, in fact, the Danish language hymn books and the Danish translation of the Bible, by Christiern Pedersen. The Christian III Bible was published in 1550 and was full of illustrations, with a fine portrait of the king at the front. Pictures were still used for educative purposes. But the text, and the explanation of it offered by the clergyman to the whole congregation, had moved centre-stage in church art, along with the many signs of the power and importance of the nobility. Jørgen Rosenkrantz transformed Hornslev Church into an effective mausoleum for his family, and designated family pews for himself and his relations during services.

In a Danish context, Renaissance art was also often secular, as in the architecture of manor houses and castles, in portrait painting and in the decoration of castle interiors. The conversion and furnishing of Kronborg (the castle of Shakespeare's Hamlet) at the end of the 16th century was the supreme manifestation of the Renaissance in Denmark. A series of historical tapestries was made for Kronborg that depicted many great deeds and merits of the Danish kings. These magnificent tapestries include portraits, symbols and emblems, as well as short biographical texts about the monarchs.

The study of history and languages was at a beginning, along with natural science, which both wittingly and unwittingly had come into conflict with the worldview of the Catholic Church. The cosmology of the Greek astronomer Claudius Ptolemy, in which the earth was seen to be the unmoving centre of the universe, was disputed by Copernicus in the 16th century, and even though the Catholic Counter-Reformation made his teaching heretical in the next century, his hypotheses could not be suppressed in the long run, and new discoveries were made based on Copernicus' ideas.

Renaissance writers were ardently interested in the poetry of Antiquity. Part of being an educated, cultured person was to posses the ability to write poetry in Latin, as well as master classical metres, conventions of imagery and stylistic figures. One had to know one's rhetoric. Occasional poems were written in Latin that could lend lustre to persons of high social rank, commemorative poems became common and beautifully formed letter poems were exchanged. But the scholars of the Renaissance were also interested in their native tongues and writing in these flourished as well. The collection of ballads written by the nobility becomes a key part of the cultural environment of the Renaissance, which in general loved collections of every kind, e.g. archaeological specimens, old words, letters, books, strange skeletons, pieces of musi and knowledge of highly educated women.[112]

The writings of Bishop Anders Arrebo (1587–1637) and Princess Leonora Christina (1621–1698) show in their different ways the connection between the Middle Ages, the Renaissance and the Baroque, which enters the picture from the mid-17th century onwards. Their writings are full of both old and new cultural material. Arrebo's work, which was written between 1631 and 1637 and published posthumously in 1661, actually looks like a medieval encyclopedia of God's creation, and it seeks in accordance with medieval thought to show how nature is God's own book. One could know God by reading the book of nature, the logic went, and there are enough creatures on earth and in the sea and air to teach us much about Him. The new feature is that Arrebo is committed to writing poetry in Danish and to transferring the classical metres into the Danish language. In this effort, Arrebo created a sophisticated Danish poetic language. For that reason, many literary historians refer to him as the first Baroque poet, with followers including Søren Therkelsen, who cultivates pastoral poetry based on Antiquity, and the late 17th century hymn-writer Thomas Kingo. Others place Arrebo in the Renaissance, because he emphasizes man and his creative talents, and because his poetry takes such great joy in colours and the senses.

A Royal Daughter of European Fame

One of the most remarkable manuscripts of the Renaissance is Leonora Christiana Ulfeldt's memoirs, *Jammers Minde* (Memoirs 1869/1872).[113] Leonora Christina (1621-1698) was the daughter of Christian IV; she was married to one of the most powerful noblemen of the time, Corfitz Ulfeldt. She visited Paris and the French court and was praised abroad for her beauty and fine manners. After Christian IV's death in 1648, the Ulfeldt-couple was suspected of high treason against the new king, Frederik III. They fled, but Leonora Christina was captured in London in 1663 and sent to Denmark, where she was imprisoned at the king's castle in Copenhagen. Her case was never tried at court, but she remained in prison for almost 23 years (1663-1685). Corfitz Ulfeldt escaped arrest and may have died in Germany. During her imprisonment, Leonora Christina started to write the memoirs of her life in prison, completing her text in the last years of her life when she had been released to the secular convent in Maribo with her daughter. Her daughter kept the manuscript and sent it to her brother in Vienna where it was kept. In 1869, it was published for the first time by the young librarian Sophus Birket Smith. The public praised the *Memoirs* for their style, and for the compelling narrative of Leonora Christina's experiences in prison, where she withstood poor conditions and humiliation. Her story is told for the most part in Danish. In the first section of the work, dealing with the free portion of her life, she often translates Low German, High German and French dialogue into Danish, merely noting in which language the conversations took place. She later begins to report dialogue in its original language, and in so doing she adds another dimension to her various character sketches. She has the opportunity to score linguistic points against her opponents by replying in a language that they either do not understand or that

The Leonora Christina memorial in Maribo, by Ejnar Dyggve, 1934

outclasses them. Her hereditary enemy, Queen Sophie Amalie, speaks High German or Danish in short, clumsy remarks; Leonora Christina's few allies speak French and use it in intimate conversations or heartening letters. In its use of language, *Memoirs* is a complex network in which the smallest detail is important to the rhetoric that Leonora Christina creates from her life. The *Memoirs* is a unique and radical version of 17th century autobiographical and humanistic literature, but also has features in common with Catholic legends of pious hermits and with 17th century existential religious writings on the soul's communion with God. In her interpretation of herself as 'Christ's Crusader', Leonora Christina is the pious hermit who endures her Passion, her sufferings and who experiences the liberation of her soul. She positions *Memoirs* as a monument to her spiritual and moral triumph over her adversaries, the evil agents of power and the flesh ungodly. Leonora Christina masters a number of different tones and habits of expression. Her work is both deeply serious, full of fear and doubt, and also illuminated by humor and a surplus of mental resources. Leonora Christina also clearly intended the *Memoirs* as a testimony to her mental strength, and she therefore tries to keep the reader in the belief that most of the work was written while she was imprisoned. Analysis of the paper and the handwriting has, however, established that two-thirds of the manuscript was written in the 1690s, when Leonora Christina was living in Maribo. She knew that the work would have a greater impact if it appeared to be a direct account written within the prison walls, and thus she chose to present a fictitious version of its genesis. She was not going to let an opportunity slip; she had to draw on fiction and rhetoric to turn her sufferings in the *Blue Tower* into literature.

Restless, dynamic writing

Literary historians often use the term 'Baroque' to describe Danish-language poetry of the period between the introduction of absolutism in 1660 and the beginning of the 18th century. According to several accounts, the Baroque starts with the learned Creation poem *Hexaëmeron* by Anders Arrebo in the year 1661 and culminates in the hymn-writing of bishop Thomas Kingo (1634–1701) and the Norwegian Dorothe Engelbretsdatter (1634-1716). The concept of Baroque, like those of the Middle Ages and the Renaissance, is imposed on the period retroactively. In the 18th century, it was a derogatory term for the exaggerated, bizarre characteristics of 17th century art – everything that irritated the classicist art connoisseurs of the time for whom simplicity and clarity were the ideal. Later, at the end of the 19th century, the term became more neutral, used simply to describe an art-historical tendency that arose after the Renaissance. As a specifically literary term, Baroque was first used in a Danish context at the beginning of the 20th century, since which time it has gained a certain footing, perhaps because it makes it possible to see the interaction between literature, music, architecture and visual art in the period from the mid 17th century until the beginning of the 18th century. The concept also gathers literary history and Danish history in general into a unified period from the introduction of absolutism in 1660 until the conclusion of the Great Northern War in 1720.[114]

The concept of the Baroque allows one to compare the powerful, complex visual art of the 17th century with the large linguistic register of hymn-writing and secular poetry belonging to the same period. One can see connections between the mythical garments worn by characters in the new secular opera and the dramatic decorations of castle walls and ceilings. While God had filled the medieval world and its holy texts with signs and significances that man could interpret, man now took up these spaces in pictures and texts with self-created themes and forms. While the empty space simply did not exist in the medieval worldview or medieval art, and the Renaissance everywhere made space for man to discover himself, his past achievements in Antiquity, his immediate national traditions and his entire surrounding world, the Baroque, in both literature and art, seemed to fear empty space and time that was neither controlled nor organized.

Natural science put forward new ideas that compared the world to a clock set in motion by God, who afterwards maintained a suitable distance. In 1584, Tycho Brahe was able to open his observatory on the island of Hven at a time when it was becoming clearer that systematic observation and measurement of nature were to be the basis of modern scientific work. The logic of medieval scholasticism, where all certain knowledge was to be winkled out of the complex maze of arguments and related to eternal ideas or purposes, was succeeded by experiments and observations and hypotheses about the laws of nature. Tycho Brahe's inventive design of instruments of measurement and his use of these to measure the orbits of the planets displayed the method of the new discipline. The formulation of natural laws on the basis of observations and experiment was also the point of departure for the English mathematician and physicist Isaac Newton, who in 1687 published his epoch-making work *Philosophiae Naturalis Principia Mathematica* (Mathematical Principles of Natural Philosophy), which formulated the three laws of motion of classical mechanics. Medieval scholastic speculations were replaced by a curiosity and eagerness to study the material world and build theories from the ground up.

The new science had made God distant from man. But art and literature could give a dynamic experience of the vast infinity that God must constitute in this newly imagined universe. Therefore, Baroque art filled its spaces with grandly intertwining vines, convoluted columns, chubby cherubs and decorative elements, and literature similarly became complex and elaborate. The spaces of the Baroque are in restless and dynamic motion. Space does not seem limited by four walls. Even the most contained spaces seem to point towards, to try to contain, the infinity of the universe. The medieval ideas that God created nature out of nothing, that nature operates on the basis of the possibilities offered it to by God, and that the artist imitates nature, still apply in some form. But God's beautiful order, which the Middle Ages saw and interpreted, has become immense and distant, even unknowable, and best shown in art by emphasizing unrest and violent motion. Man could explore and discover this order in science and in art. But the question begins to arise of whether the order being discovered is sufficient for a belief in God. Belief begins to become an act of will, of conscious determination rather than the assumption of a natural order.

It is characteristic of the period that Isaac Newton worked zealously on textual interpretations of the Bible and thought about all sorts of theological subjects: 'A sinner does evil not because he cannot do all things that he will but because he will not do all things that he can'[115] he jots down in one of the many notebooks that he filled with theological argument and whose number hugely exceeds his scientific and mathematical works. In another of these, Newton asserts that one must not introduce religious revelations into philosophy, nor bring philosophical opinions into religion. The new natural science itself hands over an area of human life to belief.

The hymns of the Baroque, too, emphasize the distance between God and man, as well as the finite brevity of earthly life. Unlike the medieval conception of human time as an in-between time, these texts contrast human time and God's time. The hymn-writers of the Baroque express a profound, fervent longing to escape from the one into the other by gaining eternal life.

The hymn-writer Thomas Kingo is only too willing to bid this world farewell. Temporal life has become a burden, and he wishes to escape from this earthly condition. Earthly time only knows one path: towards unstoppable decline and increasing misery that one hopes will soon be over and done with. But one takes one's leave of the world observing all the rules of the game and through use of a previously unseen mastery of language and style.

Kingo's main works were his devotional books *Aandelige Siunge-Koors Første Part* (Spiritual Song-Choir Part I, 1674) and *Aandelige Siunge-Koors Anden Part* (Spiritual Song-Choir Part II, 1681). He started these as a local vicar in Slangerup, but when he published the second part of the work, he had already become bishop of Funen. The heraldic beast of the poems, the winged horse Pegasus, adorned his coat of arms as a clear reminder that it was his poetry that had won him advancement in this

Kingo's and his wife Birgitte Balslev's memorial, Fraugde Church, Funen, 1702

absolutist society.

Kingo's *Siunge-Koor* (Spiritual Choir-Song) is extremely beautiful and clearly organized in groups of hymns, with morning and evening songs for each day of the week and for various occasions in religious life. The depiction of the contrast between the divine and the earthly is the basic principle of the work both formally and thematically, and Kingo imagines the universe as a chaotic and painful opposition between creation and destruction with which human beings have to live. The hymns are full of antithesis, variations on themes and sudden exclamation, as well as complex, composite images and juxtapositions of words. The poetry is ornate and expressive, and thus also a demonstration of linguistic power and the effort to create order and coherence through language. The theological understanding of time finds expression in themes of creation and providence, sin and death, as well as penance and atonement, and the religious sensibility is linked to praise for the absolute monarch and his societal edifice. The interweaving of these major themes might sound like a difficult premise for the poet to work with. But alongside his complex stylistic figures and composite metaphors, Kingo also possesses an ability to be simple and expressive, as in the sixth morning-song 'From eastern skies I now see sunlight streaming', where in the middle of the hymn we find:

My soul, be of good cheer,
Cast out all weeping,
Your body's petal here
Is in God's keeping:
He will today give me the strength and power
My calling to pursue,
To give my God His due
At every hour.[116]

The speaker of the hymn encourages himself, and even though bodily existence is transitory, there is also hope that the 'petal' of the body will arise once more, and that God will give the individual power and strength to complete his task in society. Kingo's praise for the contemporaneous absolutist order is unpalatable to modern readers, but the hymn's lovely images and simple tone also rise above these contextual details, capturing a joy in waking up in good health and thinking about one's assignment in existence.

It was a great challenge for 17th century poets to write good verse in Danish: attempts were made to follow the classical metres, but it was not until the poets Anders Arrebo and Thomas Kingo combined the French principle of fixed syllable counts in the line with the German rule of fixed stress counts (the result being identical to accentual-syllabic meters in English) that beautiful and singable poetry in Danish could successfully be written. The construction of lines and stanzas thereby became identical from one stanza to another, and the congregation no longer had to uncertainly squeeze varying numbers of syllables into each line when singing the hymn. The metre aided and supported the singing. Kingo worked precisely with alternating verse forms and made sure that his words could be sung to well-known melodies.

Kingo's Baroque hymns are intended to be used in the church by vicar

Section of the altarpiece, Egtved Church, 1425

and congregation and help give the absolutist church a uniform stamp; pastoral poetry and plays are part of the social life and ceremonies of the court; occasional poetry serves to praise people of high rank, remember the dead, celebrate a wedding, complain about someone or something in pasquinades or send a petition to the absolutist monarch.

Baroque occasional verse in Denmark culminates in Kingo's ornately composed, versified petition 'The most fervent and humble sigh and petition of the poor from Odense Infirmary to our most gracious master and king', which he probably wrote in 1682–83. Here, in the ghastliest detail, Kingo details the conditions under which the poor inmates of the infirmary live. He employs all the poetic effects at his disposal to move the royal reader and remind him of his responsibility as an absolutist monarch as regards these poor people, who cannot chew their own food, are tormented with sores and abscesses, are on the point of coughing up their own lungs, or in their insanity grunt like pigs and beat themselves until they bleed. The verses are so brilliantly conceived and executed and have such a bold built-in polemic against the decisions of the royal ruler[117] that the occasional poem transcends its own genre and stands for posterity as one of the most important works of art of the period.

With the new interest in hymn-singing, a number of the larger churches were equipped with organs, though in the village churches people still made do with unaccompanied singing. The organ came originally from the Byzantine, Eastern Catholic Church, and it was already in use in the medieval period in some churches – Lund Cathedral was equipped with an organ in the 13th century. Only after the Reformation, however, and particularly in the 17th and 18th centuries did the organ become more common on Danish soil. In the Church of Our Saviour in Christianshavn, built on the initiative of Christian V and consecrated in 1696, the organ was an integral part of the grandiose decoration. It was provided with 'blind pipes' which made no sound and served purely decorative purposes, and the king was given the place of honour with a bust at the centre of the organ facade. The Church of Our Saviour served rather obviously to honour the king and identify him as an absolute authority in a pact with God. Indeed, he can actually be placed side by side with God: 'Deo & C5 Gloria' (In honour of God and Christian V) is written on one of the large organ pipes. The organ case is constructed so that it seems to be borne by two elephants. This detail also bears witness to the king's might – in 1693 he had made the chivalric Elephant Order the most prestigious one in the kingdom.

From God's time to man's time

Many centuries have passed between the hand-written manuscripts of the Middle Ages and the Baroque celebration of the absolutist monarch

Face sticking out his tongue. The church of Dronninglund, 1520

and his partnership with God. From a life within God's time, we have moved to a more dynamic sense of God in history, in union with the reign of a human king. But for a majority of people in Denmark during all this time, many aspects of life changed very little. The life of the sizeable peasant population followed centuries-old patterns and the course

The Library of Sorø Academy

of the seasons. The stipulations of the Jutland Law of 1241 still applied up until the introduction of the absolutist Royal Law of 1663. It is in art, science and literature that we see major changes taking place. New media and genres come into existence, and man has moved into the foreground in the artistic universe. God still occupies a large place in both secular and church literature, but man has conquered time and space both in the world and in literary texts. The stable symbolism of the medieval period, which had called for interpretation and elucidation, gave way to a world and a literature that called for genius, curiosity and exploration. There was still a divine order and plan to be followed, no matter whether one studied the origins of society or the organization of nature. But God moved out to the periphery of his own creation, i.e. the limits of the visible world. When it came to organizing society, 16th and 17th century people began to interest themselves in the practical and historical motives behind social arrangements.

The Danish bishop Niels Hemmingsen (1513–1600) is one of the first important sources in this debate, which played out across the whole of Europe. Hemmingsen's *De lege naturae*, a 1562 Latin work on the laws of nature which was printed in Wittenberg, was the point of departure for the more famous natural law philosopher, the Dutchman Hugo Grotius, whose Latin work *De jure belli ac pacis libri tres* (On the Law of War and Peace) was published in 1625.

Hemmingsen argues that God has equipped all human beings with reason and a conscience that enable them to distinguish between good and evil.[118] This means that humans have the ability to organize their societies according to nature's own law. Grotius extended the idea that human reason enables people to join together in societies, while the Englishman Thomas Hobbes claimed that it was people's urge for self-preservation and their fear of each other that had caused them to leave their natural state and form societies. These debates about so-called natural law prompted the study of how civilized society had come into being, and typically suggested that absolutism was its natural culmination.

In the early 18th century, art, science and writing indicated in many ways that man's time had begun.

The century of the Enlightenment

1700–1800

'Ah! Where am I and what?'[1] It is the poet Schack Staffeldt (1769–1826), who is to become one of the most important figures of Romanticism, that has to ask himself this disconcerting question at the beginning of the 19th century. He tries to express in poetry how his world and his experience of himself have disintegrated.

Horror and dismay assault him when, in the year 1800, he enters one of the bloodiest places of execution of the French Revolution – Place de Terraux in the city of Lyon, where 6000 people had been executed. Like many of the other young intellectuals and poets everywhere in Europe, Staffeldt had nourished high hopes of the French Revolution. The Revolution, which had begun with the storming of the hated absolutist prison, the Bastille, would surely herald a new age and a new realm of freedom. Staffeldt had compared the Revolution to a tree that sought to rise out of blood, but which would soon grow and offer protection so that liberty could reach all people.

The poet Jens Baggesen (1764–1826) experienced the outbreak of the Revolution with the storming of the Bastille on 14 July 1789. In his travel book *Labyrinten* (The Labyrinth) from the early 1790s, he set down his many dramatic impressions:

> The three social orders have united in one people's assembly! Everything is prepared for war between liberty and slavery, the law of the people and despotism! The frightful anarchy, that dark, trackless, hellish labyrinth through which the path runs from *Tyranny* to *Monarchy* has started. Europe's largest political powder magazine, Paris, has been ignited. The enlightened friends of freedom are fighting; the suppressors fume; the scared, confused, incensed mob is enraged.[2]

Baggesen soon, however, started to doubt the extent to which 'the basically morally corrupt Paris' was actually suited to be 'the cradle of freedom'.[3] And to Staffeldt, doubt increased when reports of the wave of executions became known.

The figure of Bravery, section of the Liberty Column, 1797

Staffeldt's European journey of 1795–1800 gave rise to a painful reunion with the century that was ending. What he saw and thought about filled him with disquiet and doubt. What is it that constitutes a human being? Reason, in which he and other European young intellectuals had put their trust, had proved capable of leading to the worst atrocities and mockery of humanity. Reason could end up in a frightful logic, as in the last and bloodiest phases of the Revolution. And the freedom one dreamt of and placed all one's hope in could be brought to heel – even in the name of freedom itself. Staffeldt, and many like him, were appalled and shaken in every way.

One can compare Staffeldt's reflections concerning the emergence of the regime of terror that imprisoned and executed citizens indiscriminately in the 1790s with the scepticism towards the concept of the Enlightenment formulated by the German social philosophers Theodor W. Adorno and Max Horkheimer in the 20th century. After the Second World War, they started to ask themselves why the liberation of man and reason during the Enlightenment seemed to be followed by suppression and coercion.[4] Their thoughts derived from the question of how it was possible for the Nazi atrocities to have taken place in the 20th century in the otherwise so enlightened Europe.

Staffeldt tried to save something from the wreckage by recalling his old hero, the German writer Friedrich Gottlieb Klopstock (1724-1803), who wished to liberate poetry and turn it into a new paradigm for humanity, in the same way as the Revolution had made liberty and reason into principles for a pact between people and the organization of society. Klopstock had enthusiastically praised the Revolution and in 1792 had been made a citizen of the French Republic.

But to Staffeldt, the farewell to the old century was grim: 'Tarry, genius of the century! I hold you/by your bloody hair,'[5] he wrote. What, after this, still remained of emotions, abilities and strengths in man which one could hold onto? In his ode from Lyon he speaks, despite everything, of 'Faith in human dignity',[6] but his other poems indicate that precisely the inextinguishable longing for freedom, which the poet feels, but which is not directed towards a particular goal, is a guiding star in his thinking. After the French Revolution, poetry and the poet's longing for freedom assumed an even stronger position than in his early poems. It was this longing that, for Staffeldt, made a man a human being.

The 18th century, which Staffeldt looked back on with disquiet, had brought many changes, a great many new, brilliant values and conceptions, new forms of thought, science, art and literature as well as a new kind of artist and writer. There had been just as much to be enthusiastic about for young poets and philosophers as to regret and fear.

Independence and authority

Liberty and equality were not merely ideals in the French Revolution. The new ideas were the basis of the American War of Independence that began on 4 July 1776. On that day, 13 eastern American states declared themselves independent of British colonial rule. The epoch-making declaration resisted to the old European world by presenting a perspective that sought to change society radically. For the rebellious colonies maintained that all men are created equal and that their creator has provided them with inalienable rights, such as those to life, liberty and the pursuit of happiness. If these words were to be put into practice, one would have to completely change the order of society.

The American Declaration of Independence was to leave a lasting mark in the following centuries everywhere in the world where people strove for equality and liberty. Like the French Revolution, it set an agenda for society that still applies when the present age insists on human rights. In the French declaration of human rights from 1789, it says that men are born and remain free and have equal rights. Social differences can only be justified by what is for the common good.

Ideas about modern society, from the Dutchman Hugo Grotius and the Englishman John Locke in the 17th century to the Frenchman Jean-Jacques Rousseau in the 18th century were the basis of the principles of human rights. These thoughts about society were formulated within the discipline that was called natural law. Here, one philosophized about how human society had come into being. How and why have people formed societies? And how can the social pact be renewed? Natural law assumed that all human beings had been endowed by God with reason and the instinct of self-preservation, and that these two qualities had caused people to join together in societies and make a pact with each other, most recently in the form of the absolutist society.

The philosopher John Locke (1632–1704) and the writer and philosopher Rousseau (1712–78), however, put forward strong arguments against the idea that absolutism was still the right social pact. John Locke underlined the right to personal freedom and property, while Rousseau retained the idea that the social pact had to express the rights of the people and be in accordance with the people's will. John Locke believed that the people could have the right to seize power themselves if a regime made inroads into individual rights, while Rousseau spoke unconditionally in favour of the people's right to revolt against a suppressive monarch.

In Denmark/Norway, the professor, philosopher and poet Ludvig Holberg (1684–1754) and his slightly younger colleague from the university, Jens Schielderup Sneedorff (1724–64), became interested early on in modern social philosophy, especially on the basis of 17th century rationalism and moral philosophy. Holberg simply combined the various ideas he knew from natural law in his *Moralske Kierne Eller Introduction Til Naturens- Og Folke-Rettens Kundskab* (The Core of Morality or Introduction to Knowledge of Nature and the Common Law, 1716). Holberg explains here that the strongest argument one can use against people who despise and debase other people is to say:

> *I am a human being just as much as you are*; and as human nature is bestowed equally on all people, it follows that everyone ought to respect every other person as someone that is equal to him by nature.[7]

The modern thinking within natural law invited change, and the 18th century was full of changes – also in the literature.

The century gets underway

In Denmark, absolute monarchy was introduced in 1660 in connection with the country's unfortunate wars against Sweden and, at the dawn of the 18th century, absolute monarchy was still the form of government in the dual monarchy of Denmark - Norway. Absolutism was abolished in 1848 after a peaceful agreement between the king and the people.

In a Danish-Norwegian literary context, the 18th century stretches from Thomas Kingo to Ludvig Holberg, Hans Adolph Brorson, Charlotta Dorothea Biehl, Johannes Ewald, Johan Herman Wessel, Jens Baggesen, Peter Andreas Heiberg and the young Schack Staffeldt, who began writing poetry in the 1780s. The 18th century starts off in Danish with hymns, mocking satires, occasional poems and elegant pastoral songs and is enveloped in smoke from the last witch-burnings, which took place in 1693.

The literature of the 17th century ended with the publication of *Dend Forordnede Ny Kirke-Psalme-Bog* (The Ordained New Church Hymn Book) in 1699, the same year that Frederik IV came to power. The hymn book was to have a very long life, and it came to be known as *Kingo's Hymn Book*, even though Kingo had been removed from his position as editor by the time the hymn book was finally published. But many of Kingo's hymns were still included in the work, and their poetic power and fervour became part of the religious life of the population in general. When an extremely reason-dominated theology gained support among

Memorial column for A. Ch. Arreboe, Andreas Bording, Thomas Kingo, C. Bravn Tvllin, Johannes Ewald and Johannes Wiedewelt's sculpture park, Jægerspris, 1784.

clergymen and officials at the end of the 18th century and a new hymn book was introduced in 1798, a number of congregations continued to use *Kingo's Hymn Book* in protest.

In the Faroe Islands, Kingo's hymnbook remains very important. A special performance of the hymns has developed in some of the villages where church organs have never been installed.

Hymns, however, were only one of several genres that triumphed in the transition from the 17th to the 18th century. Anders Bording (1619–77) made elegant use of the Danish language in his pastoral songs, odes and occasional poems while strictly observing the rules of Danish-language literary poetry for imagery, metre and style:

> My Danish pen gained life and strength
>   To write verse sweetly rhyming.
> At court I graciously was told
>   At almost every turning:
> My style was valued and extolled
>   By those of rank and learning.[8]

Bording, however, relates in verse that his idea of promoting and disseminating his 'forefathers' tongue' is proving to be more difficult in practice than he had envisaged. He makes fun of the fact that his jaw drops from time to time and that his ink grows thick.

Bording addressed the king in Danish in this poem, but the languages of the court were, in particular, German and French, and in Copenhagen the king sought diversion with specially called-in theatre troupes and French opera, while at the university people spoke Latin.

In the latter half of the 17th century, academics had been interested in studying the potential limits of human knowledge. The French philosopher René Descartes (1596–1650) had looked critically in the mid-17th century at human potential for obtaining firm knowledge about the world and had given science a modern philosophical basis with his ideas that we humans gain knowledge when we critically derive rules and conclusions from facts that are known as certainties. His dictum 'I think, therefore I am'[9] is the pithiest formulation of his critical, rationalist thought.

At the end of the 17th century, John Locke had formulated the idea that knowledge is attained through the examination of phenomena. His empiricism led to an elementary interest in investigating and describing the outside world, and his idea that human consciousness is, at birth, like a clean slate on which things are subsequently written inspired many writers in the 18th century to see man's potential.

Academics were also interested during the second half of the 17th century in history and language. Grammar books were written, runes were studied and songs and sayings were collected in 17th century Denmark, and the study of man, history and language went in new directions in the 18th century under the influence of ideas about educating and instructing a wider cross-section of the population. But there are also large differences between 17th century rationalism and 18th century Enlightenment: While the rationalist concept of reason is linked to abstract systems of thought, the Enlightenment connects the possibility for man to gain certain knowledge through concrete experience and experiments. Here, reason is directly linked to experience and emotion, and making the individual an autonomous, thinking human being is a major issue.[10]

Precisely this idea of the emancipation of the individual, his powers of judgment and experiences is what we find in Staffeldt when he considers how he experiences himself and his own age: 'Ah, where am I and what?' he exclaims in the poem in which he looks back at the century. It is important to note that the question is not 'Who am I?' but 'What am I?' For it is not so much a question of personal identity but of what sort of entity a human being actually is, and how one experiences one's humanity. 'What am I? ' – 'What makes me a human being?' – it was precisely that which preoccupied 18th century Enlightenment and which Staffeldt asked himself as the 18th century drew to a close.

Between optimism and a crisis mentality

The innovative literature and thought of the 18th century seeks in general to imbue man with new courage, a trust in the ability of the individual to ask, know, believe, feel and think, even if that courage, emotion or critical sense can lead to where there are no answers, or one can scarcely recognize oneself.

The philosophical discussions of the 18th century opened with the German mathematician and philosopher Gottfried Wilhelm Leibniz's (1646–1716) work on the theodicy problem *Essais de théodicée* (Theodicy, 1710), which claimed that man lives in the best of all possible worlds, one where God has reduced evil to a minimum. God is the basic cell, the basic monad that is the source of all being and thought. Leibniz's optimism, however, was contested less than half a century later by the earthquake in Lisbon in 1755, which many people at the time interpreted as God's punishment on humanity.

In Denmark the bishop and hymnwriter Brorson wrote about the catastrophe in his didactic poem 'Lisbon's pitiful demise' (1755), which interpreted the earthquake as a pronouncement from God to man and as evidence of the fact that humanity was approaching the Day of Judgment.

In Lisbon, man's iniquity, pride and self-indulgence had got completely out of control and therefore precisely that city and its Catholic institutions were singled out for destruction.[11] 'Folk strut about on earth so cock-sure and so bold,/ As if there were no doom and no God in heaven above'.[12]

The philosopher Voltaire (1694–1778) gave a stinging reply to Leibniz in his philosophical novel *Candide* (1759), in which he asserts via the use of satire the imperfection of the world. The young student Candide, who has been brought up with Leibniz's teaching, experiences personally the Lisbon earthquake and starts to doubt his conviction about living in the best of all possible worlds:

> If this is the best of possible worlds, what then are the others? Well, if I had been only whipped, I could put up with it, for I experienced that among the Bulgarians; but oh, my dear Pangloss! thou greatest of philosophers, that I should have seen you hanged, without knowing for what! Oh, my dear Anabaptist, thou best of men, that thou should'st have been drowned in the very harbour! Oh, Miss Cunegonde, thou pearl of girls! that thou should'st have had thy belly ripped open! It is almost more than I can bear![13]

Voltaire's satire was aimed at man's convenient relinquishing of his own responsibility to God, fate, teachers of tradition, and it was a call to human beings to behave responsibly.

The catastrophe actually proved to be a turning point in Enlightenment thought. It caused Voltaire to say that hope is a special human capacity. It is, in fact, hope that can liberate man from religious interpretations of existence, and the experience of the earthquake also caused Kant to state that man has been torn away from his natural basis and has freedom as his life's purpose.[14]

While people later in the 18th century thought in terms of the concepts of hope and freedom as human aims, Ludvig Holberg level-headedly and on a rationalistic basis introduces his work on natural law by stating that it is simply reason that makes man a human being: 'Man's glory in comparison with the tongueless beasts can especially be seen from the fact that he is endowed with a reasoning soul from which there comes a glorious light to understand and judge things (...][15] to be able to understand and adopt a position on things.' By means of this, according to Holberg, he is equipped to adopt a critical attitude to the world and its ingrown prejudices and unreasonableness.

In 1783, Immanuel Kant (1724–1804) defines the concept of Enlightenment in a way that can be directly connected to that of Holberg:

> Enlightenment is man's emergence from his self-incurred immaturity. Immaturity is the inability to use one's own understanding without the guidance of another. This immaturity is self-incurred if its cause is not lack of understanding, but lack of resolution and courage to use it without the guidance of another. The motto of Enlightenment is therefore: *Sapere aude!* Have courage to use your own understanding![16]

Even though the concept of enlightenment is transparently and clearly defined by Kant, in a historical reading of the Enlightenment texts it is important to remember that the Enlightenment period is a title used for a series of tendencies that can hardly be synthesized.[17] The leading 18th century historian Roy Porter discusses in his thesis the relation between a narrow and a broad conception of Enlightenment. He is critical of the German Ernst Cassirer's concept of Enlightenment in *Die Philosophie der Aufklärung* (1932), in which Cassirer sees Enlightenment as an essence of the ideas of the radical French philosophers: Voltaire, Diderot, d'Alembert, d'Holbach and Rousseau, and omits taking the English Enlightenment thinkers into consideration. Porter instead emphasizes the necessity of seeing the Enlightenment as many-sided and with players in various countries:

> [...] the Enlightenment should be viewed not as a canon of classics but as a living language, a revolution in mood, a blaze of slogans, delivering the shock of the new. It decreed new ways of seeing, advanced by a range of protagonists, male and female, of various nationalities and discrete status, professional and interest groups.[18]

The British historian Jonathan Israel, in his major studies of the Enlightenment *Radical Enlightenment* (2001) and *Enlightenment Contested* (2006), sees the Enlightenment as being divided into a moderate Enlightenment that supports the monarchy and the church, and a democratic-republican, radical Enlightenment. The moderate form of Enlightenment is the predominant one:

> Of the two enlightenments, the moderate mainstream was without doubt overwhelmingly dominant in terms of support, official approval, and prestige practically everywhere except for several decades in France from the 1740s onwards. Nevertheless, in a deeper sense, and in the long run, it proved to be much the less important of the two enlightenments.[19]

According to Israel, moderate Enlightenment does not have any major importance because it is problematic, philosophically and theoretically, because of its mixing of rationalistic thoughts and theological and traditional concepts. Israel finds an important prerequisite for radical Enlightenment in the thinking of Spinoza (1632–77), whose concept of tolerance meant that he emphasized the freedom of the individual and of speech rather than the cultivation of faith and the worship of God.[20]

In Israel's opinion, the conception we now have of modernity as being the basis of fundamental values such as tolerance, personal freedom, democracy, equality in relation to race and gender, sexual freedom and a universal right to acquire these values derives exclusively from radical Enlightenment. It is also one of Israel's important conclusions that one has to study as a totality the interactions between Enlightenment in England, France, Italy and the Netherlands. A national study of Enlightenment distorts the picture of the many European exchanges. This conclusion is correct, but Israel's conception of the two types of Enlightenment does not leave much room for such thinkers as Holberg and Sneedorff. They are not republicans and philosophical radicals, but rather monarchists and reason-thinkers, influenced by both 18th century Enlightenment and 17th century rationalism. The entire Nordic variant of modernity is – when it comes to ideas of tolerance, freedom, morality, social considerations and the common good – strongly influenced by Holberg's thinking in terms of reason. Holberg and Sneedorff use such thought to challenge institutions, customary social conventions and inherited ideas and, for example, to formulate their ideas about religious tolerance and equality between men and women. When it comes to precisely this subject, Holberg – and the Swedish Enlightenment poet Hedvig Charlotta Nordenflycht (1718–63), who herself refers to Holberg – displays a radicalism that Israel does not include in his presentation.[21]

Various terms for the Enlightenment period

If one takes a look at Danish histories of literature and whether or not they use a concept for the Enlightenment period, one will quickly be able to single out Ludvig Holberg as the main figure of the period in question. The repeated use of the word 'if' indicates that it is far from self-evident to use the concepts of Enlightenment and Period of Enlightenment as a main heading in the Danish literary history, even when writing about Holberg.

Certain presentations restrict themselves to using 'the 18th century' as an overall term for a review of ten to fifteen of the best-known oeuvres;

other make use of ideological, consciousness-historical or culture-historical terms such as 'public servant culture under absolutism' or 'Age of patriotism' when the 18th century is to be treated.[22] In volume one of *The History of Danish Literature. 1100-1800*, edited by May Schack and Klaus P. Mortensen, 'Enlightenment' is the main title for two sections bearing the titles 'The Age of Reason. 1700–1770' and 'The Age of Individualism. 1770–1800'. The concept of Enlightenment is briefly defined as a 'widespread European tendency that Danish culture was also part of, and if it is to be dated, it must be – as far as Denmark is concerned – from the introduction of absolutism in 1660 until 1700, which was a troublesome time of incubation with contradictory signals.'[23] Enlightenment is linked here to the development of the absolutist system of government that develops from being an outer coercion to a kind of inner reason, the guiding principle of which is consideration of the common good. Reason and individualism thus become the main captions for Enlightenment in a Danish context, and this is mainly due to Holberg's thoughts about natural law. In this interpretation, there is a toning-down of Holberg's – from an international point of view – original contributions to the 18th century discussion of gender and culture, the diversified emergence of a literature of periodicals, thoughts about the nation state in Sneedorff and several of the other sources of international inspiration in Danish literature.

In Per Thomas Andersen's *Norsk litteraturhistorie* (History of Norwegian literature, 2001) the concept 'modernity' is used as an umbrella term for the 18th century since, inspired by the German Jürgen Habermas' theories, he focuses on the coming into existence and development of the bourgeoisie as well as the emergence of a double authority: the absolutist monarch and critical public opinion. According to such an analysis, the tasks of literature become to develop enlightened popular opinion through books, periodicals, the school system and other fora for public debate.[24] Later on, in Per Thomas Andersen's presentation, the term Enlightenment period is also used in connection with a European contextualization of Norwegian-Danish literature. The point is made here that Holberg is more influenced by 17th century rationalism than by the encyclopedists and radical Enlightenment thinkers of the 18th century. This is a fair point, but it must be mentioned in the same breath that Holberg's comedies and historical writings acquire their own radical edge, since he links reason and experience with a critical reasoning about social life and a wish for progress. Otherwise, one does not get a proper grasp of Holberg's originality.

Research into the 18th century has especially emphasized the patchwork, composite nature of the Enlightenment, as is clear from the title of

Thomas Bredsdorff's study: *Den brogede oplysning. Om følelsernes fornuft og fornuftens følelse i 1700-tallets nordiske litteratur* (The variegated Enlightenment. On the reason of the emotions and the emotion of reason in 18th century Nordic literature, 2003). Here, the concept of Enlightenment is broadened to comprise both reason and feelings, the focus being on the Enlightenment as a break with accepted truths and hierarchies – a tricky, difficult and manifold entity, hard to grasp but exciting to study – and the work is full of good, fascinating Enlightenment histories from literature, society and culture.

Even though scholarship in a Danish context has hitherto been reticent about using the concept of the Enlightenment period, we have not yet arrived at any outright rejection of the existence of Enlightenment literature on Danish soil, as has been the case in Sweden, where the Swedish historian of ideas Tore Frängsmyr in his thesis *Sökandet efter Upplysningen* (The search for the Enlightenment, 1993) has discussed various definitions of Enlightenment and Enlightenment period and has reached the conclusion that, in Swedish the context, there is no Enlightenment that can be understood as French-influenced intellectual struggles.[25]

In his presentation, Thomas Bredsdorff makes a critical examination of Frängsmyr's conceptions of the Enlightenment and the Enlightenment period and demonstrates that the concept of Enlightenment can be used and that it can be localized to the 18th century, but that it must also be regarded as being a broader set of conceptions and ideas that are of importance for the coming into existence of the modern world and that are still present in present-day culture. Bredsdorff, like the English 18th century historical Roy Porter, avoids a narrower historical reading and demarcation of the Enlightenment. In this optic, we are still living in the Enlightenment.

The definitive discussion of Enlightenment literature and the Enlightenment period can easily become sophistic, and as a reader one needs to have a more concrete point of departure for the study and definitions of the many-sided concept. One can gain this by making a visit to the Academy of Sorø, founded by Christian IV and renewed 1747 by Frederik V, assisted by Ludvig Holberg, and delve into the literary activities of the academy both before and after the 18th century. Such a study also has the advantage that the Enlightenment period cannot be enclosed in a separate literature-historical box with a label on it. It is simply impossible to unequivocally define the Enlightenment – one is constantly obliged to think both forwards and backwards, to see things in terms of long lines and striking breaks, to listen to the language of the Enlightenment and see the many players involved.

The habitats of the Enlightenment

Recent scholarship has underscored that the Enlightenment involved man having the courage to feel and to rely on the right to feelings.[26] Imagery to do with light and enlightenment is everywhere in the choice of words used in the 18th century in connection with belief, reason and feelings.

But the person who has the courage and maturity to know, believe and feel, also gains the courage to make decisions and to demand some influence on the outside world.

The absolutist monarchy and government that had been introduced in 1660 was, characteristically enough, based on a constitution that was kept secret for several decades. But absolutism acquired an increasing need for a certain degree of Enlightenment thinking and initiatives to be able to function and to centralize its machinery of power, even though one was wary of every hint of criticism of the form of government and the monarchy.

Holberg and Sneedorff were supporters of enlightened despotism. Sneedorff regarded it as characteristic of an enlightened monarchy that the relation between monarch and subjects was articulated and linguistically staged.[27] The relation between monarch and population in particular was important, and the relation between monarch and population should further be demonstrated by marks of distinction being given to faithful subjects. The monarchy lived on eloquence, and metaphors. Enlightened despotism, to Sneedorff, is thus to a great extent a question of language and communication. Sneedorff was appointed professor at the Academy of Sorø 1751, but the court employed him in 1761 not as a 'spin doctor' but as something similar: as a tutor for the crown prince, Frederik. The present-day Danish royal divorce and the Norwegian marriage between a crown prince and a former drug abuser and single mother would hardly have made a good impression on Sneedorff. He would see it as an advantage that the royal family could also in such matters set a good example that people could talk about and refer to.

From Sneedorff's point of view of society, the art of public speaking and literature were important. There are preconditions for people to be able to follow nature's reasonable law, which enable them to distinguish between good and evil. And God has not reserved reason for Christian men – all humans by definition share in it, even heathens and women. Women were, in fact, ascribed a very particular role in society as regards language – in principle and on paper, at any rate. Women also had the advantage that they mastered the mother tongue, which was something the learned men could have difficulty with, since the profes-

Liberty Column, Copenhagen, 1797

sional language, since the Middle Ages, had been Latin. Nor were the absolutist officials proficient at speaking Danish, nor was the absolutist court where people spoke German or French. The fact of the matter was that there were two governmental languages: Danish and German. A German-speaking administration, a German Chancellery, was responsible for governing the duchies and taking care of foreign policy, while the Danish Chancellery took care of domestic policy. French was often used at court and by the top-ranking officials.

Holberg regarded women as his ideal readers and emphasized this early on in one of his satires in the description of the talented Zille Hansdotter, who is not allowed to read, study and make a career for herself because old prejudices exclude her from the university and officialdom:

> The law which women does exclude
> From office and profession,
> Is strict as one that would preclude
> All twins without exception,
> Or anyone with curly hair,
> A wart upon his forehead,
> Whose legs were not an equal pair
> And who thus leant to starboard,
> Who had been born on Christmas night,
> Or any man whatever,
> Though wise, from having any right
> To be a judge wherever.[28]

Later, intelligent girls appear in Holberg's comedies, and often it is a Pernille or a Marthe who leads the intrigue against ignorance and caprices. Holberg's defence of women is striking, also in a European context, where the men of Enlightenment seldom thought about equality between the sexes. Holberg's portraits of women are without any parallels in Voltaire, where women most often are portrayed as victims of their own and others' conceptions.

Author and public

> The comedy is great fun, but it is written for the gallery. From time to time I am of course obliged to keep my desires under control and put the bait on the hook that I know will attract the public that/sits in the theatres/and enthusiastically clap their hands,/every time the actors/and actresses fall on their backsides.[29]

This is what Holberg wrote about his comedy 'Den 11. Junii' (June the Eleventh, 1723), which, with a good grasp of his public, he had

Ludvig Holberg, The Royal Danish Theatre, sculpture by Theobald Stein, 1875

performed on the very same date so as to further attract a large audience. But neither a large audience nor a host of readers sat ready to read and discuss the Danish-language literature that Enlightenment writers so dearly wanted to promote. In the theatre, it was necessary to give those assembled there bait on the hook in the form of the comedy known from the grammar school comedies and Lent plays of the 16th and 17th centuries. The idea was to create a public willing to discuss with a competent audience that could benefit from what they saw and read. The literature was full of regular role models in the form of gifted readers who commented on thing. The hope was that reality's readers would 'take a leaf from their book'.

'Publico' was Holberg's concept for the public and the public forum he wished to promote. Prose and poetry, drama, essays, historical writing, philosophical writing and letters were seen in light of the common good and were the cornerstone of the first contours of a public arena with newspapers, periodicals and book publications. Perhaps it is the crucial significance that literature and drama gained with the coming into existence of a 'publico' that gives rise to the fact that many Danish critics still link 'real' literature with works that have to do with society and that deal with social issues.

In the 18th century, a new kind of author emerged in the form of university people and officials who wishes to benefit and amuse a 'publico' with comedies, essays, letters and articles in the vernacular language. Occasionally, an enlightened woman also shared in the stipends and financial favours distributed by the court to authors and writers, and to women the Danish-language theatre became an important Enlightenment environment, a simple opportunity to be artistically active. Charlotta Dorothea Biehl (1731–88) tells in her autobiography *Mit ubetydelige Levnets Løb* (My Insignificant Life, 1787) about the important contacts she made via her contributions to the stage repertoire, but also about the financial straits and defeats she encountered. She did not give up, because she felt it was her duty to use the talents she had been endowed with for the common good.

While Sneedorff was a professor in Sorø, he participated in the founding of the important *Det Smagende Selskab* (The Tasting Society) in 1759. This society, which consisted of senior officials, would promote a new bourgeois literature, enhance the taste and develop a new literary culture for new readers and writers. The society was responsible for publications and awards and both Biehl and her competitors Johan Herman Wessel and Johannes Ewald received awards. The Tasting Society became a prime mover for a modern literary culture, becoming visible on a larger scale in the middle of the 18th century, where Sneedorff's Danish language journal *Den Patriotiske Tilskuer* (The Patriotic Spectator, 1761-1763), also gained many followers. The most important magazine of the latter part of the century was Knud Lyne Rahbek and Christen Henriksen Pram's *Minerva*, which began to appear in 1785 and continued until 1808. *Minerva* followed the tradition of *Den Patriotiske Tilskuer*, publishing both literary narratives, Danish and translated poems and essays on social and economic topics. Literature and social debate have a common platform here. The new civil society should in the publishers' opinion be founded on law, social science and literature. A young audience in the form of Copenhagen students also began to take part in the life of literary clubs and societies. In 1772, Norwegian students founded the lively and literary important Norwegian Society, which in 1775 began to publish its *Poetiske Samlinger* (Collected Poetry), defending a classicist line of the Norwegian Johan Herman Wessel (1742-85). The society was a sworn opponent of Johannes Ewald's and the German poet Klopstock's odes.

The Danish Theatre

Visits by French theater troupes were regular events at the Danish court, and also performances by more popular German troupes took place in Copenhagen, but in 1722 the first Danish-language theatre opened in the capital. The new theatre's management consisted of two Frenchmen, Etienne Capion (1670-1757) and René Magnon de Montaigu (1661-1737). Both of them were members of a French troup that Frederik IV dissolved in 1721. The new Danish speaking actors were recruited among Copenhagen students, and the opening performance was Moliere's *The Miser*. Senior courtiers asked Ludvig Holberg, who was a professor at the University of Copenhagen, to write for the theatre, and he was seized by a true drama frenzy where he was inspired by the Italian comedia-del-ar-te and of Moliere. In a few years he wrote a series of comedies, which were staged in the Danish theatre in Lille Grønnegade. Many of them are classics that are still performed on Danish stages.

Holberg succeeded in creating a dramatic genre where every day experiences and moral issues could be addressed. His comedies gave the audience a new access to reality and to an open thematization of moral and reason. Morality was no longer closely connected to religion and faith.[30]

Many themes are treated in Holberg's total of 33 comedies and he brings the genre to live with linguistic humour, shifting between low-brow scenes and philosophicaly sharp discussions.

Among the most beloved classics is *Jeppe på Bjerget* (Jeppe of the Hill, 1722). Jeppe is a tenant farmer in a fictional village in Zealand and his life is hard - he is caught between the demands of his wife, Nille, and the demands of the Baron. In addition, he is socially humiliated by his wife who sleeps with the parson. He has stooped very low and he displaces his problems by means of heavy drinking - and a very vicious circle is etablished. Jeppe lies drunk and miserable on the dunghill most of the time. His most famous line is the following: 'They say that Jeppe drinks but do they ask why Jeppe drinks.' [31] There are obvious reasons why Jeppe drinks - but the comedy does not give any easy solutions – or any characters that have the morality or ability to change the social order. Jeppe is surrounded by villains but he turns out to be a villain himself when he – as the plot shows - obtains the power of a baron.

Youth and education are important issues in all of Holberg's writings and this is also the subject of the comedy *Erasmus Montanus*. Generations of Danish pupils and university students have read and/or seen *Erasmus Montanus* (1723, first performed in 1747). The play has simply attained the status of classic of all classics in the Danish educational system.[32]

Erasmus Montanus has the advantage that the themes of teachings and dissemination as well as discussions of the relation between educational institutions and society never seem to loose actuality

The comedy's status as a classic also emphasizes how Danish fiction and drama are linked to educational themes pertaining to school, learning and upbringing. One can draw a clear line of literary history through Danish literature from Holberg to one of the 20th century's leading authors, Klaus Rifbjerg (1931-2014), who also criticizes the institutions of education.

Erasmus Montanus is an artistic testing of some of the issues Holberg knew from his own experience as a student and a professor. The play portrays a pompous student, Erasmus Montanus, who returns to his home in the country after studies at the University of Copenhagen. He masters both logic and metaphysics and has knowledge of the earth's spherical form. When he returns he boasts to his parents, his fiancée and his brother with his new knowledge and teases them with his ability to use and abuse logical deductions, the so-called syllogisms. Erasmus ends up being punished and made a victim of his own syllogisms.

However, it is a matter of interpretation whether the play should be perceived as a comedy where the fool is punished, or a tragedy where the hero is forced to renounce the obvious truth about the round shape of the earth.

The author and philosopher Søren Kierkegaard (1813-55), who repeatedly refers to the comedy, mentions how he cries when he sees the play. There was in the 19th century a tradition of perceiving Erasmus as a sympathetic character, suffering defeat in the self-sufficient and confined Danish village.[33]

But perhaps the uncertainty of the tragic and the comic is solved if one grasps the fact it is not only Erasmus who is pictured as foolish. The play goes to the edge of the comic genre and becomes a play with more than one fool.

Most of the characters are foolish: Both the boastful and snobbish student Erasmus and the unlettered parish clerk Per Degn, who deceives money from the peasants for his very poor prayers in Latin, the awed parents admire the spoiled Erasmus' new but useless skills and the skeptical in-laws with a limited horizon seem more or less foolish. Representatives of common sense are not merely pictured as good: Erasmus' gifted peasant brother tries to make Erasmus look more ridiculous than he is, and the lieutenant, who finally punishes Erasmus and enrolls him as a soldier, is a rough farmhand.

Erasmus Montanus, performed in 2012 by the theatre company Pulchra Semper Veritas at Gammel Estrup

The play has none of the cheerfully, intriguing characters that often stage the intrigue. Erasmus Montanus is not only a play on useless and oldfashioned studies, but on the need to use and develop a modern knowledge sharing and knowledge flow between different areas of society.

Holberg simply uses his own favorite motto: 'Let's examine' in comedy form. The comedy becomes an examination that seeks to get still further into the subject and thus enlighten contemporary issues.

The second Holberg comedy that thematizes youth and education is *Jean de France*, written and performed in 1722. Jean de France portrays a student, Hans Frandsen, who has lost all of his common sense and a good part of his father's money on his study tour to Paris. He has become a Francophone fool who is brutally punished and put out of the way so that his fiancé can marry the loving and reasonable young man, Anthonius. The comedy is a hilarious demonstration of Hans Frandsen's French infatuation, including a long discussion between his father and his fiancee's father on youth and education.

The humour of *Jean de France* is gritty, and some scenes become independent of the main plot. Holberg himself emphasizes that he intends comedies like *Erasmus Montantus* and *Jean de France* to 'entertain and teach'.[34]

But it is clear that, with *Erasmus Montanus,* Holberg tries to approach the topic of learning in a new way, while in *Jean de France*, that has a very well known topic on harmful foreign travels, he more randomly gets hold of some important side issues. Several scenes are loosely tied to the plot, which means that more side themes can be developed. The comedy frequently occurs in the imbroglio between French and Danish and creates coarse language satire.

The main side theme relates to the maid Martha, who is the master of the plot. She compares herself several times with a comedy writer inventing a new intrigue. While her male fellow servant Espen is plotting against the father Jerominus trying to trick him out of some money, as in Plautus' old comedies, Martha tries to make Jean even more crazy than he is. Their friend Antonius asks her: 'But what do you gain by disgracing him in this way?' – and she replies: 'What I gain is that his father – in – law-to-be will prefer to marry his daughter to a chimneysweeper instead of to him. But I don't know how the plot will develop. What happens to me is what happens to every dramatist: writing the comedy they find out how it shall develop and how it shall end. '[35] Marthe improvises and says that success in terms of plot is in fact, as with most of the world, due to 'a simple twist of luck'.[36] The character Marthe is Holberg's own improvisation. She looks like a major cultural surplus that society ought to use much better – she says to Esben: '(...) There will come a time when the public values brain higher than gender, expertise higher than name and then I will be nominated chair of the county and you will become an seller of ables'.[37] Marthe rescues Elsebet from the forced marriage to Jean/Hans, but in fact the comedy ends with a marriage that neither Marthe nor Elsebet wishes: the fathers agree to marry Hans' brother Jochum to Elsebet's sister Lisbet.

The thought-provoking endings of *Erasmus Montanus* and *Jean de France* show that Holberg has started an artistic examination of the outdated education system, the lack of knowledge flow and women's education rather than submitting crystal clear morals. He follows the artistic possibilities of his characters and his idea to get the audience to think and judge for themselves.

Holberg's successor at the theatre was Charlotta Dorothea Biehl (1731-1788), who was inspired by the French bourgeois comedy of Philippe Destouches, by the works of Jean-François Marmontel and by the Italian playwright Carlo Goldoni. She had taught herself French by reading and listening to spoken language, and although it was very unusual for a woman to come forward as a writer, she managed to attain a certain status at the theatre. Her comedies did not manage to establish any performance tradition at the Royal Theatre and are not played today; only one of her comedies, *Den listige Optrækkerske* (The Crafty Lady Swindler, 1765), has occasionally been performed. This comedy depicts a woman who cheats lustful, decitful men out of their money and it is very witty and, if women authors and dramatists had not been neglected in the late 18th and the early 19th century, this comedy would probably have survived. The main character represents an interesting dramatic challenge to a leading woman actor.

The new star of Danish theatre was Johannes Ewald; he introduces the Nordic mythology as a new interesting topic for expressing feelings and individuality, and in his tragedy containing songs *Balders Død* (Balder's Death, 1778) he uses the story of Nordic half-god Balder to develop a conflict between duty and passion. Ewald also contributed to the patriotism of the late 18th Century with his play containing songs *Fiskerne* (The Fishermen, 1779). Ewald based his play on one of the stories in Ove Malling's newly published *Store og gode Handlinger af Danske, Norske og Holsteenere* (Great and Good Deeds by Danish, Norwegian and Holstein Citizens, 1777). One of these deeds was some Zealand-fishermen's heroic rescue of an English captain whose ship was stranded during a violent storm. The rescue had happened in 1774, so the story was still remembered and on opening night, which was the king's birthday, the rescuers themselves were present and saluted the king from their loge.

Charlotte Dorothea Biehl's main work is her autobiography, *Mit ubetydelige Levnets Løb* (My Insignificant Life), first published in its entirety in 1986. The fine narrative provides a powerful insight into how difficult it was for her to educate herself and work as a dramatist and author. The autobiography also gives a vivid picture of life in Copenhagen, the visiting cultural figures and the young woman's ambitions to achieve recognition. Her self-portrait has a deep understanding of how her isolated upbringing made her a kind of 'old child' [38] for whom it was difficult to act on her own, even after the death of her dominant father.

As mentioned, the script was not published in her own lifetime; she had written the story of her life for her bosom friend Johan Bülow, a prominent courtier (1751-1828) and it was intended to circulate in his circle of friends. Bülow asked her also to report on conditions at the Danish court. The result was her historic letters about Danish kings from Frederik IV (crowned 1700) to Christian VII (crowned in 1766). Dorothea Biehl had grown up close to the court and had been following several events. Bülow provided her also with confidential material so she could write about Crown Prince Frederik's coup against the conservative government in 1784. Bülow chose Biehl as his chronicler, because he knew her ability to create an elaborate story with inlaid anecdotes and of a certain freedom and frankness. Biehl does not hold back when it comes to the portrayal of the changing kings' excesses of drunkenness and adultery. Her historical letters have been heavily criticized and described as gossip from the court, but they have also been used by both historians and writers in the depiction of the relationship between the insane Christian VII, his queen Caroline Mathilde (1751-1775) and his physician-in-ordinary, Johann Friedrich Struensee (1737-1772), who became the queen's lover.

Freedom of the Press

Government took an unexpected turn in Denmark when the physician of the king, Struensee, became the de facto ruler in Denmark and instigated a large-scale reform programme. Struensee issued over 2000 orders in council during the period from 1770 to 1772. The introduction of freedom of the press and poor relief, the abolition of torture and various privileges were among the many reforms. The changes received immediate response. Denmark was quite simply the first country in Europe to introduce unrestricted freedom of the press, and Voltaire himself send a long poem of praise to Christian VII, paying homage to him as a courageous and virtuous monarch. In well-turned verse and making good points, the king is praised for his courageous and sensible disposition which, according to Voltaire, could serve as an example to other monarchs. In the poem, 'Epître au roi du Danemark', he says, among other things:

> I throw myself at your feet, in the name of humanity.
> It speaks through my voice, it benefits from your mercy,
> You give its rights to mankind, and you allow one to think.
> Sermons, novels, physics, odes, history, opera,
> Anyone can write anything – and whistle if he pleases![39]

The fall of Struensee in 1772 led to restrictions being imposed on the free-dom of the press decree. The dramatic story of his execution was a subject in newspapers and periodicals, especially in the form of derogatory illustrations of Struensee and his friend Brandt and of Caroline Mathilde's departure from Denmark. Later, several dramatists and novelists have portrayed those colourful figures and events. Maria Helleberg and Per Olov Enquist offer very different views of history in their respective novels. Helleberg's *Mathilde, magt og maske* (Mathilde, power and mask, 1991) sees the events from the point of view of the very young queen, while Enquist's novel *Livlægens besøg* (The Royal Physician's Visit, 1999/2002) focuses on the zest for life, eroticism and emancipation that Struensee brings with him, and all the political underhand dealings surrounding the insane king. Dario Fo has written the tale, *Der er en skør konge i Danmark* (There is a Mad King in Denmark, 2015) on the drama and the young comic book writer, Karoline Stjernfelt has published the graphic novel, *I Morgen Bliver Bedre* (Tomorrow Will Be Better, 2015 and 2020) on Christian VII. All of these tales and novels are inspired by Charlotta Dorothea Biel's historical letters about Christian VII and Caroline Mathilde. In Biel's interpretation, the relation between Caroline and Christian VII is strong and loving in the beginning of their marriage. But the courtiers disturb their relation and under their influence Christian becomes more and more mentally ill. In Biehl's opinion, Struensee's reforms are carried out to quickly and this causes his fall.

Even though freedom of the press was reduced after the fall of Struensee, singing still took place in the many literary clubs and associations that were founded in the latter half of the century – both convivial drinking songs and political songs that criticized absolutism and the nobility. Later, even the influential German aristocracy of officials was the target of criticism by such writers as the Norwegian translator and poet P.A. Heiberg. The first signs that patriotism was changing from love of the common good in the kingdom of an absolute monarch to a national sentiment were becoming apparent.

In the latter half of the 18th century, German and European influence and import of culture start to clash with young writers' new ideas about a Danish identity. This takes place in a dynamic, conflicting and dramatic way. A series of showdowns with German dominance occurs in connection with the violent events related to the fall of Struensee, the introduction of the Rights of Citizenship (*indfødsret*) in 1776 and the coup against the nationally minded, conservative Queen Dowager, Juliane Marie, the Crown Prince and the leading minister, Ove Høegh-Guldberg, in 1784. The early manifestations of Danish identity are seen in young academics and citizens who are born in the country and speak Danish, but who feel themselves hampered and disregarded in their career opportunities by the ruling aristocracy of officials. Language, birthplace, history, popular community, loyalty to the king and a certain feeling of inferiority regarding German dominance are elements in this early feeling of Danish identity.[40]

One of the statues in Nordmandsdalen, begun in 1764 by the sculptor Johann Gottfried Grund, based on the realistic wooden figures of Norwegian and Faroese farmers and fishermen by Jørgen Christensen Garnaas

P.A. Heiberg (1758–1841) defended Danish language and identity, but he did so, it should be noted, on the basis of ideas from the French Revolution. In a critical article called 'Sprog-Grandskning' (Language Studies, 1799) – which contributed to his being sent into exile – Heiberg defines the word Danish with a satirical sting in the tail: 'a stain on a well-brought-up individual that makes him incapable of holding any important office in Denmark. Can be washed off to a certain extent, but only in foreign water, always leaving a discoloration.'[41]

When a French delegation visited Copenhagen in 1792, it was received with enthusiasm not only by such writers as Heiberg but also in Copenhagen bourgeois homes and business houses. It was perhaps especially the amount of money that could be earned from dealing with the French delegates that counted most. People in Copenhagen quickly learnt to sing along with the Marseillaise in Danish and French, and bourgeois girls and married women fell in love with both the Frenchmen and their ideas, as is described in the novel *To Tidsaldre* (Two Ages, 1845) by P. A. Heiberg's wife, Thomasine Gyllembourg.

In some of the many literary societies of Copenhagen, critical discussion was the order of the day, and after Struensee's fall, the somewhat reduced freedom of printing was challenged by numerous writers. P. A. Heiberg went further in his criticism of the absolute monarchy in some of his songs than did the more policially cautious writer Knud Lyne Rahbek (1760-1830)

In 1790 Heiberg published his famous 'Selskabs-Sang' (Song for a social event) where in he criticized the king for only awarding representatives of the nobility and paying no attention to the work of gifted ordinary citizens, writers and civil servants such as Ove Malling, Peter Frederik Suhm and Tyge Rothe:

> [...] Often on idiots orders hang squarely,
> Ribbons and stars only noblemen grace,
> Though to the Suhms, Roths and Mallings will rarely
> newspapers ever devote any space.
> Those though with wit
> can well omit
> orders and stars from their kit.
>
> Wealth from the cradle all noblemen savour,
> and, as a shoemaker's just made the claim,
> Plutus and Fortuna will only favour
> those with a *van*, *von* or *de* to their name.
> Though we're not rich,
> we've nothing which
> we from the state tried to snitch. [...] [42]

The young Malling, whom Heiberg mentions for his merits along with Peter Suhm, was a great admirer of Sneedorff and was the author of the important dissertation *Store og gode Handlinger af Danske, Norske og Holstenere* (Great and Good Deeds by Danish, Norwegian and Holstein Citizens, 1777) while Suhm worked for a patriotic renewal of history writing. The author Tyge Rothe also contributed to the contemporary debate on bourgeois patriotism and advocated the idea that one's homeland is the country one feels comfortable in, contrary to the idea of the connection between place of birth and nationality, which was expressed in Chr. VII's Native Law Act of 1776. The discussion and debate that Sneedorff had opened gradually became more critical than he himself would have liked. But it is interesting that Heiberg delves into the metaphor that Sneedorff considered crucial to the monarchy of monarchy: the decorations and medals as metaphors of honour. He used Holberg's old dictum of man's ability to know and judge to criticize the absolute monarchy.

Heiberg's political criticism finally led to him being banished from Denmark on Christmas Eve, of 1799. He had previously been given warnings and fines for his works, but following the new harsher censorship laws by the ruling Crown Prince Frederik in September 1799 he was accused and sentenced retroactively to banishment. In the courtier Johan Bülow's letter book we find a brief description of Heiberg's departure from Copenhagen. It is not known who sent this letter to Bülow, but he inserted the letter as one of the important historical testimonies to his letter book, which he considered to be a kind of secret history writing:

> 11th February CPH: A large number of fops and a literary mob were present to escort this Martyr of Truth. Rahbek and his wife as well as the citizen Wedel Jarlsberg sat with him in the car and followed him to Roskilde, from where the journey continued to Hamburg. They shouted hurray in the street and wanted to pull his wagon through the town, which he refused. The Chief of Police was unaware of this.[43]

Heiberg settled in Paris where he lived until his death in 1841.

The enlightenment of the sentiments

Heiberg and his friends in Copenhagen dreamt of an emancipation of the individual and of a society ruled by a reasonable and just monarch who allowed freedom of speech.

But the emancipation of the individual was also important to the Pietist movements that gained a footing in Denmark in the first half of the 18th century. Holberg and the writers of the Enlightenment were not enthusiastic about the religious fanaticism that Pietism introduced. Holberg regarded the Pietists as being religious Titans who had completely abandoned the golden mean. He was annoyed at seeing drama forbidden as the work of the devil in 1738, after Pietism had become the state religion of the absolutist Christian VI. The religious revivals took hold of common people, theologians and high-ranking citizens, and the movement was difficult to control, despite the fact that a Conventicles Placard, i.e. a decree prohibiting religious meetings that took place outside the church, in 1741 put an end to lay preachers' religious meetings. Although Pietism was quickly removed from the official programme of absolutism after the death of Christian VI in 1746, it lived on as a popular movement that was renewed in the 19th century by religious meetings and the strongly evangelical Home Mission.

Pietism focused on the religious experience of the individual, and the right way of exercizing religion became more important that the right dogma. The Christian individual had to undergo a personal conversion, confess his or her faith, read the Bible for himself or herself and preach the Gospel to others. The hymn writer and bishop Hans Adolph Brorson writes in a brief story of his life, preserved in a transcript from 1770, about his Pietist conversion. It took place in 1717 while he was a private tutor in Løgumkloster:

> At that point in time he began to gain greater insight into the true nature of Christianity, amidst various temptations, in unceasing prayer and spiritual contemplations to taste the sweetness of the gospels, and it such a way yet more joyfully to continue his theological studies, from which source his well-known Hymn Book known as The Rare Gem of Faith derived, for the resuscitation and refreshment of many souls.[44]

With the Pietist revivals, the authority of the church and the clergy began to waver, since perfectly ordinary common folk simple refused to accept the church's monopoly on reading and explaining holy scripture. The Pietists were 'readers' – readers of the Bible, of course. But it soon transpired that sons and daughters of prominent Pietists started to make their mark on new secular literature. Pietism became a source of literary Romanticism. The pietist reader anticipated the modern writer and poet who is driven by his or her own personal talent and who breaks free of his or her obligations in relation to church and king. The young successful poet Johannes Ewald, who was the son of a prominent Pietist, regarded himself as an artist who followed his own passion, his ability to experience and express himself in poetry. 'The poetic spirit will awaken itself – it becomes refractory when at all times it has to obey the first command that comes along,'[45] he explains in 1780.

Prayer meetings and gatherings of professing and hymn-singing men and women appeared in both the capital and around the country, especially in North and South Schleswig. Here, there was lively contact with the German university town of Halle, a centre for a strong branch of Pietism. A kind of grass-roots movement existed there, one that reacted against the growing rigidity of belief and outer orthodoxy, i.e. an approved, correct doctrine. But lay preachers also emanated from the religious community in Herrnhut, which was under the protection of the charismatic Count Nikolaus Ludwig von Zinzendorf. The count was a pupil of the Pietists in Halle, and he had opened his estate of Herrnhut to a group of persecuted believers who called themselves 'Brethren of the Law of Christ'. They were disciples of the preacher and clergyman Jan Hus, who was burnt as a heretic in 1415. Hus' preaching had many similarities with Luther's Reformation, and after his death his disciples had founded their own church in Bohemia. They were persecuted almost to extinction, however, in the 17th century. In secret, the faith was now passed on from father to son. One of the clandestine believers, the carpenter Christian David, met Zinzendorf in 1722 and asked for protection for himself and his fellow-believers. But the Moravians (as they are known in English) fell into disfavour in Denmark when the Pietists from Halle brought the king over on to their side. Zinzendorf was stripped of his Order of the Dannebrog, and theologians who had visited Herrnhut were unable to obtain any office in Denmark. Contact with the Moravians could quite simply lead to losing one's property.

But nevertheless Brorson, who had become bishop of Ribe in 1741, sent for a Moravian brother to help him when he feared that he had sinned against the Holy Spirit. Brorson's most important song book was *Troens Rare Klenodie* (The Rare Jewel of Faith, 1739), in which he collected the hymns he had previously written and added translations of German pietist hymns as well as hymns by some of his acquaintances. The book ended up consisting of 283 hymns, 81 of which are Brorson's own, original hymns, while more than 190 have been translated from German, based particular on the so-called *Tøndersalmebog* (The Tønder Hymn Book), published by the Tønder vicar Johan Herman Schrader in 1731.

H. A. Brorson's residence, Taarnborg, Ribe

Troens Rare Klenodie (The rare jewel of faith) is organized in a such a way that the drama of faith, doubt, conversion, penance and victory is being experienced by the believer in the seven sections of the work: 'The Joyous Feast of Faith', 'The Growing of Faith', 'The Means of Faith', 'The Fruit of Faith', 'The Battle and Victory of Faith, 'The Glory of Faith' and 'The Conclusion of Faith'.

Brorson does not, as Thomas Kingo, follow the church year but the various phases and themes of religious life. The believer experiences both walking in danger 'where I tread'[46] and walking with Jesus, the angels and God himself.

In the early hymns, God's creation wonders and enchants the individual. The hymn 'Op al den Ting som Gud har gjort' ('Up! Everything that God has made') contains a series of images of the boundlessness of creation and the individual's enchantment, but also demonstrates the incapacity of the human being to verbally express of this enchantment:

[...]What shall I utter, when I see
The woods with life abounding,

The many birds that leap with glee
Beneath the heaven's rounding?

What shall I utter, when I walk
Among the meadow's flowers,
When all the birds in song do talk
Like a thousand harp-string showers?

What shall I utter, when my mind
Down on the seabed merely
So little in its depths can find
And many mouths see clearly? [...][47]

Troens Rare Klenodie (The rare jewel of faith) is particularly intended for private devotion outside of the church, at the vicarage, in the home and by the individual who constantly has to fight to retain his faith and receive the mercy of God. In Brorson's most famous Christmas hymn 'Den yndigste Rose er funden' ('The fairest of roses'), faith is linked to emotion and to spiritual sensitivity:

[...]
You, Jesus, will be beyond measure
My rose and my glory, my treasure,
    My heart you have captured completely,
    Your sweetness does nourish and feed me.

My rose is my jewel and my treasure,
My rose is my joy and my pleasure;
    My poisonous lust you have beaten
    The cross you deliciously sweeten
[...] [48]

Faith is internalized and individualized, and it expresses itself in poetical visions and images that can be used by the individual believer outside of the church institution. Brorson was an enthusiastic lute-player, and at the bishop's residence in Ribe he used to accompany his family when they sang hymns together.

During his short period as *de facto* ruler, Struensee – who was himself the son of a Pietist from Halle – managed to invite the Moravian Brethren in Herrnhut to establish a colony in the open fields of Christiansfeld in southern Denmark. The Moravians acquired their own court of law, and their craftsmen were not forced to join the old guilds. They were even excused from customs and military service. The Moravian Brethren resembled a social experiment, an attempt to kick-start a modernization of the country by simply importing innovation. The industrious people from Herrnhut regarded their handicraft as a testimony to their faith. Good work helped them to be sanctified. One should be able to see and notice from the artefact that it was part of working with the faith. The Moravians brought new handicraft and small-scale factories to Denmark, and even to this day Christiansfeld the honey-cake baker as well as the stove builder are reminders of the Moravians' many skills.

Holberg, Sneedorff and the Moravians had different views about faith and church, but there was one thing they could all agree om: the emancipation of women. And some writing, hymn-writing and preaching women were in the right place at the right time to grasp the opportunity and make themselves heard. But as the 18th century drew to a close, the view of women in literature changed. The poetry of the Romantic period did not like to see women as independently active. Instead, they could be a source of inspiration for male writers.

Early on, Rousseau had placed great emphasis on underlining the differences between men and women – and on pointing out women's physical and mental inferiority. Kant further developed this by viewing the sexes as different and complementary. In his opinion, both sexes were endowed with reason, but man's reason was rational and profound, while that of women was beautiful and tasteful. Women had a sense of the beautiful, while men were preoccupied with the elevated. He concludes that the differences must have consequences in terms of upbringing and education. Women have just as little use of earning geometry, history or geography as they have of the smell of gunpowder![49]

In Kant, there are two kinds of Enlightenment: that of women and that of men. Kant's conception of the crucial differences of reason and soul between the sexes is – on the threshold between the 18th and 19th centuries – part of the world of ideas found in the Romantic salon culture.[50]

Literary tendencies and positions

One of the early poetic attempts of the 18th century was Tøger Reenberg's *Ars Poetica*, which was probably written around 1703. Young Reenberg's verse on the art of poetry takes ideas from the French classicism, which develops in the second half of the 17th century in such dramatists and poets as Molière, Racine, Corneille and Boileau as well as with letter writers and salon ladies such as Madame de Sévigné.

Reenberg (1656–1742), who was a student from Viborg, had as a newly qualified graduate of theology visited both France and England and had lapped up the new literature and literary discussions to be found there. He now published his poems as single prints that could be included in libraries and collections. The Frenchman Nicolas Boileau-Despréaux had published his poetics in 1674, in which he challenged the Baroque under the headline 'simplicity and clarity' and Reenberg unhesitatingly embarked on the same genre. Like his French colleagues, he advocated writing poetry in the mother tongue – first and foremost with clarity and taste, but also with great perfection and elegance. According to the French classicists, perfection could be attained by imitating ideas from poetry of Antiquity. The ancient Greeks and Romans were and remained models. As a poet, one had to keep on writing and rewriting – preferably more than twenty times, Boileau warned. The point was that the reader would not be able to notice any trace of the poet's efforts and work if the art was to live up to its objective to please and benefit. Reenberg also emphasized perfection, saying that Anders Bording in person stood watching over one's shoulder. Anders Bording's light, well-turned verses were – along with those of the Frenchmen – a model for Reenberg. His injunction to the poet was unequivocal and inspired by the rhetoric of Antiquity:

> Be brief, though quite distinct and clear,
> No brimful cup inserting
> That with your aim will not cohere
> And from it is diverging. [51]

He also remarked that a poet must think carefully about who he is speaking to, so that every word can make an impression: 'squeeze, press, bind', as he put it.[52]

Reenberg was one of the first to promote ideas about literature and the art of poetry that were to leave many visible traces in the 18th century. In the form of a French-inspired classicism that stressed imitating the poets of Antiquity and their use of genre and sets of rules for these genres. Classicism attained a high status and was renewed by Holberg, who also re-interpreted the classical genres with which he worked.

In a Danish context, authors imitated their French, German and English models as much as they imitated the masters of Antiquity. Holberg's comedies are far from being stylistically consistent with the comedies of Antiquity. They are often a combination of various literary impulses from the French classicist Molière to the Italian popular *commedia dell'arte* tradition, in which fixed figures such as the servant Harlequin, the merchant, the doctor and the captain improvise on a loosely based plot. The literary researcher and Holberg expert Billeskov Jansen was of the opinion in his analysis of 18th century literature that there was a kind of double imitation in Danish classicism: The Danish poets had the imitation of a foreign model as their point of departure, but they also took the poetry of Antiquity into account.[53]

We also find classicism in another literary tendency in the 18th century within pastoral poetry, hymn writing and landscape poetry. The concept of Rococo is later used for this literature. The concept of Rococo is really an artistic stylistic term from the 18th century, but we can use it as a kind of umbrella term for German-inspired pastoral and hymn writing, mastered in particular by such writers as Ambrosius Stub (1705–58) and H.A. Brorson, and English-inspired landscape poetry, which the Norwegian Christian Braunmann Tullin (1728-1765) sought to promote. A characteristic of Rococo literature is the elaborate thought which is expressed in light, elegant and amusingly pointed verse. The nature scenery of the Rococo often has its point of departure in the opposition found in Antique poetry between town and country. Here, one sees nature as a universe full of gaiety, grace and a splendour that always reminds one that nature is God's creation and a pure miracle. 'So let us rise/And now apprize/How sweetly nature does beguile – and smile', Ambrosius Stub proposes elegantly in his aria 'Den kiedsom Vinter gik sin gang' ('The Tiresome Winter Now Is Gone')[54], which was written for use on social occasions in 1740/41. Stub was also the master of Rococo allegories in poems to do with age and transience, such as 'Du deilig Rosenknop' ('You Rosebud Sweet and Fair'), and he likes to portray himself with a witty blend of frankness and self-irony, as in the aria 'Uskyldig Tidsfordriv' ('Innocent diversion'):

> Innocent diversion's mine
> In music, dance and song,
> While others like to quaff their wine,
> I nimbly dance along;
> The clavichord I love full well,
> and at it dearly would excel;
> An aria I often sing,
> And melancholy put to wing.[55]

Weis' Inn, Ribe. Ambrosius Stub's arias were sung here

Belonging to the picture of the various tendencies and aesthetical positions in the 18th century is inspiration from the new, bourgeois English and French prose, from Daniel Defoe's *Robinson Crusoe* (1719), about a man stranded on an island who basically proved himself to be a bourgeois, society-creating and rationally-acting individual, to Voltaire's already mentioned philosophical novel *Candide* (1759) and Jean-Jacques Rousseau's educational work *Émile, ou De l'éducation* (1762), where the child and nature are cultivated. Defoe's and Rousseau's works, along with Laurence Sterne's *The Life and Opinions of Tristram Shandy, Gentleman* (1760–67), were important prerequisites for Johannes Ewald's autobiography *Levnet og Meeninger* (Life and Opinions, 1774–78), written down in 1774–78, but which first appeared in instalments in the periodicals *Den danske Tilskuer* and *Ny Minerva* at the beginning of the 19th century (1804, 1805 and 1808). Also Jens Baggesen's travel novel *The Labyrinth* (1792–93/1827–32) about his journey through Germany and Switzerland, on to Paris and back to Copenhagen linked up with Rousseau and Sterne.

Johannes Ewald (1743–81) and Jens Baggesen, then, found inspiration in a German and French sensitive literature and poetry that stretched from the German Klopstock (1724–1803) and the Anglo-Irishman Sterne (1713–68) to the Frenchman Rousseau. It is characteristic that, here too, one cultivated and was interested in the poets of Antiquity, but now wished to be inspired in order to be able to express oneself with originality and create sublime art. Sensitive poetry thus broke with the aesthetics of classicism.

The concept of the elevated and the sublime has a profound influence on the discussion of art in the 18th century, from Edmund Burke (1729–97) to Kant, who gives the discussion new dimensions with his *Kritik der Urteilskraft* (Critique of Judgment, 1790). Kant understands beauty as a question of the experience of the single individual, and the elevated and sublime in art give the individual intimations of a world that lies completely outside his comprehension, as well as of the freedom that is man's individual purpose.

Charles de Montesquieu's *Lettres Persanes* (Persian letters, 1721) were of key significance to Holberg's generation, while Samuel Richardson's novel *Pamela, or Virtue Rewarded* (1740) about the virtuous servant-maid was for important to Charlotta Dorothea Biehl and her contemporaries. Voltaire's oeuvre was familiar to Sneedorff and also made an impression on a slightly younger generation about the periodical *Minerva*. Goethe's letter and diary novel *Die Leiden des jungen Werthers* (The Sorrows of Young Werther, 1774/1779) was famous and notorious, it was forbidden in Denmark, but naturally also eagerly read and discussed by both men and women. The novel was a topic in Charlotta Dorothea Biehls moral tale, 'Den unge Wartwig' (The young Wartwig, 1782), where a young man has become totally bewildered by reading Goethe's novel and ends up being cheated by a prostitute.

Nordmandsdalen, Faroese woman on her way to a wedding

In prose, the entire classical literature inheritance was not only used as a model and inspiration – the classics were also parodied and re-used in the style of Sterne and Rousseau. In a Danish context, it was in particular Johannes Ewald who successfully led classicism out in this parodying direction, while Charlotta Dorothea Biehl used the English letter novel and the French sensitive, bourgeois art of comedy as her springboard for writing stories and plays where virtue winds its way through every sentence and is invoked in every other line.

Danish literature and culture, with their strong French, English and German relations, were part of a European literature and culture. Even though Holberg also published in Latin and Jens Baggesen had a large oeuvre in German, the language of literature was increasingly Danish. But inspirations and prerequisites – indeed, the entire horizon of literature – had to be sought in modern European literature and the poetry of Antiquity.

One can ask oneself if any of the Danish 18th century works can measure up to the best books from Europe. Today, the answer has to be yes, even though disseminating the books internationally has not been successfully achieved. Ludvig Holberg's utopian novel in Latin *Niels Klim* (1741), Jens Baggesen's travel novel from 1792–93 and Charlotta Dorothea Biehl's autobiography *Mit ubetydelige Levnets Løb* (My insignificant life, 1787) can now be seen to deserve a place as important works of European 18th century literature. But the best Danish works often had no contemporary history of reception, because they were only known in narrow circles. The works were simply not published because the writers did not immediately regard them as literary works or texts that were intended for publication. This applies, for different reasons, to the autobiographies of both Ewald and Biehl. Others were sporadically or negatively mentioned, such as Holberg's *Niels Klim*.[56] Holberg believed that a critical German review of *Niels Klim* was the work of one of his Danish opponents.[57]

Niels Klim was a great venture; the work is a utopian travel novel in which the Norwegian student Niels falls through a hole in the ground and ends up in foreign and strange worlds. He experiences different types of governance and Holberg's criticism of the church and the absolute monarchy is evident. Holberg uses the novel to develop his ideas on common sense, morality and the common good.

Even though translations of individual works and selections continued to appear in the 20th century and up until the present day, Holberg's works have not gained any significant history of European reception. Recent editions of *Niels Klim* now exist in English, German and French, and when one presents *Niels Klim* at international research conferences nowadays, Holberg's works arouse considerable interest.[58]

The history of European reception of the most important Danish-Norwegian 18th century writers does not have to be a finished chapter.

Baggesen's *The Labyrinth* has been translated into German and appeared most recently in 1986.[59] But as far as Johannes Ewald is concerned, we practically have to start from scratch.

Ewald's authobiography *Levnet og Meeninger* (Life and opinions, 1774-1778) has not been translated, his drama *Balders Død* (The Death of Balder, 1773) was translated 1889,[60] and only a few of his poems are available in English.

Levnet og Meeninger (Life and opinions) is a witty tale of love and poetry and of the art of writing. It is a joyful and amusing narrative mixed with philosophical knowledge and with an awareness of death and of the transistoriness of life. In the opening of one of the famous chapters of the book, Ewald describes a young woman whom he loves, Arendse. 'Did I own an Arendse? Or was it a Dulcinea, whom my imagination created because I needed one? No, by Cupido, I owned or rather I was owned by a lovely, fine and cleaver, noble, regal Arendse – one of those shady beauties, whose smile is like the gleams of the sun on a rainy sky, whose gesture is penetrating and unresistably gleam of sad virtue – one of these demanding, powerful and enchanting brunettes, whom you cannot look at without a dread and hardly love without admiration'.[61]

The poetic language is both embedded in bodily experience, poetic tradition and philosophical discourse, and the book becomes a very special reading experience of humanity and artistic sophistication.

Ewald's poem 'Rungsteds Lyksaligheder' ('The Delights of Rungsted', 1775) praises the power of poetic language and the strong sentiment of the poet:

O poet most blissful,
        That gladness bade come to his dwelling;
To duties most cheerful,
        To freedom, through virtues compelling! –
        All cherubs while winging
        His bold voice hear ringing,
And heavens are gathered around him; and joy
        Unfolds in man's breast, ne'er to cloy. [62]

God and his cherubs are listening, but it is not God, but the reader who appears at the end of the poem as a figure that is crucial to the poet and his experience of nature. This exit does not mean that Ewald relinquishes his belief in God, but the relation of the believer to God is undergoing change, and the human self-reliance of the poet is increasing. This is also true for the hymn that Ewald wrote on his deathbed, just a couple of hours before he passed away. He himself offers God his saved spirit:

To arms, hero of Calvary!
  Lift high your bright-red shield;
For sin and death - as you can see –
  By force would have me yield.

In righteous ire your sword outstretch
  'Gainst those whom you defy!
Hurl from the light – and me poor wretch –
  Such foes before I die.

Safe in your hand I then will view
  My death without dismay;
And my saved spirit offer you
  On its now unmade clay.

…………………………

Oh Lord! Rest and relief vouchsafe:
  Though if you would chastise me,
Teach me endurance – prayer – and faith,
  Let my heart CHRIST suffice me. [63]

The modern moment

In one of his epistles, Holberg discusses the chronology of the almanac as opposed to his own physical experience of time. The whole discussion begins with Holberg, together with his addressee, an unnamed gentleman, being vexed about the official calendar, which is full of saints' days that the user finds totally irrelevant. It ought to be enough just to write Monday, Tuesday, Wednesday, etc. And one cannot actually be completely sure about time and moments of time:

> I recall an occasion when a fine official at a gathering once asked what the time was; he was told that according to the hands of the town clock it was three o'clock, but in addition that the clocks of the town did not show the correct time, so that they differed almost half an hour from the time shown on the sun-dials. The man replied that he did not at all doubt the correctness

of the sun's motion, but that he could not arrange his life accordingly, for when one is obliged to attend a court of justice or a meeting, one has to observe the time as shown on the town's clocks, no matter how incorrect the time shown, and cannot excuse oneself by referring to the course of the sun, should one arrive late.[64]

Holberg is not happy with the time calculations of the saints' day calendar, which is devoid of any practical importance in a modern society, and he makes fun of the possibility of there being a disparity between time as calculated by nature and by culture. He himself speaks in favour of his own sense and calculation of time, based on the needs of the body. He knows what time it is when he feels hungry, and he knows what day of the week it is according to what he has decided to eat: meat on Mondays and fish every Tuesday. So he does not need to speculate about what day of the week it is, or what he is to eat. He believes that the regularity that he observes in his life on the basis of his personal needs has contributed to his living to be as old as he is (65 at the time of writing). The point is that the personal experience of time and measurement of time is the most important – it gives one a good and long life – but that one naturally has to fall in with the time-calculations of society, even when the clocks show the wrong time!

To Holberg, time is a personal sequence that is structured in both a linear and a circular fashion, according to time of life and advancing age and the recurring needs of the body that one ought to deal with rationally and practically. Holberg's time forms a modern, enlightened contrast to the overall, authoritarian sequence of the old calendar with its recurring saints' days.

The individual relation to time which Holberg writes about becomes an important theme for a number of 18th century writers, but the ideas about time quickly move in completely different directions than Holberg's Enlightenment thinking and linear concept of time. Both Ewald and Baggesen attempt in poetry to establish a personal moment in time, an instant when the I-figure gains mastery over time, or when the I-figure's experience is stressed. Ewald writes grandiosely about the time of the emotions and the soul in his poem 'Haab og Erindring' ('Hope and Recollection'):

HOLD fast your Now, my soul! Attempt to savour
The instant's presentness!
Oh, bind the fleeting, taste its flavour
Through feelings' ferventness.

Pond of the Graces, with a sculpture by Johannes Wiedewelt, Fredensborg Palace, 1760-1769

Oh this! – 'tis great – and pure – unblended
With sorrow – virtue-warmed!
Will e'er time's Father send one such, distended,
So with his joy transformed?
Oh grasp, oh feel it, ere it vanishes![65]

The monument Ewald's Barrow, Rungsted Strandvej, 1876. In the park at Rungstedlund there is another Ewald's barrow marked by a monument. At the foot of this barrow Karen Blixen lies buried

Paradoxically, the moment is not really present for a person until it is already past. When the moment is gone, the person recollects its greatness: 'its birth and its death',[66] as the poem says. The sublime time of the moment, however, opens up mysteriously in the poem in shapes and colours about which one can only remain silent: there are no words for it, even though the work of art, paradoxically, is itself language and song.

In Baggesen's *The Labyrinth*, the moment is of special importance. In the winding sequence of the journey the moment stands out and is quite simply a temporal form of experiencing that characterizes the I-figure and the modern poetics that Baggesen develops in opposition to classicism. Baggesen's I-figure perceives the world through moments and with his personality enters into time and art via the moment. The time of the moment marks the presence of the I-figure and turns the journey into a series of turning-points where something new takes shape: a new experience, a new insight, a new mood or a new feeling. Indeed, the journey itself began at a certain moment in time: 'from the moment I entered on my journey',[67] Baggesen characteristically says.

History also manifests itself as a dramatic moment in the form of the French Revolution. One can see how Baggesen, in his attempt to describe history in terms of time, moves from the concept of age to century, from there to decade and the definition he finds most central: 'the beautiful moment':

> Blessed age! blessed century! Yes! What am I saying? blessed *decade*! for which the light of Gaul's magnificent dawn gleams! in which the world – and we – were to see actions deserving to be cast in ore, hewn in marble, and displayed in paintings for the admiration of posterity!' – Oh! Happy me! Thrice happy me, that fate allowed me to view *Europe* at this beautiful moment when reason starts to rub the long – long – long *Slave-slumber* from its delightful eyes![68]

Baggesen's *The Labyrinth* is one of the 18th century works that has gained a major Danish and German reception, and that even now is eagerly studied and discussed in dissertations and articles.[69]

Many interpretations have discussed the sources of Baggesen's inspiration and paid special attention to the labyrinthic aesthetics of the work that actually makes it relatively difficult for modern-day readers, less trained in the reading of texts, to follow what is happening. The many digressions and the long, winding sentences with dashes, exclamations and insertions confuse people. But once one is inside the universe of the work, one quickly becomes engrossed in Baggesen.

It is the aesthetics and discourse of the labyrinth itself that both makes demands and inspires. For Baggesen, as several elucidations point out, uses the labyrinth as an allegory that indicates the artistic interpretation of the journey and the writing process. It is not the surroundings but the interpretation of them that is of interest.[70] The journey, the work of art and life are all included in Baggesen in the image of the labyrinth, which he explicitly uses about the landscape, love, the Revolution and the reading of the book.

The concept of the labyrinth is immediately introduced in the pre-recollection of the work in a heated debate between a collection of readers who end up throwing away the book since it is stupid, German and tasteless.[71] But *The Labyrinth* is and remains the title, and Baggesen's literary version of this figure is what the author and philosopher Umberto Eco refers to as a network labyrinth that has neither entrance nor exit, centre nor periphery, and where all the passages are interlinked.[72]

The journey admittedly has to do with a concrete sequence of events and a movement between localizable places in Germany, Switzerland and France, but the book is mainly seen as being part of a labyrinth:

> The present journey is really a labyrinth – or even more actually: a section of the labyrinth that it is my lot to roam through from cradle to grave.[73]

One might expect it to be the experiencing of places, the movement and the arrival at places and famous localities that formed the most important structural sequence of the text, but although the presentation lists places and makes them into titles within the presentation, the temporal dimension and the experiencing of the moment are, as already suggested, of major importance. The work does move from place to place but is actually formed like an almanac[74] mixed with other genres: letter, diary, treatise, confession, verse, dialogue, maxim and travel guide. Baggesen himself calls the work a completely new almanac based on a subjective experiencing of time, where neither days nor weeks necessarily have the same duration. The various forms of time the reader can experience in *The Labyrinth* are actual time, experienced time, remembered time, the moment and time standing still. In general, the book is written in the past tense that circles round the moment when something new took place, but Baggesen also uses the present tense, not only as a historical present tense, but as a narrative tense which, like moments, are inserted into dairy entries and sequences and create a movement in the time-relation and an unrest in the experiencing of time. The present tense is used, for example, in some of the best-known passages of *The Labyrinth*: Baggesen's description of the sinister Jews' street in Frankfurt and his analysis of the rectangular classicist urban landscape of Mannheim, which he feels is killing him. The summary of his impressions is also formulated in the present tense:

> I feel that my mind, during the short time I have been staying here, has already – contrary to its meandering nature – started more to edge its way forward. Just as water, in the space of a couple of quite cold winter nights, turns to ice. How must it be for those minds that are and remain here constantly? I shudder at the thought.[75]

The leap between times and the compression and extension of periods of time and the way in which the moment is experienced in *The Labyrinth* express a subjective experiencing of time that culminates in the chapter on Baggesen's ascent of the cathedral tower in Strasbourg. Until 1874, the tower of the church was regarded as being the highest building in the

Cross-stitch embroidery picturing Jens Baggesen, the Museum of Local History, Korsør, 1960

world, but Baggesen boldy sets about crawling up to the very highest and last foothold on the spire of this *'Epic in stone'*.[76]

The church building itself Baggesen finds nauseating, an appalling monument to the Middle Ages and Catholicism. To him, it seems like a spiritual prison. The spire, on the other hand, is transparent and leads right up into the purest air and into the experiencing by the I-figure of himself as a being that alternates between point and infinity. The I-figure experiences his own abstract situation in time and space, where his imagination roams freely and all thought has ceased to exist. The moment leads into an eternally dizzying infinity.[77] It is a quite modern form of expression that Baggesen is describing here, one in which the I-figure perceives himself as liberated from his location, floating in space, in his own feeling and sensation:

Here I stand, a grain of dust, a point,
Half something, half nothing – a sigh –
A thought hardly begun –

Johannes Ewald, Ewald's Mound, relief by Vilhelm Bissen, 1876

> Lost on an atom in the space
> The omnipotence of your eternity fulfils!
> When did I become myself? where am I? and what?
> Where am I being whirled off to? – oh! do I perish? –
> [...]
>
> Is it pleasure or pain I feel in this dizzying state? Am I closer to life or death at this dustless point? I start and cease existing – am created and annihilated – triumph and swoon in one and the same sensation![78]

It is particularly interesting to compare Goethe's and Baggesen's experience of the cathedral.[79] Goethe mentions his visit in *Vor Deutscher Baukunst* (On German Architecture, 1773),[80] describing how all details cohere for him into a great, harmonious unity that transports his soul. The cathedral expresses a harmony that Goethe identifies as being true German architecture. It definitely does not belong to the then problematic term 'gothic', which refers to something overloaded, unnatural and unharmonious.

While the cathedral forms the I-figure and creates harmony in soul and art in Goethe's text, the work of art flings Baggesen's I-figure out into a modern time concept and a modern aesthetic to do with the giddy whirling of the moment between the finite and the infinite, between the dot-like size of the I-figure and its immensity. Precisely the description of the modern existential dimension of the moment here forms a tradition that stretches from Johannes Ewald's experience of the dizzying now of the soul to Jens Baggesen's experience of the opening up of the moment towards nothingness and on to Søren Kierkegaard's dizzying moment of spiritual decision.

Holberg, Ewald and Baggesen all formulate a time-dimension in their works that makes time personal and human. But not until Ewald and Baggesen does the moment become a modern, epistemological and aesthetic category, the dimensions of which are later developed in Kierkegaard in his attempt to give human existence a new spiritual verticality in the form of the moment of faith.

Turning points

When it comes to the history of Danish-Norwegian literature in the transition between the 18th and 19th centuries, one can focus on three turning points: The first is Holberg's oeuvre, especially his Danish-language comedies of the 1720s. Here, we have the first Danish-language art of comedy that helps turn Copenhagen citizens into 'publico' – a public engaged in secular art. This is where a modern literary culture with a wide-ranging European horizon has its beginnings. The second turning point comes with Johannes Ewald's epoch-making publications in 1775, the tragedy *Balder's Death* and the ode 'The Delights of Rungsted'. While Danish-language theatre marked the beginning of a modern literary culture, Johannes Ewald's publications in 1775 are the prelude to a sensitive Enlightenment literature in which writers such as Ewald himself, Charlotta Dorothea Biehl, Jens Baggesen, Friederike Brun and Schack Staffeldt include a European perspective, inspired by French, English and German literature and drama. The third turning point comes with Adam Oehlenschläger's critical rejection of Ewald in his lectures from 1810 and the poet's enthusiastic embracing of Goethe's reconciliatory Bildung thinking. This marks the end to the radical and experimental period in the transition from the 18th to the 19th century.

The ages of longing

1800–1900

The year 1867 was an eventful one in Hans Christian Andersen's life. Honours and variation jostled for position in the 62-year-old writer: two trips to Paris including a visit to the World Exposition, a trip to Switzerland, election to the post of titular Councillor of State on the silver wedding anniversary of the royal couple – and finally honorary citizenship of his native city, Odense, where Andersen was celebrated with a series of glittering festivities around the official date: 6 December. All the writer's longings for world fame and recognition seemed to have been fulfilled. Andersen himself was extremely satisfied although somewhat anxious – and furthermore plagued by a toothache about which he would subsequently tell many stories and that he actually included in one of his last and most modern tales, 'Tante Tandpine' ('Aunty Toothache', 1872).

Andersen was particularly pleased with the Titular Councillor of State honour, since he believed it exercised a kind of magic in his native country. He was titled and respected, and he could be amused at those who wished him to be named honorary citizen of six different towns, since there could now be a suitable dispute as to where the writer was actually born. Gradually, though, the dispute narrowed down to a specific house in Odense. The Andersen project was on the point of succeeding for Hans Christian Andersen: a modern celebrity with a fairytale biography had come into existence.

Andersen had shaped a modern writer's role on the basis of the Romantic idea of the creative genius and he demonstrated time after time how he saw and exploited the writer's opportunities in relation to a new international literary market. He mastered both the naive mode of expression for the really large public as well as experimental narrative style, which interpreted the new world of modernity in an original way. He created himself as an artist when he performed and read aloud for the bourgeoisie, the nobility and the royal family – as well as for the new trade unions. He used and was used by the outside world, he was disgusted, wept heart-breakingly, caused offence and was fêted. A characteristic

Hans Christian Andersen, Copenhagen City Hall Square/H.C. Andersens Boulevard, Copenhagen, statue by Henrik Luckow-Nielsen, 1961

and almost symbolic episode in the life of a modern author was jotted down in his diary entry for 17 June 1872. On that day, he visited the Nordic exhibition in Copenhagen. He compared it with the exposition in Paris, but had to do without something important, something that had also lacked in Paris:

> It annoyed me at the exhibition, here as in Paris, that my bust was absent, whereas those of the other poets and, as in Paris, that of Bjørnson, were present. I was in chocolate – so there it was also possible to *nibble* me.[1]

Modern life as an artist and writer could mean quite literally that one was exposed to being nibbled at and slobbered over by the public.

Was Andersen a celebrity whose staging of his life ended up being more exciting than his art, as happened with some of the writers of the 20th century? No one – neither now nor then – could be in any doubt that in Andersen's case there continued to be a solid artistic foundation for his fame: the fairytales, which Andersen was far from finished with in 1867. But Andersen understood how to create a synergy out of his two texts – his fairytales and his life-story – and to get them to promote each other.[2] His successful model for being a modern, self-made writer was far from unique. Women managed with great trouble to create possibilities for themselves as writers despite constraining norms and ideals for women's lives. New writers from social and geographical peripheries appeared on the scene in an increasingly patchwork literary market. Some of them also survived into the later writing of literary history and became important figures in narratives about 19th century literature. This applies for example to Steen Steensen Blicher (1782–1848).

In the histories of 19th century literature, the modernization of literary culture and role of the writer is an important chapter, linked to new departures between various poetics and aesthetical positions. One can analyze some of the new departures by looking more closely at various generations of Romantics. The generations think in various aesthetical concepts and literary themes about longing, premonition, absence, reconciliation, unity, harmony and *dannelse* (for which the German word *Bildung* is normally used in English). Hans Christian Andersen knew both the good and bad sides of such themes, and his writing often comprises investigative, critical studies of their literary potential and range.

One century – several ages

The cultural and literary situation in Denmark at the beginning of the 19th century, when Hans Christian Andersen (1805–75) was born, and that at the end of the century, when he was long since dead, were miles apart. Andersen's life bordered on the beginnings of Romanticism with the poetry of Adam Oehlenschläger and Schack Staffeldt, and he experienced the climax of Romanticism and the emergence of popular literature in the 1820s and up until the middle of the century.

In literary history, there are a number of important year dates to chose from when analyzing connections and breaks in early Romanticism and all of the modern literary culture around the year 1800. Many literary historical presentations of the Romantic period in Denmark start with the story of how Oehlenschläger is inspired by the philosopher Steffens to write his collection of poems *Digte* (Poems 1803). There is a strong literary-historical tradition for considering precisely this collection as an epoch-making breakthrough for a completely new type of poetry.[3]

The story of Romanticism can be told in several ways, and one can gain and has gained inspiration for such a presentation from both Nordic and European literary history.[4] There is, for example, a tradition in Swedish literature of seeing Romanticism as being anticipated in the 18th century by a 'Romanticism of the Enlightenment'.[5] The Danish professor F.J. Billeskov Jansen is one of the early critics of various literary-historical attempts to find anticipations of Romanticism in the 18th century. He argues in *Danmarks Digtekunst* (Danish Poetry) that one ought to include all of the 18th century under the heading of 'classicism' and see 'sentimentalism', 1784–1802, as the last poetic school of classicism.[6]

The Anglo-Saxon concept of the 'pre-Romanticism'[7] is also used in the Danish context by such critics as Jette Lundbo Levy, Klaus P. Mortensen, Erik A. Nielsen and Svend Skriver in their analyzes of Danish literary history.[8] The German concept *Sturm und Drang*, which is most often connected with the young Goethe and Schiller, is also occasionally used to illustrate the early mediation of Macpherson's *Ossian* and Norse mythology in the mid 18th century, which is regarded as an anticipation of Johannes Ewald's poetry and the collecting of popular poetry by the German philosopher of language and history Johann von Gottfried Herder.[9]

But if one has problems in terms of deciding when the Romantic period starts, and whether or not it is anticipated in the 18th century, the difficulties in that arise from attempts to reach a conclusion on the matter are no less of an issue. And the discussion concerning the beginning and end of Romanticism is further complicated by the fact that the new poets of the 19th century, headed by Adam Oehlenschläger and N.F.S. Grundtvig, adopt a highly critical attitude towards the emphasis on reason shown by the Enlightenment – and especially, as far as

Oehlenschläger is concerned, towards Johannes Ewald. Both see Ewald as a model to be avoided as much as possible. There is no mistaking their fear of being influenced by him. Ewald becomes a literary forefather who is well and truly misread. The reception of Ewald in early Romanticism is thus a living illustration of the thesis of the literary figure Harold Bloom about the fear of being influenced, where new poets try to veil the influence of their predecessors and models.[10] Grundtvig and Oehlenschläger prefer to present themselves as the beginning of the literary golden age, and they have had considerable success in getting this explanation accepted.

When it comes to the end of the Romantic period, the leading figure of the modern breakthrough, Georg Brandes, wishes to draw a clear and sharp dividing line. In 1870, he states that Danish literature must now break away from its infatuation with Romanticism and with its cramped intellectual life and open itself up to new European influences. And precisely around 1870, works are written and published in Denmark that challenge the ideology and aesthetics of Romanticism.[11]

Both the beginning and the conclusion of Romanticism end up being easier to define literature-politically than -historically. But politics is, on the other hand, also part of history. And any historical presentation that ignores the struggle about canonical literature and new departures and thereby the history of the reception of literature lacks perspective. For that reason, posterity has to put up with a historical picture that is somewhat murky. It is also possible to look more positively at the problem and claim that the concept of Romanticism becomes complex and complicated if one wishes to focus on various literary tendencies that are well and truly intertwined.

In my opinion, it is a good idea to list the following literary-aesthetical positions in the transition between the 18th and the 19th centuries and the beginning of Romanticism: First, one can point to the presence of a sensitive Enlightenment poetry with German, English and French predecessors, from Laurence Sterne (1713–68) and Edward Young (1681–1765) to Jean-Jacques Rousseau (1712–78) and Friedrich Gottlieb Klopstock (1724–1803). This poetry influences work by Johannes Ewald and Jens Baggesen, and the first generation of Romantics are both critical towards and inspired by this poetry, since they use it as a springboard. An important year to hold onto in the history of this sensitive Enlightenment poetry is 1775, the year prior to the publication of two of Ewald's works: the tragedy *Balders død* (Balder's Death), which was published in series of *Det smagende Selskab* (The Society of Taste), and the ode

A memorial for Johannes Ewald and Johan Herman Wessel in the centre of Copenhagen, by Otto Evens, 1879

'Rungsteds Lyksaligheder' ('The Delights of Rungsted'), which was printed in the Copenhagen *Adresseavis* 1775, no. 102, 28 June.

In 1775, Copenhagen and North Zealand are the places where practically all poetry in Danish is being written and published, but the literary geography starts to change radically in the first decades of the 19th century. If literary history of the Romantic period exclusively follows the nocturnal walks of Oehlenschläger and Steffens in and out of Søndermarken and focuses exclusively on the year 1802, it results in both a simplification and a distortion. The first decisive literary innovation that leaves long-lasting traces in the 19th century and into Romanticism can be pinpointed to 1775, when important works by Ewald were printed. With Ewald, a strongly formulated sensitive subjectivism finds expression and the role of the poet becomes a professional one. Ewald was, and was perceived to be, a poet – not an official who wrote poems.

Early Romanticism, the main year of which is 1803 with Oehlenschläger's remarkable debut, is a German-inspired universal Romanticism, and it has the young Oehlenschläger, Staffeldt and Grundtvig as its main figures. The second and third generations of Romantics cultivate a Bildung-poetry influenced by Schiller, Goethe and Hegel, and its representatives are in particular the mature Oehlenschläger, Johan Ludvig Heiberg (1791–1860) and Thomasine Gyllembourg (1773-1856). With these generations also follows a Herder-inspired national-Romantic poetry to which many poets contribute.

Among the second and third generations of Romantics from the 1820s and 1830s (Poul Martin Møller, B.S. Ingemann, St. St. Blicher, H.C. Andersen and M.A. Goldschmidt) there are various divergences between a reconciliatory Biedermeier poetry and a reflective Romanticism.[12] In addition, the 1820s mark the breakthrough of a new popular prose literature. A number of authorships lie in the tension between the two tendencies, such as those of Emil Aarestrup, Carsten Hauch and Ludvig Bødtcher. It was a later writing of literary history which, inspired by art history, started to call the new harmony-seeking literature Biedermeier literature. The name was taken from a naive schoolmaster who was parodied in a popular German comic paper of the 1850s. *Bieder* in German means respectable, good-natured, ingenuous, honest – and Biedermeier literature was interested in portraying literary characters and their surrounding world in a reconciliatory, poetic and harmonious light. The world of the family and the home were a central focus, as Hans Christian Andersen does so well and playfully in 'Moderen med Barnet' ('Mother and Child'), better known as 'Hist hvor Veien slaaer en Bugt' ('At the bend made by the road', 1829). He elegantly demonstrates that the Biedermeier formula is quite predictable. He even allows himself the line: 'Setting sun – you know what follows.' The reader is invited to invent even more cosy details for this genre picture of mother and child.[13]

Part of the picture of Romanticism, however, is that cutting across the generations is a radical Romanticism that very much applies to parts of the work of Andersen, Grundtvig, Blicher and Kierkegaard. Here, a sensitive poetry of longing, absence, disunity and passion is revived, known from both Ewald and Staffeldt.

If one works in a historical overview with a division of literature into three Romantic generations and uses such concepts as a sensitive poetry in the 1780s and 1790s, a universal Romanticism, a Bildung-literature, a national Romanticism, a Biedermeier literature, a Romanticism and a radical Romanticism, it becomes possible to show how authorships shift between various literary-aesthetic positions. Neither Oehlenschläger, Grundtvig, Andersen nor Thomasine Gyllembourg work from start to finish on the basis of the same fully formulated Romantic poetics. Their authorships change, also under the influence of the development of the literary culture with new publishing channels and the emergence of new literary environments. Grundtvig's long struggle with Norse mythological material and his historical studies and presentations can, for example, only with difficulty all be grouped under the concept of national Romanticism, even though this is sometimes done in literary history,[14] because the works deal to a greater extent with a theological and Norse topic than a national problematics. His *Verdens-Krønike* (World Chronicle, 1812, new version 1814 and additions 1817) is an international history of society, culture and literature that describes the various peoples and authorships on the basis of their beliefs and relations to God.[15] At the same time, Grundtvig, like many others, is a diligent contributor to both poetry about the mother tongue and patriotic songs in connection with the dramatic national events of 1807–08 (the unsuccessful Danish participation in the Napoleonic Wars) and in 1847–48 (the prelude to the three-year war with Schleswig and the abolition of absolutism). This applies to songs such as 'Kommer hid, I Piger smaae!' (Come to me, young lasses all!, 1810)[16] about the naval hero Peter Willemoes, who was killed in battle against the English Navy off Sjællands Odde in 1808, and several versions of the Swedish popular melody 'I walked abroad one summer's day to hear' (1847)[17] about the good Danish life from the Sound in the east to Dannevirke in the south.

To Grundtvig, Danishness is identical with mother tongue, humanity and popular character, and he always underlines that the human race is one and the same everywhere, since it exists as various peoples.[18] But in his opinion, Denmark has a special God-given calling in the renewal of Christian religious life, and with nationalistic zeal he emphasizes

Danishness as a living sentiment, a form of life and a linguistic identity. Nationality and language belong inextricably together in a mode of thought that one would nowadays refer to as linguistic nationalistic. The nucleus of a people, according to Grundtvig, is first and foremost the farming class, the peasantry and women.[19]

When it comes to the literary-historical analysis of Romanticism, one must not be too schematic. A literary-historical presentation and overview must make it possible to show aesthetic movements, contexts and contrasts as well as be able to describe the changes in the literary culture, the new publication possibilities, the new author roles and the various shifts between literary environments: clubs and literary associations, new periodicals, North Zealand salons and vicarages throughout the country.

When determining the literary culture at a more general level, it makes good sense to talk of the period between 1770 and 1870 as the age of Romanticism. But far more literary-historical concepts have to be used when one delves into the various oeuvres and works.

In her large novella *To Tidsaldre* (Two Ages, 1845), Thomasine Gyllembourg contrasts the radiant age of revolution at the end of the 18th century with the age around the mid-19th century. Gyllembourg relates how a new literature and new ideas from the French Revolution reached Copenhagen during 'the age of revolution' and caught the enthusiasm of the city's young bourgeoisie. By the middle of the 19th century, her friends have scattered to all points of the compass, and bourgeois homes have declined into superficial Bildung and a love of pleasure. Gyllembourg's lengthy work on writing Romantic Bildung narratives concluded with a critical text about two cultural ages, the beginning of Romanticism and its apogee in the mid-19th century. Thomasine Gyllembourg herself did not, however, manage to experience or take part in the break-away from Romanticism. Her writing culminated with *To tidsaldre* (Two Ages), and she died in 1852.

In retrospect, Gyllembourg's authorship in particular, along with that of Kierkegaard, Grundtvig, Blicher, Ingemann, Goldschmidt, Aarestrup, Ludvig Bødtcher, Hauch and Andersen were cornerstones of literature in the mid-19th century. Andersen also came, with his late tales, to prepare the modern breakthrough of a new age around 1870,[20] when Herman Bang, J.P. Jacobsen, Amalie Skram and Holger Drachmann could be counted among the most important writers, and the literary figure Georg Brandes, with dazzling eloquence, summed up his ideas that Danish literature was in need of new inspiration from European literature. He gave the new programme the title: The modern breakthrough.

The New Hans Christian Andersen House and Museum in Odense by the Japanese architect, Kengo Kuma, 2021

The 19th century included the literary ages of both Romanticism and the modern breakthrough. Longing is a central theme and concept for both ages. While Romantic authors longed and in their poetry sought infinity, freedom and eternity, the writers of the modern breakthrough focused on people's lives in the present. Here, longings were often disappointed, or they found neither time nor space. Brandes felt that the major Romantic tendencies in European literature had never really manifested themselves in Denmark. His ideas about a modern longing for freedom were thus to a great extent a transmission and updating of a European Romantic programme concerning a radical, intellectual freedom. The right to freedom and critique of Christianity were and remained the nucleus of his philosophy of man.

But while literature renewed itself and was followed by a small and, at times, indignant public that in particular came from the capital, Copenhagen, popular literature in the form of magazines and weeklies, historical novels, stories, biographies from home and abroad were being read by an increasing number of people around the country.

The many longings and dreams about life that Andersen had as a child in the poor part of Odense originally came partly from popular literature, partly from his father's accounts and partly from the fairytales and oral tales he knew from his grandmother and the other old women at Odense Infirmary. Andersen had read a surfeit of popular biographies about famous men and imagined that his life would take the form of entering into such a story. He felt that if only he considered his life to be a story of fame and intrepidly started to act like a hero, then the story would soon bring life into line. In an autobiographical retrospective look, he made fun of his childlike fantasy about the fairytale of life, but one notices at the same time that he believed in the child's yearning interpretation of life. It was precisely the child's ideas that he followed when he insisted on being the main character of his own life and tried to make life fit the story. In the developing modern society with industrialization and a new social mobility, the child's strategy was not without potential. But a brilliant, happy ending to such a modern fairytale was almost just as rare as Andersen himself.

The modern fairytale – radical Romanticism

Some of Andersen's tales have precisely to do with the fact that the longings and dreams of the main characters give them life-stories with anything but a happy ending. Here, a theme of disunity and absence that also applies in universal Romanticism is radicalized, and to get a concrete, literary impression of the tensions and range of Romanticism one can take a closer look at one of Andersen's tales about the two ages of the 19th century. There are several one could choose between, but especially well-suited is 'Dryaden' ('The Dryad'), which Andersen wrote under the impression of the manifestation of the new, modern life – the World Exposition in Paris in 1867.

The main character of the fairytale is a young female nature spirit who lives in a lovely chestnut tree. As a figure, the dryad derives from Greek mythology where her fate is linked to the life and death of the individual tree. During her childhood, the dryad lives happily and well inside her tree, which stands in a peaceful village – very much in accordance with the genre picture 'At the bend made by the road'. But the priest's teaching of the village children in the history of France and its heroes, combined with the lights from Paris, cause the dryad to long to experience 'The Magical City' and the great world exposition. She comes to

Paris, but longs even more strongly to escape from her tree and be able to move freely about the city. She prays to the higher powers to be allowed to experience a night in Paris. Her longing becomes reality. But reality turns out to be full of illusions and death. The dryad disappears like a tear in the morning sun, and with her the young chestnut tree also dies.

'The Dryad' is a fairytale about a modern culture that creates longings and wishes that cannot be fulfilled, but only result in ever more longings. The spirit has allowed itself to be tempted out of nature only to end up in the urban universe as 'a tear, rounded, disappeared'.[21] Andersen is quite unrelenting in 'The Dryad', ending with a highly ambiguous remark in which he airs a goodly portion of Romantic irony: 'All this has happened and been experienced. We ourselves have seen it, at the Paris Exposition in 1867, in our time, the great and wonderful time of fairytales'.[22]

The reader involuntarily asks himself why the narrator calls the modern age the great and wonderful time of fairytales when the tale has to do with a beautiful, young female spirit who perishes. Is modern culture spiritless? The tale of the dryad tells of a new age full of longings. But the longings are not, as in early Romanticism, directed towards an ideal, a lost mythical age, towards a new golden age, towards something divine or the eternal. Now the object of the longings is the body, movement, light, speed, change and the satisfaction of the senses through sights, sounds and images. The fairytales of modern life are delightful and fascinating, but also dangerous and destructive. They are linked to the moment, to mind and body.

Here, the spirit is tempted out of nature and is allowed to gleam briefly, while the moment is transformed into a second, and the spirit perishes, as does the dryad herself. The French poet Charles Baudelaire (1821–67), ten years before Andersen, had written about the modern urban universe in *Les Fleurs du Mal* (*The Flowers of Evil*, 1857/1906). It was a truly epoch-making book – the first modern major work of European poetry, quite simply. When Baudelaire wrote about the new times, he used both a new and a traditional poetic vocabulary about the modern taste for nothing, about the spring that loses its scent and time that eats humanity, about prostitutes and carrion. In a verse from the poem 'The taste of nothingness', 1859 he writes:

And Time engulfs me in its steady tide,
As blizzards cover corpses with their snow;
And poised on high I watch the world below,
No longer looking for a place to hide.
Avalanche, sweep me off within your slide![23]

Andersen's boldness of image and expression is different from that of Baudelaire, although they have the same artistic consistency and share a special nerve for rhythm and sound in language. Unlike Baudelaire, Andersen is a narrator, and as such he is particularly aware of the relation between the spoken and the written language and that a whole world of images is developed in the course of the narrative. As a poet, Baudelaire has his attention particularly fixed on the poetic image's potential for concentration and compression. Andersen's 'The Dryad' tells of annihilation, fragmentation and the cruel and wonderful glimpses of a second, and he uses a classical figure, the dryad, to develop the story – which he wrote, by the way, alongside visits to Parisian brothels. According to what he himself said, he was not tempted to anything other than conversations with the prostitutes.[24]

Modern culture is not spiritless in Andersen's text, but its relation to spirit takes the form of annihilation. Modern life gets people to send their consuming and thus annihilating looks in all directions: 'We saw it ourselves,' as it says at the end of the fairytale. The curiosity and desire cannot be satisfied, only nurtured by new sights. The female bel-esprit of Romanticism, the dryad, has become a modern consumer of fascinations and experiences.

Andersen uses a Romantic irony that punctures the illusion and framework of the fairytale. The narrator comments on his fairytale and calls the new age and the harsh tale great and wonderful. It is as surprising and unexpected as Andersen himself.

In 2005, the bicentenary of Andersen's birth, it was, typically enough, 'The Dryad' who was subject to one of the most stimulating artistic treatments in the one-man show 'The Andersen Project' by the Canadian artist Robert Lepage. Lepage moved the action 100 years forward to 1967. He was thereby able to show the artistic problematics of his own age at a time when a new postmodern, pornographic culture was taking form.

Each time one has the feeling of getting a firm grasp of Andersen's writing, he surprises one by letting a modern, experimental form and a modern theme, as in 'The Dryad', alternate with a naive, reconciliatory Biedermeier story as in 'The Cripple' (1872), in which all the conflicts are ironed out and only a single bird has to abandon life and die a meaningful death so that a young, pious cripple can be made healthy and rich.

Georg Brandes, who already as a young man had had a keen, appreciative eye for Andersen's tales, did not particularly like 'The Dryad'. He felt it was one of the blemishes on Andersen's art. Here, Andersen had discovered the limits of the form by going beyond them. The tale, in

Brandes' opinion, became unpoetic when the dryad left her tree. Dryads simply cannot do that! But Andersen's dryad had to leave her tree, for the tale takes place in a modern culture and deals with the relation of this age to myths, poetry and spirit. Andersen's challenging confrontation of the Romantic world of ideas and modern culture as well as his analysis of the exchanges between Romanticism and the new life were things Brandes did not have an eye for. But Brandes had a sharp sense of all the different keys and of the range of the fairytale as a genre and he appreciated Andersen's most famous fairytale 'Den lille havfrue' ('The Little Mermaid').

The character of 'The Little Mermaid' has become a national Danish Icon, due to a well-known statue made by Edvard Eriksen 1913 and due to numerous mermaid-accessories: from porcelain figures and dolls to carnival costumes. But the fairytale is not a story of Denmark and has no happy ending although the Disney film, 'The Little Mermaid' (1989), provides the story with such a device. Andersen's fairytale is, like the 'Dryad', a story of longing and of a problematic modern self-realization. The little mermaid seems to be driven to leave her realm of the sea by her love for a prince, whom she has saved from drowning. Love, however, is perhaps not as unambiguous an entity as one might think at first sight. Does the mermaid love the prince because he resembles a statue she has placed in her garden on the sea-bed? Love and longing in Andersen's work are not so simple as they first looks. The text says the following about the mermaid's garden with the statue:

> [...] while the other sisters added the most remarkable things they had taken from stranded ships as decoration, all she wanted to have, apart from the rose-red flowers that resembled the sun high up above, was a beautiful marble statue, it was of a fine-looking lad, carved out of clear white stone and left on the sea-bed after a ship had foundered. At its base she planted a rose-red weeping willow, it grew splendidly and hung with its fresh branches over the statue, down towards the blue sea-bed, where its shadow appeared to be violet and in motion, just like the branches; it looked as if the tree-top and its roots played at kissing each other. [25]

This erotically tragic scene created by the mermaid in her garden, one where the weeping willow kisses itself, she repeats later on when she saves the prince from drowning and kisses him when he is at the point of dying:

> When morning came the bad weather was over; not a shred of the ship was to be seen, the sun rose red and gleaming out of the water – it was as if this

The statue of the little mermaid was exhibited at the World Exibition 2011 in Shanghai where the Danish Pavillon became one of the most popular

brought life to the prince's cheeks, but his eyes remained closed; the mermaid kissed his lovely high forehead and stroked back his wet hair; to her he looked like the marble statue down in her little garden, she kissed him again, and wished for him to be allowed to live.[26]

The prince, for his part, loves the mermaid, but he loves her because she resembles someone else: the girl he saw when he woke up on the sea shore. A strange pattern emerges here: the mermaid and the prince are both in love with the image they have created of their beloved, and the prince does so to such a degree that he does not recognize the mermaid, indeed, he can scarcely recall the first time he saw her. He also dresses her like a boy – so that she resembles him, which is a thought-provoking image of the fact that he is bound by his own fancies. That which differs from himself he attempts to transform into his own mirror-image.

The prince marries a princess whom he meets because he believes that it was the princess and not the mermaid who saved him on the sea shore. This must be deemed to be a troublesome love, one where those in love are bound by their own fancies rather than focusing their attention on the object of their love.

When it comes to the mermaid, it is more the prince's feelings than her own which cause her to refrain from killing him and becoming a mermaid once more. When she hears the prince mention his bride's name in his sleep, the mermaid flings the knife that the witch gave her sisters into the sea. By naming her, the prince has moved from the world of his illusions: saying the name means he speaks the truth about his love, and to this truth the mermaid then submits. He says her name in his sleep – like a true romantic, for whom everyday consciousness is always a barrier that shuts the individual out of the real, spiritual world. The little mermaid gives up her plan of murdering the prince's bride and choses to try to archieve an immortal soul by becoming a daughter of the air. In an existence as pure nothing, she can at least struggle to achieve the individuality that is part of being immortal and that becomes her most sincere desire and longing, more important than her love of the prince.

"The Little Mermaid' can be interpreted as a rather cruel story about a form of individuality, narcissism and self-scarifying femine gender role that emerges with modernity and it has a parallel in the Norwegian Henrik Ibsen's famous drama, *Et Dukkehjem* (*A Doll's House*, 1879). Ibsen's drama is a realistic play about a wife who ends up leaving her husband after having tried in secrecy and by a very naive economic fraud to help him when he was seriously ill. Both Ibsen and Andersen use a female figure to express the conflicts of a modern loss of cultural tradition and a modern search for individuality and self-dependence. The female figure becomes an icon for important aspects of modernity in the way that Rita Felski has pointed out in her dissertation, *The Gender of Modernity*, 1995.

Romantic longings

Around the year 1800, Adam Oehlenschläger was becoming a model for a new type of poet, the young genius, who could be praised by connoisseurs at the writer's home of Knud Lyne and Kamma Rahbek at Bakkehuset and by the slightly older generation in the form of the mature Jens Baggesen. He symbolically handed over his Danish poet's lyre to the young man when he returned to Paris in 1800. In December 1802, Oehlenschläger's debut poem was published.

Digte (Poems, 1803) had the appearance of an epoch-making work, with programme poems, drama, ballads and poems about what poetry is. In an innovative way, Oehlenschläger had used genres, metres and themes. The three sections of the collection: romances, mixes and 'Midsummer Eve Plays' formed fascinating and varied poetic patterns.

The large programme poem was 'Guldhornene' ('The Golden Horns'). It indicated what the young poet wished and wanted. And there was no mistaking his aim: 'The Golden Horns' was a sharp criticism of a learned culture and a society that was intellectually gutted, where people had no sense of history, myth and art. For generations of readers, the poem became the incarnation of Danish Romanticism.

Adam Oehlenschläger, The Royal Danish Theatre, statue by H.V. Bissen, 1861

At the beginning of the 21st century, the picture has become less black and white, and more poems and poets have to be taken into consideration when talking about Romanticism on Danish soil. Schack Staffeldt's poem 'Initiation' (1804) is on the verge of taking over from 'The Golden Horns'. But for most of the 20th century, 'The Golden Horns' was the core text of Romanticism.[27]

Oehlenschläger's poem gave a poetically poignant interpretation of the find of the two Gallehus horns, the 'gleaming pair from days of yore' that had been discovered in 1639 and 1734 in a field near Møgeltønder. The mysterious horns had, in Oehlenschläger's interpretation, brought 'times most olden' and 'these miracles from outside time' into the present and given promises of the beginning of a radiant new age, 'in later ages dazzling'. The present day, however, was incapable of perceiving this sacred mystery which had to come from the gods themselves. People only saw the magnificence and preciousness, not their spiritual and mystical powers, and the hope of an intellectual revival dwindled when the gods took back the horns:

Sacred mystery enshrouds
ancient runes and signs.
A holy aura trembles round
these miracles from outside time.

Honour them, for fate can falter
soon maybe no more they'll rove.
May Christ's blood on God's high altar
fill them, as did blood the grove.

You see gleam as the whole story,
not what's venerable and high!
Only show their outer glory
to a dull indifferent eye.

Skies grow dark, the storms awaken!
Certain hour, your word is law.
What they gave has been retaken.
What was sacred is no more.[28]

But, but alas and alack, the golden horns are not appreciated and so they disappear! The poem describes how the gods take them back; in reality,

Elers Kollegium, Copenhagen

the horns had been stolen a few months before Oehlenschläger wrote his poem, and it was later discovered that they had been melted down. What remains today are two pairs of earrings made by the thief. They are exhibited at the Danish National Museum in Copenhagen

The Norwegian natural scientist and philosopher Henrich Steffens (1773–1845), in a marathon conversation lasting 16 hours – including a meal of beefsteak and red wine – had inspired Oehlenschläger to write 'The Golden Horns'. Steffens had come to Copenhagen in 1802 after a study trip to the stronghold of German Romanticism, Jena, where he had been in contact with such figures as the philosophers Johann Gottlieb Fichte (17621–814) and Friedrich Wilhelm Joseph von Schelling (1775–1854) and the writer Johann Wolfgang von Goethe (1749–1832).[29] In November 1802, Steffens began to give his lectures in philosophy and natural science at Elers Kollegium. Many young listeners heard his mineralogical and geological presentations. His ideas anticipated and harmonized with the new natural science that was to reach its climax in H.C. Ørsted's discovery of electromagnetism in 1820.

Steffens also spoke critically about how bourgeois life fettered individuals from birth. Time itself, Steffens said, holds man imprisoned, so he does not gain contact with the eternal and the divine. For that reason, it is the poet's task to create holy images of the eternal.[30]

All of Oehlenschläger's account of the long conversation with Steffens can be seen as the expression of a Romantic attitude to time and the experiencing of time. And the intense time spent together by the two beaux esprits breaks completely with bourgeois life's time-framework and structuring of existence in the public and private spheres. Abandoning oneself to inspiration and the special learning process of the genius takes one beyond time and space, and the narrative becomes effective communication of Romanticism and the difficult concept of the genius. Oehlenschläger's story of the Romantic breakthrough takes its strength and impact from being understandable to everyone.

In 'The Golden Horns', Oehlenschläger also worked with the theme of a captivating and liberating time, and he did so by contrasting times and spaces. He wanted to show via the poem that the stamp of eternity, which the horns possess in the right hands and with the right recipients, can create new times, ones that are linked with the most ancient times. The reader witnesses an imposing movement through times, from the present-day time and space to the time and space of the gods and into history at three points in time and in three universes.[31]

The first point in time is the time and space for the find by the young peasant girl of the first horn: One lovely morning, when the girl is thinking thoughts of love and is on her way out to the field, she stumbles and, blushing and 'amazed at the sight' and 'with hands snow-white' she lifts 'from the earth's black hold/the crimson gold'. Time and space for the

The house in Vestergade in Copenhagen where Adam Oehlenschläger lived while working on his debut collection

young man's find of the second horn during his ploughing is portrayed as a ringing moment:

> The plough seems to freeze,
> and a shiver is heard
> to pass through the trees.
> Flocks of birds
> cease to call
> Holy silence
> consecrates all.
>
> The ringing of old
> of ancient gold.[32]

Finally, the poem describes the 'certain hour' when the gods intervene in the present, shutting the heavenly gates to their eternity.

The free movement of the poem through various times expresses the longing for the divine and eternal and shows in practice the possibilities the poem has to transcend the prison of time. When, as Steffens said, the poet sings, an endless imagery spellbinds the reader. Steffens uses the concept of allegory in connection with this language. This is an extension of the way in which the concept of allegory was used in the Enlightenment. Here, one spoke of allegory as a figurative mode of expression with several meanings, while the symbol described a more abstract, non-ambiguous mode of expression. On several occasions, Goethe formulated important Romantic hypotheses concerning the allegory and the symbol. He began by criticizing the allegory, where the image – in his opinion – became an example of an idea, while the symbol could form a living, instant revelation of the idea. The idea was thus able to be living and active in the image-formation of the symbol. Paradoxically enough, according to Goethe, the idea is both expressed and yet remains unexpressed. To Goethe, the symbol was a living, momentary revelation of something unfathomable.

It was this imagery that Steffens was also on the look-out for – admittedly now using the concept of allegory. In 'The Golden Horns', Oehlenschläger attempted to use such a liberating and new imagery and to turn the horns into a living Romantic symbol.[33]

The tension between times that can be experienced in 'The Golden Horns' was characteristic in general of Oehlenschläger's Romantic poetry. In *Digte* (Poems, 1803) he worked with a historical past, a mythical ancient past, the present and the eternal. The tension between past, future and present, between mythical time and present time, is described in the following way. The present is seen as a falling off in comparison to historical time and mythical time.

> [...]
> My hope is, my hope is, my faith is great,
> the time that is past will once more return!
> Yes, the mild spark of love shall ignite
> divine fire of ancient time's light.
> From the cold ocean's night-time wave
> the sun shall arise from its grave![34]

– thus sings the harpist at the post office in one of the romances of the collection.

Before Oehlenschläger started out on the collection of poems, he had actually had a collection approved for publication at Brummer's the book dealer. The good publisher, however, was unfamiliar with the more precise content of the collection, and after his meeting with Steffens, Oehlenschläger quickly decided to write a completely new collection, which appeared at the unsuspecting Brummer's in December 1802, instead of the one already handed in.

While Oehlenschläger was busy writing new poems after his meeting with Steffens, another poet, Schack Staffeldt was busy after the Oehlenschläger publication getting his own poems published. He tried to overtake the young genius on the inside by claiming that all the poems about his *Digte* (Poems, 1804) had been written before Oehlenschläger's. Staffeldt's attempt to manipulate the time of composition shows something the new importance that the Romantic age allotted the poet's originality and the idea of being the first person to produce something new. While Oehlenschläger's deception of his publisher became an amusing anecdote in his *Levnet, fortalt af ham selv* (Memories told by himself, Vols. I-II,1830-31), Staffeldt's deception made him extremely suspect and resulted in him being side-tracked for a long time in posterity's perception of Danish Romanticism. Later, Oehlenschläger was often presented as the young man who went on to make a fine if somewhat complacent cultural career. Staffeldt, on the other hand, became the poet who stopped writing and ended his days in a dreary position as an official in Schleswig.

Both Oehlenschläger and Staffeldt had a German family background. This was problematic, as the late 18th century patriotic love of king and country in connection with the Napoleonic Wars was replaced by a cultivation of the excellence of the Danish nation as opposed to the German. Oehlenschläger did a great deal to underline that as a child he did not understand a word when his parents spoke German to him. Apparently, it was extremely important for him to show that his mother tongue was Danish. He even amused himself by writing to his fiancée in German when expressing the wish that a litter of kittens should be put down. For he believed that the true-blood Danish kittens did not understand German and therefore would not suspect anything!

Staffeldt's German mother tongue, however, proved yet another stumbling-block for how he wanted to be perceived by others – as a Danish poet. Time and time again, people complained that his language was heavy and long-winded, influenced by German. But part of the story also is that Staffeldt was later rehabilitated as the great Romantic poet of Danish literature as early as the 19th century when the literary critic Georg Brandes presented some of his poetry in a major essay in 1882.[35]

Unlike Oehlenschläger, Staffeldt focused far more in his debut book

Kalliope portrayed by Johannes Wiedewelt on Ludvig Holberg's sarcophagus, 1780

on a Romantic theme to do with space. Oehlenschläger opened up his poetry to 'new times'; Staffeldt opened up his verse to 'a second nature', a second, spiritual, invisible space behind what was visible. The tension is often built up around a conflict between visible space and the possible other space that opens up via the power of the imagination and fantasy. This can already be seen in the opening poem to *Digte* (Poems, 1804):

Initiation

I sat far out on the sound's still shore,
    The skies were smiling;
And filled with longing I gazed down o'er
    The waves beguiling.
The sun slipped into the sea's embrace,
The coast and sky joined in blushing grace.

With sweet foreboding a harp I heard,
    The clouds now rending;
The muse descended, in sunlight girt,
    Her lyre extending.
She sealed my lips with kiss of fire
And sank down into her shimmering pyre.

Then all around me the world was new:
    The winds spoke softly;
From pale clouds drifting before the moon
    Called spirits lofty;
In all creation a loving heartbeat,
My own reflection in all did I meet.

Since then the earth each thought and desire
    Does now imprison;
Though dreams ease longing, as do song's lyre
    And premonition,
The kiss consumes me, no peace can see birth
Before the skies I bring down to earth![36]

The experiencing of the second nature gives rise to longings. But how can the poet become inspired and call forth this second nature? Almost as a kind of meditative preparation, he starts to see nature as active figures: 'the skies were smiling' and the sun 'slipped into the sea's embrace' – already in the linguistic personifications a physical and spiritual space starts to come into existence. The experience of the other nature causes the earth to resemble a prison for both intellect and body. It is typical that, in the other nature – where everything speaks, calls and feels – the poet encounters himself. He senses a greater body or organism that connects all that is alive: 'In all creation a loving heartbeat'. Staffeldt depicts how the I-figure in his artistic inspiration can see through the outer nature and the habitual way in which his consciousness perceives things and thereby makes contact with a greater I, symbolized by the heart, which beats in everything. Even so, the time of this spiritual space is brief, and this makes life in the world almost unbearable. He knows 'no peace'.

In Staffeldt's poetry about the I, there are both echoes of Plato's philosophy concerning the world of ideas and of the Greek philosopher Plotinus who believed that the spiritual radiates in various forms out from one higher spiritual principle. He is also strongly influenced by the ideas of the Enlightenment philosopher Kant about the limits of cognition and the potential of the aesthetic symbol to reach out for true knowledge. The strong, thinking and feeling I-figure in Staffeldt is also reminiscent of the philosopher Fichte's definitions of the I as a striving in which the absolutely spiritual, a divine self, can act.

Staffeldt is more philosophically oriented than Oehlenschläger and his imagery is more compact. His poems even remind one of abstract art when they are inspired by Plato and Plotinus:

By the lake
– And while all the waves are borne off apace,
I feel as if I there too had my place,
And staring into the image-filled lake,
In some strange longing my parting would take.

From still azure depths me greeting, I spy
A different nature, different sky;
All is ethereal there and ideal,
Like things in their pristine form more real.

My very first I from the purest blue,
My once purer self then whispers anew:
Why did you leave me, just leave me and go?
Oh, how I do love you, I love you so!

How strangely afraid and aching I seem,
My spirit escapes to more than a dream:
There appear to be gods and humans who
Embrace and mingle in depths of pure blue.[37]

The abstraction 'pure blue' is an attempt to express poetically Plato's idea that the world of ideas is the true world. The Idea of the Blue is more beautiful and truer than all blue phenomena, and the poem therefore wants to approach a pure abstract form that points to the idea.

In Grundtvig, we find an experience of initiation that is reminiscent of Staffeldt's. The I experiences himself in a greater whole – or rather experiences how the whole awakens within him. This happens in particular in the long and uneven poem 'Strandbakken ved Egeløkke' ('The hill near the coast at Egeløkke', 1811). The poem takes the form of a violent self-reckoning, where the poet accuses himself of having relied too much on his reason, his academic studies and his own intellect – everything that had been praised by the Enlightenment. A painful unhappy love-affair, though, is God's way of teaching him a lesson where the I discovers his feelings and his heart:

In his mercy God took pity
Over me, poor and unworthy,
Taught through pain that tore apart,
That I had indeed a heart
That in cleverness and wit
I, a fool, would trust commit.
Then my spirit's eye did wake,
At the abyss did look around,
Hard and fast a gaze did take
For a saviour, and it found
Found, both here and there:
God everywhere;
Found him in the poet's rhyme,
Found him in what wise men told,
Found him in Norse myths of old,
Found him in the passing time;
Found him clearest when I looked
Deeply in his Holy Book.[38]

In the midst of all labour and learning, a spiritual eye opens in the I and sees itself placed in a dangerous mental landscape on the edge of an abyss. The other space of the spirit is to a greater extent than in Staffeldt placed in the I itself, within the boundaries of the body. The body and intellect of the I seem to be giving in to the pain of the heart, while the huge eye of the spirit opens up in an almost science-fiction transformation between I and spirit. One can mentally picture how the body of the poet is taken over by a terrified huge eye. The eye of the spirit seeks and finds a God everywhere, especially in modes of spiritual expression: poetry, myths, wisdom and in the Bible itself. Grundtvig meets the world of nature with considerable scepticism in the poem – although it finally gains a place in the spiritual context as a cosy childhood garden that the poet recalls. The poem combines a Romantic conception of the spirit with a distinctive, Christian-tinted concept of God.

Grundtvig believed that the visionary person could experience a pictorial, wordless vision that the artist was able to translate into figurative language, into imagery. The strength of the vision is underlined in the poem by the fact that the eye of the spirit is placed directly opposite the edge of the abyss. The effective repetition of the words 'Found him in' adds a further dimension to the vision and its expression. The actual experience of the spirit finding itself and its traces everywhere, precisely when it almost takes over the I, shows once more the importance Romanticism gives to human creative individuality. Strong spiritual forces can be roused and can act through the I. They can create longings that make everyday life almost intolerable, as with Staffeldt, but also bring the I to concrete assignments, as in Grundtvig, who early on felt convinced that he was a spiritual innovator.

Impulses from German idealism

Grundtvig had been a somewhat sceptical listener at Steffens' lectures in Copenhagen in 1802. According to what he himself relates, he was not all that attentive, and when he finally did hear something, he found it hard to understand. Even so, he was later in no doubt about the importance of Steffens for his generation of poets. 'Man of lightning' is what he called Steffens, an expression he also used about Jesus. On Steffens' death in 1845, Grundtvig wrote the following about the spirit he had woken in Denmark:

> Yes, that speech so strong and free
> Of what *hand* can never grasp,
> But from valleys deep we see
> Upward soar to stellar path:
> Then, by *spirit* led, the *word*
> Vision makes where voice is heard,
> Woke up, *Steffens!* here with you![39]

Steffens had presented his contribution to German idealism to the young students of Grundtvig's generation, and his lectures had caused considerable furore. The lectures dealt with the spiritual development and unity of nature and history, and it was quite obvious that German Romantic idealism was emancipatory thinking. It contained new thoughts about God, the world and mankind, since – developing the idealism of Antiquity – it viewed the world of ideas as the real and essential one in relation to the outer, material world. The new Romantic idealism was a reaction against the critical discussion by the Enlightenment philosopher Kant of reason and the limits of knowledge and his definition of the possibilities of aesthetics to symbolize the essence of things. The man from Königsberg, as Steffens called Kant, had given philosophy a hard challenge to meet by stating that man is unable through cognition to grasp things as they are *an sich*. As Staffeldt put it: Kant had stolen a precious gem from humanity, namely the idea of certain knowledge. One could no longer prove anything by referring to God or reason as the final reference. But this theft of a sure ground for thought could also contain possibilities for a liberation. It was Kant's definitions that Fichte and Schelling sought to use to liberate thinking in philosophical discussions, and to which Steffens also contributed with his philosophical thoughts and studies of nature and history. Steffens frequented the Jena circle of philosophers in the 1798–1802 period.

Fichte focused on the thinking subject, who is not to be confused with the I as generally used but should be seen as a striving in the actual thought process, i. e. the absolute, universal reason. He saw the absolute as a process in this thinking subject. This meant that he could use Kant's problem, that man cannot now things *an sich*, to re-open thinking.[40] It did, however, lead to nature appearing to be a barrier, a non-I, that had to be overcome in the realization by the thinking subject of universal reason.

Schelling – and Steffens as well – attempted to adopt a different view of outer nature. Steffens was very enthusiastic about Schelling's idea that the absolute, the universal spirit, in the thought process could be advanced as a unifying principle that linked nature, spirit and man.[41] Steffens had introduced the concept of a primeval state into his thought system. In this original state, there is no distance and division between man, spirit and nature. The unity, however, as it by some kind of Fall, has been neutralized, but in art's conveying of the experience by the creative genius of deep, mystical insight into nature's own creative force this original spiritual cohesion and totality is able to re-emerge. Art completes the philosophy of nature, which is constantly in search of the unity between man, spirit and nature. To Schelling, nature is visible spirit, while spirit is invisible nature, both in constant motion in a spiritual development towards ever higher forms. It is this insight art can realize in creative imagery.[42] Here, the artist does not imitate nature's outer forms but is controlled by the spirit itself. Steffens followed the same line as Schelling when he immediately stated in his first lecture: the spirit moves towards unity. The universe is governed by a universal and eternal 'Impulse towards unity'[43] that realizes itself as a contrasting development towards higher forms. In this process the spirit liberates itself from coercion. 'The living organization, in which all of us are intertwined, dares never to absolutely rest – any standstill would be its death',[44] was the point of view Steffens formulated, and that actually meant that society would change and mankind liberate itself. Steffens was more reticent about describing a state where all opposites would synthesize and the impulse towards unity would be fully realized. 'Our point of view' does not reach that far, he stated. But the idea of an impulse towards unity that led to freedom and change was a bold one in an absolutist society which saw itself as an absolute and eternal divine order.

During his time in Jena, Steffens also met Friedrich von Schlegel (1772–1829), whose definitions of Romantic universal poetry from 1798 linked up with Schelling's view of art. In his programmatic formulations Schlegel wrote:

> Romantic poetry is a progressive universal poetry. Its destiny is not merely to reunite all of the different genres and to put poetry in touch with philosophy and rhetoric. Romantic poetry wants to and should combine and fuse poetry and prose, genius and criticism, art poetry and nature poetry. It should make poetry lively and sociable and make life and society poetic. It should poeticize wit and fill all of art's forms with sound material of every kind to form the human soul, to animate it with flights of humour. Romantic poetry embraces everything that is purely poetic, from the greatest art systems, which contain within them still more systems, all the way down to the sigh, the kiss that a poeticizing child breathes out in an artless song.[44]

Idealist philosophy operated, as mentioned, with concepts of originality, fall and development, and Schelling saw in outer nature forms of consciousness that pointed to the developmental history of the spirit. He believed that art would return man to the original unity with the spirit.

In the dialectic of Georg Wilhelm Friedrich Hegel (1770–1831), the idea of development was continued in an extension of Schelling. Hegel's objective idealism provided definitions of both the dialectic of cognition and of history. He worked with the idea of the world spirit which, in dialectical opposites moved of necessity forwards in every more complex forms. To Hegel, history was proof of the dialectic of the spirit. In a gigantic self-moving process of opposites and the synthesis of opposites, the spirit moves itself forwards to ever greater insight. Reason is the spirit itself and in history it passes through the self-development of the spirit. Unlike Schelling, Hegel did not place art but reason and the philosophy of reason as the highest form of epistemology.

While it was Fichte, Schelling and Steffens who were particularly important to the first generation of Romantics, the Hegelian dialectic was important for philosophy, poetry and art criticism in the following generation. The author, editor and theatre manager Johan Ludvig Heiberg (1791–1860) was inspired by Hegel in all his work. Steffens had made a considerable contribution to the concretization of Schelling's philosophy of nature, and now it was Heiberg who, before the great master himself, used the Hegelian dialectic to analyze and determine the developmental forms of art in a large-scale system of genres. Here, he was able to give art criticism a new direction and acuteness, since it became possible to view the individual work in relation to ideas and thoughts concerning the characteristics and possibilities of a genre or form. Heiberg thought of art as having three parts and as being a dialectical process: An immediate form (poetry) would be filled and modify into its opposite: the mediated reflected form (prose), and out of the opposition between the immediate and the mediated reflected a synthesis would emerge: the speculative (drama). Highest in the genre system were Heiberg's own preferred genres: speculative comedy and vaudeville.

Hegelian criticism was used by Heiberg as a swishing cane in relation to the dramas of both Oehlenschläger and Andersen. And basing himself on Hegel, Heiberg also criticized the Bildung and culture of his own day. According to Heiberg, vulgarization and currying favour had spread everywhere from the amusements of Dyrehavsbakken to conversations at the bourgeois dinner table. The time was ripe for raising standards and for realizing that a true human process of Bildung had to have philosophy as its direction and its aim.[45]

In Heiberg's own poetry, inspiration from Hegel was to be seen in his *Nye Digte* (New Poems, 1841), in which various genres are represented, and which take the form of a spiritual and dialectic process of Bildung that points forwards towards the promising conclusion. Here, the seeking and striving that is described in the various sections of the collection can be dialectically elevated to a 'Striving towards the Light of Freedom'.[46]

Søren Kierkegaard received just as strong a Hegelian impulse, but unlike Heiberg, for him the acquisition of the philosophy resulted in a critique. This did not prevent him from hoping for Heiberg's recognition of his own authorship. That, however, was not forthcoming, even though Kierkegaard was received in the Heiberg home and did not refrain from showering Heiberg with his books or praising both the critic's wife, the actress Johanne Louise Heiberg, and his mother, Thomasine Gyllembourg.

Goethe divides the waters

Heiberg developed his critique of culture and literature and his concept of Bildung on the basis of Hegel's idealistic philosophy and his emphasis on the necessity of uniting poetry and philosophy. But he also gained inspiration for his ideas about Bildung from another of his great models, Goethe, whose Bildungsroman about the apprenticeship of Wilhelm Meister, *Wilhelm Meisters Lehrjahre* (Wilhelm Meister's Apprenticeship, 1795–96/1839) became the main work in the Bildungsliterature that spread in periodicals and in the theatre from the mid 1820s to the 1850s. The works were translated into Danish at the time.

The concept of Bildung, though, already had a long prehistory in the 19th century. As the German term *Bildung* (education) implies, there are precursors of the Romantic concept of Bildung to be found in the idea of Christian theology that man is created in God's image (the *image dei* teaching),[48] and that this similarity with the divine is a spark in the human soul that can be extinguished or made to gleam. Further, the concept of *paideia* from Antiquity, which denotes human self-development into a true, human form, along the lines of Plato's concept of human ascent towards the idea of the good, are part of the Bildung concept. In Enlightenment thinking, the concept of Bildung is developed out of Kant, Rousseau, Herder and Karl Wilhelm von Humboldt (1767–1835) with the conceptions of man being his own goal, that he is born free and independent and that he can change his conditions and possibilities on the basis of a general moral sense and reason. Man forms himself and his world as an order-creating subject and in this respect takes over the role of God. The old deocentrism is replaced by an anthropocentric interpretation of existence[49] that emphasizes man's freedom and autonomy. This does not necessarily mean that any kind of faith is rejected. But God's existence cannot be proved – to Kant, God remains a practical postulate about a high being. This becomes the most important point in the concept of Bildung – that man realizes the spiritual in himself when through the use of a general moral sense he finds himself as an individual. In the regular sonnet 'Natur und Kunst' ('Nature and art') from around the year 1800, Goethe uses the lines of the sonnet as an image that true Bildung and freedom constitute an insight into the general law that applies, in the same way that the lines of the sonnet promote masterly art. The sonnet concludes: 'Such is the case with all forms of refinement:/In vain will spirits lacking due constraint/Seek the perfection of pure elevation.//He who'd do great things must display restraint;/The master shows himself first in confinement,/ And law alone can grant us liberation.'[50]

Linked to the Bildung ideal are not only the idea of a union between art and nature but also conceptions of harmony and reconciliation with the outside world and society. Goethe present's individual development with this reconciliatory perspective in his Bildungsroman, where Wilhelm finally marries the woman he loves, gets involved in practical work and has the prospect of further shaping his personality on a journey to Italy.

An important feature of the novel about Wilhelm Meister is an autobiography of a Moravian woman, 'Bekenntnisse einer schönen Seele' (Confessions of a beautiful soul), which Wilhelm reads as part of his process of personal development. 'The beautiful soul' is a central figure in the concept of Bildung in Romanticism and is developed by, among others, Friedrich Schiller (1759–1805) in a dissertation about grace and dignity: *Über Anmuth und Würde* (On grace and dignity, 1793). The beautiful soul, by its very presence, has a liberating and promoting effect on the development and refinement of its surroundings. Schiller defines the beautiful soul as harmonious, graceful and dignified:

> It is in a beautiful soul that sensuousness and reason, duty and inclination are in harmony, and grace is their expression as appearance. Only in the service of a beautiful soul can nature possess freedom and at the same time preserve its form, since freedom vanishes under the control of a strict disposition and form under the anarchy of sensuousness. A beautiful soul spreads an irresistible grace over a physique lacking in architectonic beauty and often one even sees it triumph over natural shortcomings. All movements that emanate from it become light and gentle, and yet lively. The eye shines bright and clear, and sentiment gleams in it.[51]

Heiberg used the concept of Bildung for his radical critique of culture and literature and he gave it poetic expression in his *Nye Digte* (New Poems,1841). Here, he points out how man is to find God in the depths of his own soul and experience: 'The light of the spirit in the chamber of the soul'.[52]

Thomasine Gyllembourg developed the concept of Bildung in a series of innovative novellas that depict the dreams and reality of everyday life in a bourgeois Copenhagen environment. In her universe, beautiful female souls, full of grace, humility and dignity, were capable of influencing and reconciling the conflict-ridden contexts of everyday life. This meant that the Bildungsliterature also gave rise to a realistic-Romantic portrayal of the outside world and thus paved the way for a realistic tendency in literature in the 19th and 20th centuries.

Oehlenschläger became increasingly interested in Goethe and his ideas concerning Bildung. As early as in his lectures on Ewald in 1810 and 1811 he saw a poetry of Bildung as a counterpart to what he called Ewald's emotional bombast. To him, Ewald is what Schiller calls a sentimental poet, someone who abandons himself to his emotions. Unlike such a poet, a naive poet becomes an adult and is not only interested in himself but also in his fellow human beings and in real life. His poetry rises above the lyrical and becomes dramatic and narrative, and in his work the portrayal of character, composition and action become more prominent than in the sentimental poet, who only has his own emotions to work with. Ewald's poems, according to Oehlenschläger, often become bombastic: 'Bombast consists in an overwrought state where emotions and thought are lost in unsuitable, exaggerated modes of expression.'[53] As a counterpart, Oehlenschläger seeks to promote a kind of poetry that makes harmony and reconciliation its focus. Oehlenschläger met Goethe personally on several occasions during his educational journey in the years 1805 to 1809 and was fascinated by him, viewing him as a father figure.

The idea of Bildung is also developed in Oehlenschläger's famous closet drama *Aladdin* in the second volume of his main work *Poetiske Skrifter* (Poetic Writings, 1805). The drama relates an exotic, oriental fantasy about the cheerful, happy son of nature Aladdin, who plays and lazes about all day. Aladdin gains possession of a magic lamp that gives him both the princess and half the kingdom. In his overweening confidence, however, he loses the lamp, but in a painful insight into his own nature, in which he prays to nature to take him back into her arms and remould him, he regains his magic power, and the comedy ends in a popular celebration and reconciliation around the handsome young prince and his bride. *Poetiske Skrifter* was to be the pinnacle of Oehlenschläger's production. Here, he is able to challenge his characters and give the conflict depth. Aladdin as a careless young man is not an unequivocally, positive figure and his counterpart, the industrious Noureddin, who has struggled for a long time to find the lamp, is not a flat character either. The drama gains further artistic strength from the fact that Oehlenschläger allows a well-known Copenhagen setting to shine through the colourful Arabian surroundings: The audience is to experience that also those who worship Allah in a distant country are human creatures in search of God and happiness. *Aladdin* praises the idea of a higher nature that the hero manages to sense in himself, and the play expresses a humanist idea about the relation of all peoples.[54] The bold feature of *Aladdin* 'is the ambiguity of the characters and the humanist point of the connection between peoples, the dialectic between north and south that is formulated as early as in Sangvinitas' prologue:

> [...] Northern power lacks Oriental fire
> The same as a tempered demant sword
> that lacks a muscular, warm-blooded arm
> to be swung strongly. The flower, strong in seed,
> needs sunshine to be set on fire;
> and if too long a time should pass
> ere *Asians* journey to the North
> to ennoble the race, and warm it –
> then will that race be as alas you see it!
> a flower, long since brought hither from the South,
> but thriving less for every year, and withering
> losing all colour, sluggish, dull – and dying.[55]

The Norse gods, the Æsir, in this interpretation came from the East, and Oehlenschläger composes in skilfully changing metres and genres his *Poetiske Skrifter*, so that in their totality they thematize both the Christian, Norse and Muslim approaches to the higher nature and the divine: A pantheistic interpretation of Christianity in the poem 'The recurring life of Jesus Christ in yearly nature' is followed by the Norse prose tale 'Vaulundur's Saga' and the collection concludes with the drama *Aladdin*, where the concept of Bildung and reconciliation are the final point of the story of the untouched genius.

The lucky Aladdin, loved by the gods, becomes a recurring figure in several works in the 19th and 20th centuries. He is often viewed in a critical light, and the Aladdin figure himself becomes a target for Brandes' showdown with Romanticism in 1870.

There is a sharp critique of the Aladdin myth in Hans Egede Schack's novel *Phantasterne* (The Phantasts, 1857), where the dreamy, fantasizing youth in true Aladdin style believes he has been chosen to have a brilliant future. His encounter with real life is both harsh and heart-breaking. Schack simply renounces the Bildungsroman concept of the innate ideality of man. To Schack, the ideal foundation of man is an illusion. The romantic dreams and fantasies result in a disintegration of the personality and insanity pure and simple. Only in work can man find an anchorage that creates true meaning in his existence.[56]

The Bildungsroman genre has as its Danish main work M.A. Goldschmidt's 1000-page long novel *Hjemløs* (Homeless), which was published 1853–57. It is modelled on Goethe's *Wilhelm Meister* and refers in every way possible to Goethe's work. The theme of the personal development of the tradesman's son Otto is painted on a large canvas and takes the reader through both Danish and European environments and to political and cultural hotspots where art and religion are eagerly discussed and where Otto is confronted with a range of different interpretations of existence. The main idea of the novel is that Otto as a human being is to seek meaning not so much in his own soul as in an all-embracing moral law, a nemesis, that rewards the person who loves with yet more love: 'There is in existence a surplus of love, which means that we are awarded slightly more than we humanly have deserved, and are punished slightly less that we have deserved, and that is what maintains the world,'[57] as the author's mouthpiece explains.

Otto had imagined he would have a brilliant future as a writer or politician, but finally he has to realize that his task is to become a teacher and work in obscurity rather than in the public eye. An ingenious structure of repeated actions, meetings and mix-ups gradually brings Otto onto the track of the law of love and thereby of himself. Even so, he dies relatively young after heroically having rescued some of his friends and loved ones. At the moment of death, he experiences himself as a child, resting in his mother's lap. He has been, in terms of the novel, reunited with himself. His dying remarks are:

> 'I am marvellously happy... ... if only the child came closer.'
> 'What child, Otto,' his mother asked.
> 'The one inside me... ...it is hovering in front of me; it has never wanted to come really close.'[58]

The inside of the synagogue in Copenhagen, built 1833 by the architect Gustav Friedrich Hetsch. Goldschmidt belonged to the Jewish community

Professor Mogens Brøndsted emphasizes in his afterword to *Hjemløs* that, unlike German Bildungsliteratur, the Danish version focuses on childhood, where the personality is ready to germinate, and the impressions are so strong that they determine the rest of a person's life[59] – an observation that is also relevant in relation to major works of the modern breakthrough. But Brøndsted also stresses that Goldschmidt's Bildungsroman gains an extremely wide, European horizon in its clash between Jewish and Danish culture, glimpses of European social conditions and history and insight into everything from Indian philosophy and mythology to Swiss and Italian localities. Bildungsliteratur opens up for a literary thematization of both the Danish and the European outside world. Goldschmidt himself felt that his novel had become too long but, considered as a whole, it was what he was capable of and what he wanted.[60]

Goethe's influence on Danish literature around the mid-19th century was decisive. The young Kierkegaard hurried to buy Goethe's complete works, which totalled 55 volumes, when he was trying to enter the leading literary circle around Johan Ludvig Heiberg, and he was highly enthusiastic about the figure of Faust. He was taken up with the character of Faust as an expression of innate personal doubt. But he distanced himself from the redemption of Faust at the end of Faust II via the intervention of the beautiful Grethe. He simply felt that the continuation of Faust was a mistake. He had a more positive view of *Wilhelm Meister*. In a notebook entry from 1836 he writes:

> If I were to state briefly what I really regard as masterly in Goethe's Wilhelm Meister, I should say that it is the capacious governance which pervades the whole work, the entire Fichtean moral world-order, even more doctrinairely developed in the novel, which is inherent in the whole book and gradually leads Wilhelm to the point theoretically postulated, if I may put it that way, so that by the end of the novel the view of the world the poet has advanced, but which previously existed outside of Wilhelm, now is embodied and living within him, and this explains the consummate impression of wholeness that this novel conveys perhaps more than any other. Actually, it is the whole world apprehended in a mirror, in a true microcosm. *March 1836*[61]

From the mid-1840s, when Kierkegaard definitively breaks with Heiberg's Bildung conception, Goethe and the idea of Bildung are often given some verbal broadsides.[62] Kierkegaard's philosophy and psychology become a radical Romanticism which thinks in terms of disunity, absence and paradox rather than reconciliation, Bildung and harmony.

Nor did Grundtvig ever become an avid supporter of Goethe. He was much interested in Goethe's early medieval drama *Götz von Berlichingen* (1773), particularly because of its large historical canvas, but already in connection with Steffens' lectures on Goethe, he expresses himself critically. He is dissatisfied with what he calls Goethe's reconciliation with existence. What becomes of the world when the existence of the I is only inside the I itself? he asks. He later distances himself from Goethe's 'midde path':

> Goethe wanted to follow a middle path, lend the earthly a higher gleam and then imagine that things were then satisfactory; his later works are, artistically seen, masterpieces, but a high price has been paid for their roundness, and they seem more suitable for lulling an age into sleep than rousing it; that is why he has heaped just as much excessive praise for them as he was censured and ridiculed for the early ones[63]

– he writes in *Verdens-Krønike* (Chronicle of the World, 1812).

Hans Christian Andersen also adopted a somewhat cooler attitude to Goethe than the enthusiastic Oehlenschläger. Early on, he expresses his admiration for Goethe's contemporary, the writer of tales Johann Ludwig Tieck, whom he visited in Dresden and writes about in his travel account *Skyggebilleder* (Shadow Pictures, 1831). He says about him: '[...) Germany's *Tieck*; the man who stands as a master of an entire school, Romantic poetry, the writer closest to *Göthe* in age, value and esteem among his fellow-countrymen'.[64] Andersen's emphasis of Tieck at the expense of Goethe was, from a contemporary point of view, striking[65] and his enthusiasm for Tieck is accompanied – according to the Andersen researcher Johan de Mylius – by an increasing scepticism regarding Heiberg's formal genre aesthetics.

In the understanding of various lines and positions in Danish Romanticism, Goethe parts the waters: Grundtvig and Kierkegaard are both sceptical regarding Goethe, and Andersen has his reservations, while Oehlenschläger pays homage to him and a whole string of writers continue to develop the Bildung conception in the wake of *Wilhelm Meister's Apprenticeship*. The radical Romantics are no disciples of Goethe.

Three famous figures

In the middle of the 19th century, the tiny capital of Copenhagen could count three writers who later became world-famous among its approx. 130,000 inhabitants: Hans Christian Andersen, Søren Kierkegaard and Nikolai Frederik Severin Grundtvig. They were not particularly popular with the Heiberg family Parnassus, and they did not particularly like each other either, even though they were preoccupied by almost the same subjects and issues and even though all three of them gained inspiration from popular poetry and tales. The Norwegian Bjørnstjerne Bjørnson saw lines of connections between Andersen and Grundtvig when he referred to them as the only true folk writers who had made an impression on the common people. But Andersen did not rate Grundtvig as highly as some of his friends and female protectresses. He polemicized against both Grundtvig and Kierkegaard in his philosophical novel *At være eller ikke at være* (To be or not to be (1857), where a character resembling Grundtvig is labelled by the narrator as 'completely intolerable because of his colossal vanity',[66] whereas the talented young heroine, while reading Kierkegaard, states that she is 'tired of crawling over the cobblestones of language to reach the temple of thought',[67] where she incidentally did not discover very much fresh greenery. Andersen did, however, cite Grundtvig's poetry in a friendly way in one tale, but actually rarely mentioned him at all. In a diary entry he expressed a slightly veiled displeasure in certain remarks about Grundtvig's diction: 'Grundtvig speaks clearly but thrust the words out.'[68]

N.F.S. Grundtvig, Vartov, Copenhagen, statue by Niels Skovgaard, 1932

The atmosphere between Andersen and Kierkegaard was below freezing point after Kierkegaard's lambasting of Andersen's novel *Kun en Spillemand* (Only an Fiddler) in 1838.[69] Kierkegaard hardly had a good word for Grundtvig either. As a clergyman, Grundtvig reminded Kierkegaard of Dyrehavsbakken and vaudeville, and he was sceptical about Grundtvig's emphasis on the spoken word rather than the written. In his periodical *Øjeblikket* (The Moment), in which Kierkegaard dealt harshly with the state church as an institution, Grundtvig also got what was coming to him. His enthusiasm and struggle for a renewal of religious life had, according to Kierkegaard, more to do with bourgeois civic rights than belief. Grundtvig appears to be enthusiastic, but he is actually lukewarm and indifferent, Kierkegaard claimed.

It would seem that the three gentlemen kept as good a distance from each other out of mutual scepticism as was possibly in such a small capital. But this policy has perhaps also something to do with the fact that their three oeuvres came into existence in the wake of the Romantic ideas concerning the creative individual, ideas that had already been incarnated by Ewald's conception of the writer's role. All three of them were strongly influenced by ideas of early Romanticism concerning the poet as the lone creative figure, whose human individuality forms the basis of his mental activity. And each of them was certain that he had an epoch-making intellectual assignment to carry out:

> I know very well that at this moment I am the most talented of all young men, but I also know that this can be taken from me tomorrow – indeed, before I have ended this sentence[70]

– Kierkegaard wrote, with a mixture of self-assurance and humility in his journal in 1843. Even though Kierkegaard, Grundtvig and Andersen all wrote about their own importance, they were reserved in their attitude to the concept of the poetic genius that Steffens had disseminated.

Andersen gave the poetic figure a slightly different perspective than Oehlenschläger's model: the young Aladdin figure who is saved. While the core concept for Oehlenschläger's character was youth, to Andersen it was nature. In his artist novel *Improvisatoren* (The Improvisatore, 1835), he underlined that a new kind of writing had to have its origins in the natural popular language and an orally improvisational culture. This was here the poetic gold in the form of the natural poet came from, and it was such a writer the culture had to open up to, offer caring, educational guidance to and create possibilities for development for in a modern, international literary market. One senses that Andersen's own career as a writer as well as his dreams formed the basis for his depiction of the forming of a writer in *Improvisatoren*.

In Andersen's version, the writer can be anywhere in society, and he has access to as well as experiences from widely differing social environments. For that reason, being made a titular councillor of state suited him admirably. For it was not an office as such, it was an honour bestowed on an individual, mainly business people, and now on a self-supporting writer. While Oehlenschläger had gained recognition for his success as a writer by being given the office of a professor of aesthetics, i.e. an occupation, one saw with Andersen writing being regarded as a profession among other professions.

As a young man, Grundtvig grappled with all sorts of deliberations about his possibilities and prospects and found himself in what he referred to as 'Schelling intoxication' before positioning himself and his task as a hymn-writer and mental innovator in a field where art, the mediation of history and theology mingled. He was more interested in Steffens' ideas about history than about the writer. In his diary entries from September 1805, he turned various conceptions of the writer over and over in his mind. It seemed to him that he ended up in contradictions, and he was particularly worried about poetry possibly becoming too narrow and limited. The new poets wanted to see the culmination of poetry in their writing. Grundtvig himself wished to consider everything that had the stamp of the eternal about it as poetry, and he was afraid that such new thoughts would become too high-flown and too far removed from common life. Here, too, people should be encouraged to strive for an approach what he called the 'primeval substance of poetry'. In his own works he used 'mermaid blood' as a strong symbol of the mixture of myth, history and creative writing. This mermaid's blood was his poetic primeval substance. He arrived at the conclusion that it was his social task to spearhead the renewal of Christian religious life that he felt was underway. In 1805, he reflected that it was actually strange if the way of reaching that objective should be via becoming a writer:

> Were I to become a writer and a writer of the North, then fate would have dealt strangely with me, for it has placed me at a point where it is almost impossible, and yet allowed me to see that the only path to that end was through that particular point.[71]

On several occasions, Grundtvig was involved in hard, exhausting conflicts with the church authorities while serving as a clergyman in various callings, from 1839 onwards as vicar at Vartov Hospital. In 1861, however, he gained the title and rank of bishop.

Søren Kierkegaard often referred to the Romantic figure 'the poet' in his writings, and he criticized the idea of 'the young poetic genius'. He himself lived as a freelance writer, financed by an inheritance from his father and the income from his books, and he staged a quite large gallery of author and writer figures, narrators and writers with their separate assignments and approaches to the existential, psychological and religious themes he dealt with in such depth in his writings. On his path through life, the writer chooses the aesthetic stage – a stage the individual ought to move on from. Kierkegaard sees all the talk about the eternal in the continuation of Romantic writing as a demoniacal trait in contemporary society. In his opinion, the problem of his age was that many people simply refused to connect man with the eternal and tried to destroy the eternal by turning life into moments – as in Andersen's tale 'The Dryad'. Other people turned eternity into something completely abstract, rather like blue mountains that formed the boundary for life in time. But Kierkegaard was also sceptical about the attempts of Romantic writing to penetrate the eternal by means of the imagination, to fold eternity into time, as he put it. To look at eternity in that way, according to Kierkegaard, resulted in never knowing if one found oneself in dreams or in reality:

> [...] eternity peeps sadly, dreamily, roguishly, into the instant, as the beams of the moon peep tremblingly into a lighted grove or into a hall. Thought of the eternal becomes a fantastic occupation, and the mood is [...]'Am I dreaming, or is it eternity that is dreaming of me?' [72]

– he explained in his dissertation *Begrebet Angest* (The Concept of Dread, 1844).

In his psychological analyzes, Kierkegaard often dealt with the suffering and despair that were connected to the existence of a writer. The writer relates to God with a burning longing for the religious, but he refuses to be humble and primitive and simply believe in God. The writer does not want to do away with his own pains and tribulations for which he finds relief in his art. He finds himself in a vicious circle, one he has no desire to break.

Kierkegaard called a series of his publications from the time up until 1849 his 'oeuvre'. The texts differed considerably, comprising fiction, edifying discourses and psychological analyzes, and Kierkegaard underlined that he had always been a religious writer, one striving personally to become a Christian. He referred to and had always referred to 'the single individual', the individual reader and person who to him was the core of Christianity. '"The individual" - with this category the cause of Christianity stands and falls, since world development has come as far in reflection as it has. Without this category, pantheism has definitely won the day,'[73] he writes in the journal *NB3* (1847). He believed that the intellectual development and formation of concepts which, on the basis of the definitions of the philosopher Hegel, he calls 'reflection', make personal, subjective acquisition of belief an absolute necessity. Subjectivity had to be a defence against a common urge towards spiritualism and the animating of the outside world, the pantheism that had been so strong a feature of Romanticism.

In modern literary culture, too, Kierkegaard was on several occasions critically involved in the discussion. Only briefly, after the publication of his major work, *Enten – Eller (*Either/Or, 1843) did he write in disgust in his journal about the literary scene:

> Being a writer has gradually become the most wretched occupation of all. Generally speaking, one has to come forward like a gardener's assistant in a vignette in the newspaper, with one's hat in one's hand, bowing and scraping, full of good recommendations. How stupid: the one who writes must understand what he is writing about better than the person reading it, otherwise he ought to refrain from writing.
>
> Or one has to make sure of becoming a sly pettifogger who knows how to trick people. – I will not do so, not do so, oh no, no, to H★★★ with it all. I write as *I* want and I wear the breeches, and others can go and do whatever they want, refrain from buying, reading, reviewing, etc.[74]

Andersen, Kierkegaard and Grundtvig worked in their separate ways through Romanticism and radicalized themes such as creation, absence, disunity and paradoxicality that lay in the concepts of the human spirit and the writings of in Romanticism and German philosophy. And they reflected on modern literary culture and on how they could work within or on the edge of its framework. Their personal deliberations and work resulted in world-class art.

Hans Christian Andersen's wrote novels, travel books, drama as well as memoirs and fairytales. His fairytales have now been published in all the major languages and show the full range of his linguistic mastery, his humour, irony and deep understanding of human joy and suffering. He found out how to combine oral folk tradition and modern literary aesthetics and discover stories and especially stories of modernity every-

Søren Kierkegaard, garden of The Royal Library, statue by Carl Aarsleff, 1918

where, even in a bin as in the opening of 'Autie Toothache' (1872):

> Where we've got the story from? –
>
> – Would you like to know that?
>
> We've got it from the bin, the one with the old papers in it.
>
> Many a good and rare book has entered the victualler's and grocer's, not as reading matter but for practical purposes. They must have paper to make cornets for starch and coffee beans, paper to put round salt herring, butter and cheese. Written material is usable too.
>
> Often things not meant to be binned get binned. [75]

Nikolaj Frederik Severin Grundtvig renewed the religious life of Denmark and introduced revolutionary ideas about a liberating education of children, young people and adults. The strong tradition for dissemination of knowledge, free access to education and a welfare society where few have too much and fewer too little is strongly influenced by his thinking. His hymns possess a wonderful, poetic tonality and are still loved in the 21st century, even by non-religious Danes. The opening stanzas of Grundtvig's Whitsun hymn describes the early Danish summer landscape and expresses his joyful interpretation of Christianity:

Now gleams the sun in all its splendour,
o'er mercy seat life's light to tender –
now whitsun lily's time is here,
now we have summer mild and clear –
will more than angel's voice proclaim
a golden harvest in Christ's name.

In summer night's brief coolness ringing
the forest's nightingales are singing,
so all that God will ne'er forsake
may sweetly sleep and gently wake,
may sweetly dream of paradise
and wake their God to glorify.

And o'er the dust sighs heav'nly breathing,
and through the leaves wind's gently heaving,
and 'neath the clouds a breeze that blew
from paradise is charged anew,
and in the meadow at our feet
from life's own stream comes murmur sweet.[76]

Søren Kierkegaard gained world fame for his existentialistic philosophy and his deep analysis of human 'angst', a concept that has its origin in Kierkegaard's thoughts and German and Danish language. The concept is later used by Sigmund Freud and the French existentialist philosophers. Angst describes an intense feeling of anxiety with no clear or open cause. Angst differs from 'fear' that always has a cause. Kierkegaard describes the human being as a synthesis of the psychical and the physical, but the synthesis needs a third part: the spiritual. Angst comes from our relation to the spiritual:

That anxiety makes its appearance is pivotal. Man is a synthesis of the psychical and the physical; however, a synthesis is unthinkable if the two are not united in a third. This third is spirit. In innocence, man is not merely animal, for if he were at any moment of his life merely animal, he would never become man. So spirit is present, but is immediate, as dreaming. It is in a sense a hostile power, for it constantly disturbs the relation between soul and body, a relation that indeed has persistence and yet does not have endurance, inasmuch as it first receives the latter by the spirit. On the other hand, spirit is a friendly power, since it is precisely that which constitutes the relation. What, then, is man's relation to this ambiguous power? How does spirit relate itself to itself and to its conditionality? It relates itself as anxiety. Do away with itself, the spirit cannot; lay hold of itself, it cannot, as long as it has itself outside itself. Nor can man sink down into the vegetative, for he is qualified as spirit; flee away from anxiety, he cannot, for he loves it; really love it, he cannot, for he flees from it. Innocence has now reached its uttermost point. It is ignorance; however, it is not an animal brutality, but an ignorance qualified as spirit, and as such innocence is precisely anxiety, because its ignorance is about nothing. Here there is no knowledge of good and evil etc., but the whole actuality of knowledge projects itself in anxiety as the enormous nothing of ignorance.[77]

In Kierkegaard's thoughts 'angst' comes from our human condition of being able to choose for ourselves, our difficulty in understanding the true moral nature of our own deeds and our sense of the limits of our knowledge and of never knowing the deeper meaning of life.

Kierkegaard's concept of the stages of life are also some of his most important concepts that have been inspiring to authors as well as philosophers. The aesthetic stage, the ethical stage and the religious stage are the three stages that a human being might go through. Most people remain at the aethetic stage, where pleasure is the main motivation of life, and only a few decide to live the life of the so-called religious stage where you refer to something absolutely different from social life, which you might call 'God'. Kierkegaard developed his ideas on the stages in texts of art and philosophy in *Either/Or* and perhaps the most famous part of *Either/Or* is 'Forførerens Dagbog' ('The Seducer's Dairy' where the reader follows Johannes and is a witness of his sophisticated seduction of the young Cordelia.

How Cordelia engrosses me! And yet the time is soon over; always
my soul requires rejuvenescence. I can already hear, as it were, the far
distant crowing of the cock. Perhaps she hears it too, but she believes it

heralds the morning. – Why is a young girl so pretty, and why does it last so short a time? I could become quite melancholy over this thought, and yet it is no concern of mine. Enjoy, do not talk. The people who make a business of such deliberations, do not generally enjoy. However, it can do no harm to think about it; for this sadness, not for one's self but for another, makes one a litle more attractive in a masculine way. A sadness which darkens like a veil of mist deceptively over the manly strength, is one of the things contributing to the masculine erotic. [78]

Modern literary women

During the first decades of the 19th century, Oehlenschläger had known success, Staffeldt had ceased to be a poet and Grundtvig had been a thorn in the public's flesh. In the 1820s, new writers appeared on the scene. Andersen and Christian Winther had their debut, Blicher published his first prose book and Poul Martin Møller had read aloud from his work in progress, *En dansk Students Eventyr* (The adventures of a Danish student, 1824/1843) at the Students' Association before leaving for a post in Norway. What most authors shared was being enthusiastic about a new writer whose prose tales had appeared anonymously. Søren Kierkegaard wrote a remarkable and very long review of one her books, *To Tidsaldre* (Two Ages, 1852) which he praised because of the writer's critique of the contemporary age, where humans had become shallow and materialistic. The author in question was a woman, Thomasine Gyllembourg who, in accordance with the Romantic view of women, felt that writing was a male not a female occupation.

Literature was part of the public sphere where women were not assert to themselves. Women could be or become readers or muses, mothers of writers and other kinds of inspirational bel-esprit in the private sphere. Women did, however, create a space for themselves in a new conversational salon culture. Here, such literary talents as Friederike Brun (1765–1835) and Kamma Rahbek (1775–1829) find genres and modes of expression. These two women had their differing types of literary salon: Friederike Brun resided from 1792 at Sophienholm in a salon that was international in style; Kamma Rahbek had a much more modest salon around her tea-table at Bakkehuset. It was here that Hans Christian Andersen as a very young, newly arrived child of nature from the provinces was allowed to attend.

While the Enlightenment had to a certain extent – and in a Danish context particularly as a result of Holberg's efforts – shown an interest in

The park of Sophienholm where Friederike Brun had her salon. She meet with some of the poets in the pavilions of the park

mental and intellectual equality between men and women, Romanticism was interested in the differences. The French philosopher Jean-Jacques Rousseau had in the 18th century formulated a new programme for children's upbringing that focused on the child's self-development and on the differences between the sexes. To Rousseau, gender was admittedly the only difference, but he believed that gender – as far as women were concerned – decided most things and quite obviously determined the framework and in particular the limitations for women's development and their whole life. Rousseau wanted to emphasize how the differences between men and women gave them opportunities to complement each other and be united in the ideal figure – the child. But both in his work and during his own time the characteristics and qualities one ascribed to men were seen as the incarnation of the human and that which upheld society. Women had to fulfill and assume the role of the second person in a life linked to children, the man's sexuality and his existence in the family.

When a literary public sphere began to take form, and the structuring of life by the bourgeoisie into a public and a private life-sphere became prominent in the urban communities, the lives of women were linked

Thomasine Gyllembourg's inkpot. She used her young son's inkpot and published her books anonymously. Bakkehuset, Frederiksbergmuseerne, Copenhagen, photo by Stuart McIntyre

to the private sphere and were seen as subject to male power and dominance. This took place everywhere in Europe in the period from the end of the 17th century to the mid-19th century. It took more than an average amount of drive for a woman to arrogate other roles to herself than those allocated to her by culture and society. To move outside the narrow confines was to move outside general opinion and social relations.

Thomasine Gyllembourg, when she made her debut at the age of 52 in 1827, had long since set off on a collision course with society's norms for a woman's life and behaviour. In 1801, she had divorced her first husband, the Enlightenment author and patriot Peter Andreas Heiberg. She had lacked love in her marriage. She now wanted a new kind of marriage, one based on love, not on reason and economic considerations. And she got her love marriage when that same year she married her lover, Carl Fredrik Gyllembourg Ehrensvärd. He was a friend of P.A. Heiberg and had fled from Sweden on account of his complicity in the murder of the Swedish king Gustav III in 1792. But when it came to making a public appearance as a writer, Thomasine Gyllembourg was incredibly careful. Even though most writers and critics knew the identity of the popular everyday writer, she herself maintained her anonymity very strictly, perhaps also because the machinations also had an inspirational effect on her own creative work. Here, she had the possibility to play at empathizing with both male and female identity, and as an anonymous person she avoided being limited by her age's view of women.[79]

Among those who did not know the author's identity was the young Mathilde Fibiger. In the midst of the great new enthusiasm for the fatherland in connection with the victories of the First Schleswig War in 1848 and the abolition of absolutism with the constitution of 1849, she published her letter novel *Clara Raphael* (1851). She was assisted by the son of Thomasine Gyllembourg, the trend-setting critic of the time Johan Ludvig Heiberg, who was very enthusiastic about her style. He kept completely out of the picture, however, when the great literary feud concerning Mathilde Fibiger's ideas about female emancipation and social involvement broke out. Heiberg's wife, Johanne Louise Heiberg, and Mathilde's family made sure, in their separate ways, that the connection between the critic and the young writer did not grow, either publicly nor privately. It is clear that any relation between the two would be interpreted as more than just plain interest and maybe even the start of an extra-marital love affair. A young woman and an older man could, seen from the conception of the sexes at the time, only be viewed as his sexuality and her infatuation.

Despite the limitations and obstacles, women came to make a strong contribution to a new prose literature that focused on everyday life and was interested in ideals and realities in society, family and marriage. The female writers in the North and the rest of Europe were among the front figures in a new, psychologically analytical and realistic prose.

Thomasine Gyllembourg was on the scene early, in a Danish context, with her *En Hverdags-Historie* (An Everyday story) in 1827, and her authorship culminated with the critical novella *To Tidsaldre* (Two Ages) from 1845. In Norway, Camilla Collett, with *Amtmandens Døttre* (The District Governor's daughters, 1855) became the author of the first realistic novel about society and family based on the theme of forced marriage, while Fredrika Bremer in Sweden published her first *Teckningar ur hvardagslifvet* (Sketches of everyday life) in 1828. In the final volume, *Familien H**** was included, and in 1856 *Hertha eller En själs historia* (Hertha or the story of a soul) appeared, whose bold analysis of patriarchal society makes it a main work in the history of the novel in northern Europe.[80] In a larger European context, prose in general counted a number of female writers who helped make the novel an extremely important and wide-ranging genre. Their narrative art often draws on Romantic ideality and irony, their brilliant art of portrayal and preference for dark, mysterious characters. But the works are also typified by an openness to a realistic depiction of the outside world and characterization. Realism and Romanticism alternate in an exciting and innovative way.[81] This applies for example to the English Jane Austen's *Pride and Prejudice* (1813), the French Madame de Staël's artist novel *Corinne ou l'Italie* (1807) and the English Emily Brontë's *Wuthering Heights* (1847).

In a Danish context, Gyllembourg's popular tales strengthened the formation of a female reading public and the development of a modern literary culture. As a mother of the leading arbiter of taste of the age, Johan Ludvig Heiberg, and as a favourite contributor to his popular periodical *Kjøbenhavns Flyvende Post* (The Copenhagen Flying Post), she found herself at the centre of the literary environment and was one of those setting the literary agenda. She was severely criticized for her intrepid heroine Sophie, who in the novella *Ægtestand* (Matrimony, 1834) insisted on love, but was roundly praised by both Poul Martin Møller and Søren Kierkegaard, who stressed the perfect form of the tales and their sure interpretation of life. According to Kierkegaard, Gyllembourg – unlike Hans Christian Andersen – was able to structure her material and her narrative. The novellas were read as an important contribution to the debate of the time on existence, philosophy of life and Bildung to which also Kierkegaard and Andersen themselves contributed. Thomasine Gyllembourg assigned important social tasks to her female characters as bearers of Bildung and human understanding.

Kierkegaard's praise, however, fell into oblivion, and the writing of literary history only gave her her rightful place when research in the latter half of the 20th century liberated itself from a narrow national optic. Only then did it become clear that Gyllembourg's oeuvre could be placed alongside that of Camilla Collett and Fredrika Bremer and be viewed in both a Nordic and a European context.[82]

Gyllembourg is a very skilled storyteller, who knows how to catch the attention of her reader and describe Copenhagen localities, that her readers know. Here is the opening of her shortstory 'Drøm og Virkelighed' ('Dream and reality', 1833) and the mixture of romanticism and urban realism characteristic of her style. A young man describes how he visits a former housemaid whom he loves and who expects his child:

> Dear reader! If, on a dark and stormy winter's evening, your path should occasionally have taken you through the Nyhavn precinct, you will, I am sure, agree with me that this street, under such circumstances, is a gloomy place in our otherwise bright and lovely Copenhagen. The Charlottenborg side, dingy, never visited by the sun and seldom by humans, its vessels abandoned by sailors, guarded solely by an unhappy ship's dog, whose howling and whining is accompanied by the creaking and crashing of masts in the gale, answered by the hoarse screeching of some hungry crow or other perched in its deserted rigging – all of this lends a distinctive and sinister ambience to the location. On such a December evening I was hurrying dejectedly through this street, one that for some time I had secretly been visiting. It has unfortunately grown quite late, I thought to myself, as I hastened over to one of the few streetlamps, the dim light of which swayed in the wind, so as to consult my watch as to the time. – It had stopped! – Annoyed, I continued on my way. – 'I pretended back home that I was going to the theatre,' I said to myself: 'I only hope the performance isn't long since over! What must my uncle be thinking?' [83]

Modern literature from the fringe

Steen Steensen Blicher also made a vital contribution to the renewal of 19th century literature, and although he – like many of his contemporary fellow-writers – was a clergyman, his path to literary public exposure and recognition was a difficult one.

Blicher's first book of prose, *Brudstykker af en Landsbydegns Dagbog* (Diary of a parish clerk, 1824), was practically only noticed by Ingemann, to whom Blicher personally sent a copy. The diary was published in the

The vicarage of Spentrup where Steen Steensen Blicher once resided

modern provincial magazine *Læsefrugter*, which was full of entertaining reading and unknown in the literary circles of Copenhagen. The periodical was an example of the fact that modern literary culture was becoming commercial, targeting a new public who had purchasing power, and was interested in good entertainment of a more or less sensational nature. Blicher enjoyed a brief public success with his own periodical *Nordlyset*, which appeared in 1827–29. Among the more than 20 novellas he published were such later classics as 'Sildig Opvaagnen' (Tardy awakening, 1828), 'Ak! hvor forandret' ('Alas! How changed!', 1828), 'Hosekræmmeren' ('The Hosier and his daughter', 1829) and 'Præsten i Vejlby' ('The Rector of Vejlbye', 1829).

It was actually a cunning move by a publisher that granted Blicher a breakthrough with readers and critics. He had a flair for the new interest in the market and took the initiative of publishing Blicher's collected novellas. The work started to appear in 1833, and by 1844 it had reached its total of seven volumes. The authorship was read from a national point of view, and the reviewer in *Dansk Litteratur-Tidende* praised Blicher as early as 1833 for his portrayal of Danish characters, Danish landscapes and Danish customs.[84] Johanne Louise Heiberg read 'Hosekræmmeren ' ('The Hosier and his Daughter', 1829) aloud at an evening entertainment at The Royal Theatre in 1834, which in itself was a mark of considerable recognition. 'The Hosier and his Daughter' tells the tragic story of the young daughter of a hosier, who does not allow her to marry the young man she loves. The father has other marriage plans for her, and the story takes a deeply tragic turn. In the opening of the short story, we listen to the author who introduces the Jutlandic moor, that to most readers was an exotic place, a strange and unknown romantic landscape:

> Sometimes when I have wandered across the great moor with nothing but brown heather round about me and blue sky above me; when I have strolled far from human beings and the marks of their piddling here below - mere molehills that time or some restless Tamerlane will level with the ground; when I have flitted, light of heart, proud of my freedom like the Bedouin whom no house, no narrowly bounded field ties to one spot, who possesses all that he sees, who lives nowhere but roams as he pleases everywhere; when in such a mood my roving eye has caught sight of a house on the horizon which arrested its airy flight unpleasantly, then I would sometimes wish - God forgive me the passing thought, for after all it was nothing more - would that this human dwelling were not there! For it harbors trouble and pain; there people quarrel and wrangle about mine and thine. Alackaday, the happy desert is both mine and thine, is everybody's and nobody's.[85]

There were critical voices against Blicher's stories. The erotic scenes in 'Diary of a Parish Clerk' were referred to as salacious in the first review, while 'Tardy Awakening' was labelled filthy and revolting in the influential periodical *Maanedsskrift for Litteratur* and said to be a disfigurement on the author's entire work. The theme of infidelity did not accord with the taste of the Biedermeier culture.[86]

While the life-philosophy debate had given Gyllembourg's novellas a good reception, in Blicher's case it was the growing national enthusiasm around 1848 that paved the way for his authorship on the literary scene. His dialect poetry was appreciated by the critic Christian Molbech as early as the publication of the periodical *Nordlyset*, and his later cycle *Trækfuglene* (Birds of passage, 1838) also had a good reception.

The Himmelbjerg Tower, raised in 1875 in memory of Frederik VII, who gave Denmark its constitution

Blicher's own conception of national involvement resulted in his initiative to hold popular festivals on the hill of Himmelbjerget. The festivals, the first of which was held in 1839, were to strengthen love of the fatherland and were conceived of as a kind of Olympic Games, with sport, singing and speeches. Here, one was to prepare the rebirth of the fatherland, cultivate a Nordic community and pave the way for a free constitution. Blicher died in 1848, the same year that absolutism was done away with, but no poem or words in memory of him came from either his friend Ingemann or from Grundtvig, who had been in contact with him concerning the Himmelbjerg festivities.

Blicher's works appeared in several editions during the 19th century, and they inspired both Hans Christian Andersen and the new so-called school-teacher authors who started to appear in the 1860s. The school-teachers were a further example of the fact that 19th century literary culture was becoming more diverse, with new groups of readers and types of authors emerging from all sides and outer areas. C.A. Thyregod came from the village of Thyregod near Vejle and became one of the school-teacher authors. He made his debut in 1864 with *Historier og Sagn* (Stories and legends) and wrote educative and entertaining popular literature about life in the country past and present. 'The old passes, the new comes into being' from 1868 is characteristic with its message that one must take care not to ruin good, traditional values during a time of change of customs and habits, life and production. What is new can easily lack heart. In 1874, Thyregod was involved in establishing the Danish Teachers' Association.

An organizational interest and a desire to communicate and educate is also typical of Anton Nielsen, who had his debut in 1859. He became principal of the folk high school at Vester Skerninge and later Ollerup on Funen. He also had plans of starting a folk high school for Danish emigrants in USA and in addition he wrote travel books, sketches of popular life and songs. The once so popular 'At Whitsun, when the woods are turned to green' is one of his best-known songs. One should not underestimate this aspect of Biedermeier literature either then or subsequently. It was particularly here, among these authors, that a popular image of Denmark after the defeat in the Second Schleswig War of 1864 assumed its form. Here, the small and familiar is consistently assessed as being positive, as opposed to the large, unlimited and unknown – a mind-set that also recurs in the 20th century.

Anton Nielsen's connection in Vester Skerninge, the farmer and musician Mads Hansen, who took the initiative to establishing the local folk high school, was also the writer of the children's song 'En Have' ('A Garden') from 1870. It is a fine little piece of 'utility art' for children, and the verses came to appeal to generations of both children and adults and to be the epitome of the Biedermeier image of Denmark as the lovely little garden:

Look out over dale, over field, over sound
and you'll see a garden with bowers all around,
with flower-beset meadows and waters so clear:
that garden is Denmark, our fatherland dear.[87]

Blicher had successors among the school-teacher authors, but neither he nor the school-teachers interested the new writers of the modern breakthrough – or the leading new literary figure Georg Brandes. He only mentions Blicher in passing.

Blicher was only rediscovered at the beginning of the 20th century, when new popular poets took him as a stepping stone for their own work. Jeppe Aakjær (1866–1930) and others praised his authorship in works about Blicher's life and writing, and were particularly sensitive to the exciting and tragic aspects of his life-story. An academic interest arose later in the 20th century, especially in connection with the studies during the 1960s of novella theory, narrative structure and focalization (use of point of view). Blicher's oeuvre seemed in this connection to anticipate new hypotheses about the role of the narrator. His narrative skill also opened up in a completely new way regarding the usual biographical story of the failed clergyman with the unfaithful wife.

Poems for the writing-desk drawer

As with Blicher, the reputation of Emil Aarestrup has grown since his own time. Aarestrup (1800–56) only managed to publish one collection of poems, urged on by his friend, the poet Christian Winther. The poems were greeted with total silence on the part of literary critics and sold a mere 40 copies, which did not encourage any sequel. Poor publisher Reitzel, Aarestrup wrote even before the collection appeared. Aarestrup himself had not considered either starting or continuing to publish. It was all 'a secret urge' while Aarestrup took care of his profession as a doctor. In 1849, he became the county medical officer of Odense, a post he held until his death in 1856.

When one reads the first poem of his sole publication, one notices how the poet asks the reader just to gaze 'For some moments at these pages,/ Without sternness, and with eye well-willing!' The formulation sounds modest, shy even. But one should make no mistakes here. To Aarestrup, the moment was the real time-dimension of poetry, and the reader should not make do with leafing through the poems but actually look closely. 'Gaze then' is the writer's imperative to the reader, and if one 'looks' and 'sees' the introductory poem, one immediately notices the construction with the many repetitions and then begins to hear the alliteration and the rhythm[88]:

Origin

As its dull-brown ling the empty surface,
As its spikes so light the floor of greenness,
As its flying foam a slender naiad,
As a bulb, in blackest soil, its lily,
As the polyps sponges and frail leaf-blades,
As the soft-fleshed mussel its shell-casing
Has my mind been forming these few pages
By some secret urge, and almost will-less.

Gaze then – as at ling's brown empty surface,
As at brome-grass spikes o'er floor of greenness,
As at flying foam of slender naiad,
As at bog-floor's waving yellow lily,
As at coral's sponges and frail leaf-blades,
As at sea-shore's colourful shell-casings –
For some moments at these pages,
Without sternness and with eye well-willing![89]

In his poems, Aarestrup allows pleasure to take the place of the Romantic contemplation and longing for eternity.[90] It is precisely the certainty of cessation, disappearance, annihilation and death that compacts the moment, the short meeting, the short time of sweetness, or the erotic situation. The theme of annihilation is also expressed by the fact that Aarestrup not only writes about the ideal figure of Romanticism, the young girl, half-child and half-woman, as favoured by Oehlenschläger, or the formidable demanding muse with snake-like hair that Staffeldt conjures up. Aarestrup's erotic gallery of female figures comprises both young and mature characters, whose erotic voices go from the Romantic 'silver-pure sound' to an almost realistic 'broken' sound. The poetic I-figure, disguised as a pirate, also desires 'the runic script of wrinkles'.[91]

It is important to make clear that the poet's ambition is not to reproduce reality. Poetry is and has to be the art of using words. But when the poet focuses on the moment, the body assumes greater physicality in the world of the poem than in the ethereal dream material of Romanticism. The body is talked of as it actually is – something physical – and the poem can therefore also be what it actually is, i.e. a work of art, an aesthetic form. The Romantic idea of art's images of the holy and eternal, as formulated by Steffens, disappears in favour of a conception of the work of art as art and pleasure. In Aarestrup, Romantic symbolism is replaced by a seductively fragmented, lightly distorted formation of images, where parts of the body indicate the desired physical totality. Lips, forehead, eyes, hands, locks of hair and fingers are in focus. In his notes, Aarestrup expresses the idea that he precisely wants to refrain from using his poems to formulate a Romantic longing for the eternal. He is interested in the fleetingness of time:

> Time we only have once.
> the transient, interesting
>
> Eternity is assured us,
> the lasting, enduring,
> long-drawn-out
>
> To enjoy time costs an effort,
> so make haste –
> Eternity praises ease and
> rest; but does not hasten it.[92]

There is an urgency about the poem – the pressure of fingers, the moment and eroticism's secret realm of freedom that can open up at a brief glance in the middle of the living-room of Biedermeier culture. Aarestrup's eroticism perhaps expressed more of a wishful thinking for the gaze of a woman who sees possible cracks and routes of escape from tight-lipped respectability than the desire of the male ego. The point of view is admittedly that of the male ego, but it is the woman's fingers that press and her gaze that speaks silently in the poems. The poems allow the man to see and enjoy and become melancholy at his enjoyment, but the poems create real female figures who, before the man, has eyed the possibilities and initiated the erotic sequence of events – often via the language of the body: a glance, smile, pressure of fingers. Aarestrup's poems with their sudden erotic cracks and possibilities are seen as a universe where the characters are entwined in a particularly erotic-linguistic logic via the choice of words and the rhymes. Striving (*stræbe*) rhymes with lip (*læbe*), breast (*bryst*) with desire (*lyst*), glow (*glød*) with lap (*skød*). Heiberg could not refrain from making a playful parody of the super-elegant Aarestrup and in 1839 wrote these lines:

Emil Aarestrup's living room, the Emil Aarestrup Museum, Nysted, photo by Henning Jørgensen

À l'Aarestrup

Love the all-exclusive. Amor exclusivus.

> God grant that I were a horse!
> My tail I'd then swish unceasing,
> As best I could of course,
> Summer's heat for you appeasing,
> And fan all the flies that flurry
> Around your red cheeks so fair,
> And chase them off till they scurry
> Into other ladies' hair.[93]

Aarestrup himself stressed that it was the interesting that fascinated him and that he wished to pursue. The interesting became a central aesthetic concept during his age, and a later writing of literary history has often connected it in particular with Aarestrup's writing. The concept actually derived originally from the aesthetics of the German philosopher, author and literary critic Friedrich von Schlegel. In a dissertation on the study of Greek poetry, he had in 1797 used the concept of the interesting in an analysis of modern literature. He felt that modern Romantic literature represented a falling-off in comparison with classical Greek literature. Schlegel saw the aim of art as being the attaining of the harmony and clarification found in the Greek tragedies. Here, an objective beauty was realized. Unlike Greek poetry, modern poetry cultivated subjectively beautiful effects: tension, disharmony, the interesting and the problematic. The great importance of the interesting was to Schlegel a symptom of the crisis in the culture. While Greek poetry bases itself on nature, modern literature bases itself on art principles, seeks special forms in nature and involves the reader personally and individually. In Schlegel's opinion, Goethe's poetry showed a way out of the crisis, since it positioned itself between the beautiful and the interesting and offered the prospect of a 'new dawn' in art.

In a Danish context, Kierkegaard dealt extensively with the interesting in his famous 'Diary of a seducer', which is part of his *Enten – Eller* (Either/Or, 1843). Here, the aesthete Johannes attempts precisely a thoroughly premeditated seduction of the young girl Cordelia in order to realize the interesting as an aesthetic and existential category.

The author and professor of philosophy F.C. Sibbern dealt with the interesting in his dissertations *Om Poesi og Kunst* (On Poetry and Art, 1834–69), dividing the interesting into three different types: firstly, *the pursuitful*, which represented a refined and reflected style that appealed to the intellect; secondly, the *senseful*, which represented novelty and boldness of material; and thirdly, *the expectationful*, which represented an exciting organization. Søren Kierkegaard was one of Sibbern's pupils, and his analyzes of art and psychological studies were of key importance to Kierkegaard.

Sibbern's most important contribution were his psychological studies, and he incidentally wrote a psychologically analytical double letter novel, *Efterladte Breve af Gabrielis* (Posthumous letters of Gabrielis, 1826) and *Ud af Gabrielis's Breve til og fra Hjemmet* (From Gabrielis's letters to and from home, 1850) as an extension of Goethe's *Die Leiden des jungen Werthers*, 1774). Here, the interesting occurs especially in the form of a 'pursuitful' thorough revision of a young man's Werther-like story.

The interesting in texts by Aarestrup, Kierkegaard, Hans Christian Andersen and Blicher and in such poets as Ludvig Bødtcher and Carsten Hauch helped to motivate writers of 20th century literary history to start using the concept of romantism as a term for this aspect or phase of

Sculpture of Carsten Hauch by H.V. Bissen, Sorø Academy, 1858

Romantic writing. The concept comes from the French term for Romanticism, but it is well-suited as a search-concept in connection with Danish literature, because characteristics of romantism can be opposed to the idealizing and harmonizing tendency of Biedermeier literature.

The concept of romantism can be used as a term for an analytic and reflecting literature that opens up for portrayals of realities in people's outside world and psyche and thereby also for the interesting and the disharmonious in man and his world – and with the concept of romantism one can also draw attention to the new impulses from French, English and German literature, from Lord Byron (1788–1824) to Heinrich Heine (1797–1856) and Victor Hugo (1802–85), which gradually and on a modest scale reached Danish literature.

Biedermeier literature and romantism were both impulses in the age of Romanticism, but both tendencies were screened off from social involvement and the feeling of rebellion and change that epitomized Heine and Byron with their critical and freedom-seeking poetry and that helped to change literature everywhere in Europe. In Denmark, Poul Møller wrote the long programme poem 'The artist among rebels' under the impression of the social unrest in Norway and the revolution in Paris in 1830, and his message was clear: The artist does not belong among rebels. The artist is admittedly tragically involved in the struggle against the rebels, but refuses to accept the monarch's thanks for his efforts and bids the world farewell:

In my workshop, now silent,
I say my farewell to the world,
Will never play at being judge
Nor kill my fellow-man.
On the black board of memory
Will the exploit of today

Crawl like a spectre
With repulsive script.[94]

The strong Romantic longing for freedom and the ideas of change that had characterized European and Russian Romanticism from Percy Bysshe Shelley (1792–1822) and Alexander Pushkin (1799–1837) to Byron and Heine were not particularly strongly represented in Danish literature. While Heine depicted a divided Germany in his epic *Deutschland. Ein Wintermärchen* (Germany. A Winther's Tale, 1844/1982), and advocated human rights, various Danish writers were irresolute or kept at a distance from the events around 1848. Andersen was cautious, but did function as a custodian during the popular procession that approached the king on 21 March 1848, demanding a free constitution. Grundtvig was shocked at the sight of the procession, but quickly changed his mind and with a certain amount of difficulty became a member of the constitutional assembly. Kierkegaard was an opponent of the June constitution and the new nationalism. He believed that the conception of a Danish people would end up suppressing the individual. If there actually existed a Danish people, he thought it was a people where those who are to govern are frightened and those who are to obey are brazen!

Even though inspiration from English and French writing also came in the form of such great story-tellers as the Frenchman Victor Hugo and the Scottish writer Sir Walter Scott (1771–1832), German idealistic philosophy from the end of the 18th century and the beginning of the 19th century left the longest-lasting and most important mark on Danish Romanticism, and this influence became increasingly national in its orientation. The Biedermeier culture consolidated itself.

In the eyes of the most reflective writer of the century, Søren Kierkegaard, German idealism – and Schelling and Hegel in particular – were the foundation. But in extension of his teacher in philosophy, the writer and philosopher Poul Martin Møller, Kierkegaard criticized Hegel's system with its spiritual and historical necessities for not giving enough room to the single individual, its actions and beliefs. It was just as difficult and unsuitable for the individual to navigate, on the basis of Hegel's analyses as if one were to use a world map to find one's way around Copenhagen. Kierkegaard was also critical of the fact that the dialectic system moved of its own accord. It was thinking without a thinker. For the person thinking and shaping the system cannot describe and explain himself from within his own system.

All of Kierkegaard's terminology and form of discussion nonetheless was and remained deeply influenced by the Hegelian dialectic. But to Kierkegaard, God was absolutely different from man. The contrast between God and man could not be mediated, as Hegel believed it could, or be harmonized, as Goethe had imagined. In the relationship between man and God, man ends up, according to Kierkegaard, in the paradoxes of faith, because man can only believe or not believe that the eternal and divine in the shape of Jesus has entered earthly life and time.

Hegel was also a source of a sharp religious criticism and the Marxist philosophy of history and society. David Friedrich Strauss, in his dissertation on the life of Jesus, *Das Leben Jesu, kritisch bearbeitet* (The Life of Jesus Critically Examined, 1835–36/1854), had also given a critical historical account of the Christian conceptions of Jesus, and Ludwig Feuerbach continued the critique of both Christianity and Hegel's system of thought. In his main work on the nature of Christianity, *Das Wesen des Christentums* (The Essence of Christianity 1841/1860), he defined Christianity as a product of man's own longing and narcissism. Man places his ideals in God. When man liberates himself from his belief in God, he does not need to approach his fellow-man with a need to convince and proselytize, but can instead realize his ideals in interpersonal relations. Karl Marx also had as his point of departure a critique of Hegel: He imagined a way of reinstating Hegel, seeing the class struggle, not the spirit, as the driving force of history.

The modern breakthrough

The young Georg Brandes (1842–1927) was particularly interested in Kierkegaard and wrote sympathetically and intensely about his work,[95] even though he was unable to follow Kierkegaard in the great and paradoxical leap into belief in God. Brandes' analysis, however, founded a modern study of Kierkegaard in which attempts are made to free Kierkegaard's existential and psychological analyzes from his religious dogmatics.

Kierkegaard's world of thought and his in-depth psychological analyzes of the standpoints of modern man in relation to existence and the experiences of anxiety and despair were of importance to many other authorships at home and abroad, from Friedrich Nietzsche (1844–1900) to J.P. Jacobsen (1847–85), Henrik Ibsen (1828–1906) and August Strindberg (1849–1912). This was especially because of Georg Brandes' mediation and reading of Kierkegaard's writings. In J.P. Jacobsen's contemporary novel *Niels Lyhne* (1880), the title figure tried to question a Christian interpretation of existence. The depiction of Niels' mental struggle and the relation of the other characters to existence drew on material from Kierkegaard's psychological analyzes. When the main character of the novel, Niels Lyhne, is mortally wounded in connection with the defeat of 1864, he refuses to see a clergyman, and the impressive final words of the novel are a strong and direct reference to Kierkegaard's dissertation *Sygdommen til døden* (Sickness unto Death, 1849):

> The last time Hjerrild looked in on Niels Lyhne he was lying there raving about his armor, saying that he wanted to die on his feet. And then finally he died the death – the difficult death.[96]

'To die the death' was, in Kierkegaard's words an expression of man's desperate attempts to gain control over himself, become himself and escape faith and the relation to God. To embark on that path is to die the death, since one must constantly wipe out the possibility of faith in oneself, get the possibility of faith to die and thereby face death time and time again.[97]

The blue corridor at Sorø Academy where Herman Bang obtained his high school diploma in 1875. Part of the story of his first novel takes place at Sorø Academy

The writers of the modern breakthrough related to both the Romantic world of ideas and the new thoughts and ideas of their own age. They spent a lot of time escaping from Romanticism and depicted in detail their own farewell to its ideals.[98] In his epoch-making introductory lecture on the main currents of 19th century literature in 1870, Brandes had insisted that the writers make a definitive break with Romanticism and began to open up to new impulses.

> Agreement will without difficulty be able to be reached that Danish literature has at no time in this century been in such a moribund state as it is now. Literary production has virtually come to a standstill, and no general question concerning human life or society is capable of awakening any participation or producing any other discussion than that of the daily press and ephemeral literature. We have never possessed a strong, original urge to produce, but now an almost total lack of a desire to acquire any mental impulses from outside has come about, and this intellectual deafness, like that of the deaf-mute, has led to muteness.
>
> Proof of whether literature is alive in our age is that it is prepared to debate issues. George Sand, for example, made the relation between the sexes the subject of debate, as did Stuart Mill property and Turgenev, Spielhagen and Emile Augier social conditions. If literature does not make anything the subject of debate, this is the same as saying that it is in the process of losing all significance.[99]

The authors, for their part, had started to find new paths in literature, inspired by a new natural science, the critique of religion and the social and psychological interest.

The defeat of 1864 marked a traumatic crossroads in social life, culture and literature. Herman Bang's novel *Tine* (Tina, 1889/2000) portrayed realistically and symbolically the searing defeat and those involved. Bang's debut novel, *Haabløse Slægter* (Hopeless generations, 1880), likewise had the evacuation of the entrenchments at Dybbøl as one of its fateful events. The novel describes the contrast between a family's golden age during the Enlightenment and its decline in the 19th century up until the collapse in the final generation. Modern despair, which Kierkegaard had described, and Romantic day-dreaming, which Egede Schack had analyzed and distanced himself from in the novel *Phantasterne* (The Phantasts, 1857), were things that Bang's characters were unable to be liberated from, either by an existential choice or a reason that could sever the ties with the world of dreams.

Bang's main character, William, is the product of his father's sins and debauchery and his mother's weaknesses. His desperate attempts to take on and gain control of the old family ideals are doomed to failure because of is social and biological legacy. The insane and tuberculous generation of his parents from the middle of the century have already frittered away everything, and the arrival at a new age also heralds the family's perdition.

He also had excellent capacities and much of the elegance that inherited high birth grants. [...] But quite soon it was clear that Ludvig belonged to 'the sons of the great virtues' – he was extremely weak, nervous, strongly melancholy from an early age. With him it was clear that one had arrived at a new stage in the family history.

The strength was gone, the brains were no longer as strong, eccentricity had taken over.[100]

– was Bang's characterization of William's father.

Brandes had imagined a longing for freedom, passion and 'light' as well as 'air' and a debate of modern issues in the new literature, but it was to a greater extent depressive, naturalistic elements and realistic revelations of reality that typified the literature of the modern breakthrough.[101] Brandes himself had used the term naturalism about the depiction in English literature of popular life, nature and the longing for freedom from William Wordsworth (1770–1850) to Lord Byron, although he of course also connected the term with the new French writers, such as Émile Zola (1840–1902).[102] Zola became the leading theorist of French naturalism and worked with a fearless deterministic revelation of reality. He emphasized that literature should allow itself to be guided by the new natural and social sciences. According to Zola, the definition of a work of art could not be anything other than 'a corner of nature (or 'creation' as he first wrote) seen through a temperament',[103] and he explained how the novel had become the genre for a scientific investigation of man '[...) my objective was first and foremost a scientific one.'[104] he wrote in the preface to the second edition of *Thérèse Raquin* (1867), in which he ventured to give a modern investigation of human temperaments and characters. The novel deals with a married woman and her lover, who murders her husband – and it gave rise to much indignation. Zola defended himself by declaring that it was a question of showing reality, not of agitating in favour of immorality: 'The group of Naturalist writers to which I have the honour of belonging is courageous and active enough to produce powerful works containing within them their own defence.'[105]

In a Danish-Norwegian context, it was in particular Amalie Skram (1846–1905) who was able to create masterpieces out of the aesthetics of naturalism, both in the form of marriage novels and depictions of family sagas. Skram, who was Norwegian but who thought of herself as a Danish writer, painted penetrating and revealing pictures of the suppression of women in marriage. The repulsive became a layer of her universe, linked to the profound humiliation of her sex, and her naturalism placed her in a partially problematic light with Brandes, who increasingly distanced himself from the aesthetics of naturalism. In his obituary to her in 1905, he did, however, write that she had orchestrated the 'natural notes' of all human life, from the screeching to the melting, harmonious and contrapuntal, without any jarring sounds. In his essay 'Dyret i Mennesket' (The beast in the man, 1890)[106] Brandes broke definitively with Zola and what he felt was his mechanical and badly digested Darwinism.

Brandes himself had promoted J.P. Jacobsen and Holger Drachmann (1846–1908), but he displayed greater scepticism and was more reticent about Amalie Skram and other female authors. He perceived Herman Bang directly as an opponent and competitor to the project of his brother Edvard to introduce new European literature and literary criticism to Denmark. Henrik Pontoppidan, who made his debut in 1881, was an author Brandes only subsequently came to appreciate.[107]

Brandes' work on the new literature, *Det moderne Gjennembruds Mænd* (The Men of the modern breakthrough, 1883), provided portraits of Bjørnstjerne Bjørnson, Henrik Ibsen, J.P. Jacobsen, Holger Drachmann, Edvard Brandes, Sophus Schandorph and Erik Skram. Even though it was only part of the new Danish literature that Brandes sought to promote, his critique of society, morality and religion as well as his introductions to European literature were of the utmost importance for a new cultural orientation and an opening up to the modern. Brandes had asked the authors to show an interest in natural science, in positivism and Darwinism, in the question of the position of women in society and marriage, in the break with religious interpretations of existence and in social issues that the emergence of the new working class was making increasingly pressing.

And poetry and prose were in fact written about the subjects Brandes had emphasized. Drachmann wrote poetry about the workers who had started to organize themselves, and about the Paris commune in his large poem 'English Socialists' from 1872. As a debut writer, he punctured the self-sufficiency of the Biedermeier culture and its refusal to see a world full of change, and he dedicated his poems to 'My friend', Brandes.[108] When it came to feminist issues, Brandes himself had translated *The Subjection of Women* by the English philosopher John Stuart Mills in 1869, and opened up a debate and literary thematization of the whole feminist issue. But the cause he most of all wanted to have as his patent was one that the more conservative and Christian women of the Danish Women's Society were not to 'bungle', as he patronizingly wrote.

J.P. Jacobsen translated Charles Darwin's *The Origin of Species by Means of Natural Selection* (1859) in 1872, and Brandes also referred in his lectures at the University of Copenhagen to the Frenchman Auguste Comte, who in 1830–42 published his writings on positivist philosophy. The positivist Comte, with his insistence that science is to deal with the observable and seek for connections between cause and effect, also paved the way for a new literary criticism. Here, one studied and presented such connections between the work of art and the artist and was interested in a psychological and historical consideration of literature. From his stay in Paris, Brandes knew the leading new critics Hippolyte Taine (1848–93) and Charles Auguste Sainte-Beuve (1804–69), and he combined their ideas in forming his own literary criticism. He did, however, distance himself from Taine's ideas that the work of art should be a simple résumé of the artist's age and environment.

Running parallel with Georg and Edvard Brandes, Herman Bang had started to introduce the new French literature. His work *Realisme og Realister* (Realism and Realists) was published in 1879. The Brandes brothers were not at all pleased about this initiative. Bang worked for the conservative press, which was always attacking Brandes, and Edvard expressed his irritation to J.P. Jacobsen that Bang's book had ruined subjects that he himself had otherwise thought of dealing with. By the conservative camp Brandes was criticized for promoting a grubby literature. French literature resembled a dissection room, pure and simple, where corpses were cut up. Bang replied by claiming that the poets of the new age had stopped being gods – they were human beings who lived and wrote amid the struggles of life. He insisted that realism was a form, not a conception and interpretation of existence. As a realist, one had to know society, just as a botanist knew his discipline, not only the plants but also the soil and its composition, Bang wrote, using highly characteristic botanical imagery. Bang continued his critical activities and his discussion of ideas about a modern narrative art. In 1890, he formulated, in a debate with Erik Skram, hypotheses and thoughts about impressionist art as an art that shows living, acting human beings rather than protracted descriptions. The impressionist creates illusions of the movements of life. Here Bang, once more discussed the renewal of prose that he as a writer was always involved in – and which resulted in masterpieces such as his short prose pieces and the somewhat longer *Ved Vejen* (Katinka, 1886/1990). The short novel tells the story of Katinka Bai, her marriage to the narrowminded station manager, Bai, and her unhappy love of the superintendent Huss. Katinka watches the trains pass by the railway station and the years elapse. The novel depicts how a somehow endurable

A late 19th century interior, The National Museum, Copenhagen, photo by Arnold Mikkelsen & John Lee

marriage is all that most women of Bang's age can hope for. Katinka's marriage is unhappy and her love of Huss can never be carried out. Bang is a master of showing, instead of telling – as when we see Katinka arrange her old wedding veil:

> In the top drawer of her desk, under the silver chest, lay her bridal veil and the withered wreath of myrtle.

She would also pick them up and smooth them out and put them back again.

And she could sit for half an hour at a time in front of the open drawer not doing a thing, as was her custom.

Once in a while she would just smooth the veil with her hands.

It had begun to turn quite yellow, her bridal veil.

But time was passing too. It was already ten years ago. [109]

Several women authors of the modern breakthrough have been rediscovered in the late 20th and the early 21st century. Often, their novels and short stories describe the suppression of women, their longings, hopes and their despair. Some of the women are hospitalized with mental illnesses, and the women authors describes, how the patriarchal society regards female gender as a departure from the 'normal', and how women and especially women artist are sickened. Amalie Skram and Helga Johansen (1852-1912) wrote remarquable novels about their own experiences with mental hospitals. Amalie Skram's novels, *Professor Hieronymus* and *Paa Sankt Jørgen* (Professor Hieronymus and At Saint George's Hospital, 1895) describe a woman painter who is hospitalized by the doctor and her husband against her will. Helga Johansen's novel *Hinsides* (Beyond, 1900) is an autobiographical story of the young woman, Hannah, who seeks tranquillity and rest at a mental hospital, but the treatment makes her seriously ill and her mind collapses.

More modern impulses

During the last decades of the 19th century, Brandes found new sources of poetic and philosophical inspiration. His thinking broke new ground, still based on a critique of religion. Among other things, he was fascinated by the attempts made by the German philosopher Arthur Schopenhauer (1788–1860) to bring Western and Oriental philosophy closer to each other, and even though he was critical of Schopenhauer's cultural pessimism, he emphasized that it was at least not a question of some superficial mood-pessimism and in addition a good cure for the insipid optimism of his own age. Of greatest importance, however, was Brandes' reading of the philosopher Friedrich Nietzsche. This passionate showdown with a religious view of life and his conception of the visionary lone figure and the importance of the great forward-looking individual aroused Brandes' enthusiasm, and his introductions made Nietzsche known throughout Europe. Nietzsche himself was pleased with Brandes' concept of a new cultural current *Aristocratic Radicalism* (An Essay on the Aristocratic Radicalism of Friedrich Nietzsche, 1889) which was the title of his dissertation on Nietzsche. He wrote to Brandes that he and Brandes had met like two people walking along a path who could please and encourage each other, and he regretted being unable to read either Danish or Swedish. Via Brandes' introductions, Nietzsche also became acquainted with August Strindberg, who warned him about having too high expectations of the translation of his works into 'Greenlandic', i.e. for a Nordic audience. Here, people tried to lock up artists in mental asylums and force people like Brandes into exile. Nietzsche himself gave an indication of the strong critical impulse that emanated from his authorship when, in a state of insanity, he wrote to Brandes in 1889:

> After you had discovered me, it was no particular feat to find me; the difficulty now is to lose me ...[110]

Nietzsche's critique of Christian morality, of the conception of objective, eternally valid values and his discussion of how culture and science are interpretations that can be disputed and unmasked, proved to be epoch-making:

> Is language the adequate expression of all realities? [...] We believe that we know something about the things themselves when we speak of trees, colours, snow, and flowers; and yet we possess nothing but metaphors for things – metaphors which correspond in no way to the original entities. [...]What then is truth? A movable host of metaphors, metonymies, and; anthropomorphisms: in short, a sum of human relations which have been poetically and rhetorically intensified, transferred, and embellished, and which, after long usage, seem to a people to be fixed, canonical, and binding. Truths are illusions which we have forgotten are illusions – they are metaphors that have become worn out and have been drained of sensuous force, coins which have lost their embossing and are now considered as metal and no longer as coins.[111]

– Nietzsche wrote.

With such ideas about language, Nietzsche opened up a new view of literature that was to be of great importance in the postmodern age of the succeeding century. The deconstructional critique of the latter half of the 20th century viewed – with a reference to Nietzsche – the literary text as indefinable and ambiguous. The deconstruction showed this trait by deconstructing the formation of meaning in the literary text.

For Brandes, however, it was first and foremost the modern and Romantic traits in Nietzsche that stood out. He was interested in the modern critique of religion and the idea of the importance of the great man for historical progress, which can be perceived as an echo of the Romantic idea of the genius. Nietzsche's ideas of the superman were, however, used and directly inscribed into the suppressive ideology of Fascism in the first half of the 20th century. For sections of the German Nazi party and for Benito Mussolini's Fascists, Nietzsche was one of the chief ideologists. Nietzsche himself, though, had little to do with German nationalism, which the Nazi party also built on, and what is more, he was dead and gone before the new century had hardly got underway. He died on 25 August 1900 in Weimar, the city that Goethe and Schiller had made world-famous. Writers and philosophers had made pilgrimages to the city at the beginning of the 19th century. It was here that Duke Carl Alexander had wished to install Hans Christian Andersen as Goethe's successor in the 1840s. But the Schleswig wars of 1848 and 1864 also put an end to such plans.[112]

The modern breakthrough became a literary sense of the realities of loss and of the new cultural possibilities it could perhaps lead to. The Nordic cultural community that the Romantic period had cultivated and that had culminated around the First Schleswig War of 1848 was reformulated in the age of the modern breakthrough into lively and critical exchanges in Norway, Sweden and Denmark. The break with the Romantic view of women led to a great Nordic feud on morality with trenchant contributions concerning both bourgeois and free-thinking double standards. Amalie Skram's marriage novel *Lucie* (1888) showed, for example, how both the upper middle class and an environment that is enthusiastic about broad-mindedness and radicalism are hypocritical and have double standards when it comes to a sexually experienced woman from the lower class. As did other female characters in Skram's works, Lucie ends up committing suicide.

Nordic writers and artists met in Copenhagen, Berlin and Paris on educational journeys or in more or less voluntary exile. Herman Bang's homosexuality placed him in a number of difficult and dangerous situations where he had to travel from town to town to avoid being arrested and confronted with the police.[113] But journeys and meetings around Europe were not only evidence of flight – they also offered opportunities to pass on and to receive artistic impulses and ideas. Hans Christian Andersen's appearance as a European writer found new parallels in Brandes' lecture tours, travel accounts and contributions to European periodicals, and in Henrik Ibsen's and August Strindberg's European fame. Strindberg actually praised Andersen on the centenary of the latter's birth in 1905, simply by referring to himself as 'August Strindberg, pupil of Hans Christian Andersen'.[114] As an adult, he was pleasurably surprised when reading Andersen's novels and re-reading his fairytales.

Younger literary travellers were also on their way around Europe in the closing decades of the 19th century. Herman Bang's young colleague and friend Sophus Claussen (1865–1931) travelled to Paris in 1892 and wrote one of his first major works *Antonius i Paris* (1896) about his meeting with the metropolis. Here, letters, poems and essays all found room in a conflict between Romantic longings and dreams and the new forms of experience the big city offered. Claussen's book was an extension of the travel letters he published in *Politiken*. Like Herman Bang, he created a connection between literature and journalism, which was to become highly characteristic of the 20th century. From Johannes V. Jensen's generation to that of Klaus Rifbjerg, the author often worked at the same time or periodically as a journalist.

The meeting between Romantic and new forms of experience are dealt with in many ways in *Antonius i Paris*. This takes place, for example, in the complex relationship between the narrator and his main character, Antonius, and the theme is also developed in the depiction of the meeting between the narrator/Antonius and the leading poet of French symbolism, Paul Verlaine. The meeting takes place on a mild, damp January evening, when the gas-light causes the outside world to lose its familiar contours, and one seems able to 'reflect oneself in the Unknown'. On such an evening the I-figure meets 'the young, literary 'King' of France, the symbolist Paul Verlaine:

> There was a touch of concern about his features, older than everything now living. But in his posture and about his whole figure there was a strange unconcerned transfiguration that made one think of an ancient Greek philosopher – of Socrates, whom he reminds one of with his large forehead, small upturned nose and grey full beard. Beautiful clothes and white linen were apparently unknown to him. His clothing was shabby, with torn button-holes without corresponding buttons, and around the white, full neck one could see a not particularly clean sports shirt of grey wool. As he stood there, surrounded by a group of admiring disciples and in the middle of a conversation that did not interest him, he seemed only to be listening to the blood in his own veins, which, to use a Verlaine-like turn of phrase runs 'as fine as poison'.[115]

A sculpture of Sophus Claussen by Arne Bang, 1928

Claussen sees Verlaine as both a wise man of Antiquity, a genius of Romanticism, a Parisian proletarian and a completely new poetic myth. A dreamy, experiential modern literature that stood on the threshold between two centuries was finding its forms and genres in Claussen's poetic universe. In a poem to Georg Brandes, he tried to express the connection, and differences between the aims of the 1870s and those of the 1890s:

Beautiful propaganda
To Dr. Georg Brandes

To raise the issues to a new debate,
pronounce the new truth everywhere one goes,
replace lie's words with those that are life's own –
that was the aim which you then had proposed.

The new truths can be worn until threadbare,
but for the idea I will raise my hat:
to raise the issues to a new debate,
pronounce the new truth everywhere one goes.

You set research up against reveries,
the present age establishes new dreams...
A change? The school of fencing stays the same:

to raise the issues to a new debate,
to make divine what was inanimate,
and then ... to trust in the fortune of war.[116]

In the 19th century, time and space had become boundaries beyond what poetry could and had to transcend. A second nature and a golden age, or a new realm of freedom could and should be brought about by the holy images of the eternal in poetry. Poetry was to heal all divisions and bring about a spiritual wholeness.

The experience of the powers of imagination and their limitations made the flashing moment, where time and space seem to glide into each other and eternity to open up, a new object of poetic longing. But the flash and opening of the moment could also point to paradox, loss, disappearance and annihilation as well as a desire for new moments, new experiences that could never be made to stop.

Danish literature portrayed, in fascination and melancholy, the moment and the loss that allowed the realities and the real to become visible. In the modern breakthrough, a new longing for freedom was involved along with a hope of mentally and artistically being able to match the modern outside world. The world opened up, also to the new abysses, as Nietzsche claimed, and to the present dreams about which Sophus Claussen wrote his poetry.

NOTES

From God's time to man's time 1000-1700

1 See the chapter 'Refleksioner over litteraturhistorisk teori og metode' (Reflections on the theory and method of literary history), Mai 2010 II, p. 212-229.

2 Peter Skautrup notes in *Det danske Sprogs Historie* (History of the Danish Language, 1944–70), Vol. I, p. 80 ff. that the growth of the church and gathering together of the kingdom are concomitant. The actual name Denmark is used for the first time around 900AD in the translation by Alfred the Great of the world history by the Christian Roman historian Orosius.

3 Moltke 1976, p. 80.

4 In her PhD thesis *Runer og runeindskrifter* [Runes and runic inscriptions] 2007, p.141, Lisbeth M. Imer argues extremely convincingly that the inscription mentions the owner, to whom the name and nickname both refer.

5 Finn Rasmussen provides this interpretation of the inscription in *Guldhornenes tydning. Forhistoriske billedsymboler, runerne og den gamle nordiske religion* (Interpreting the Gold Horns. Prehistoric pictorial symbols, runes and the old Norse religion) 1990, p. 177. An interpretation that emphasizes the literary-historical contexts is to be found in Hans Bekker-Nielsen's *Fra runeskrift til trykte bogstaver* (From runes to printed letters, 2002), p. 11 ff.

6 In his history of Denmark, Saxo Grammaticus mentions Odin's victory over Oller or Ull, the knowledgeable magician who has mastered the art of scratching sinister magic formulae on bones, but is killed by the Danes, cf. Saxo 2000, Vol. I, p. 121.

7 See, for example, the chronological table in Hvass and Storgaard 1993, p. 169.

8 Philology has given the runic alphabet the name *futhark,* after the first six signs of the system of writing. Below is the elder runic alphabet with 24 signs, from: www. kongernesjelling.dk (the alphabet is no longer accessible), cf. also Moltke 1976, p. 22:

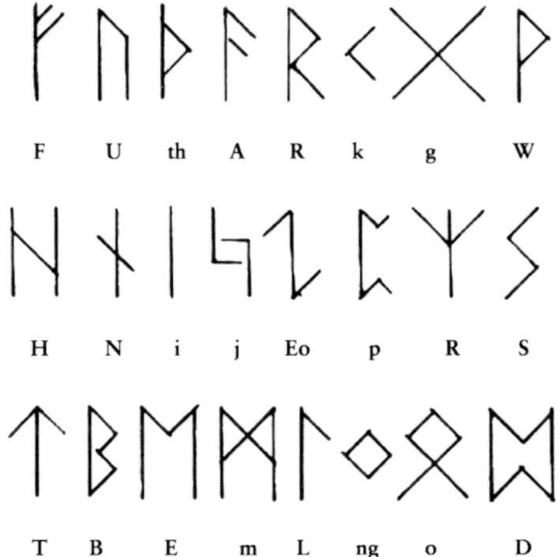

Each of the runes had its own name, as can be reconstructed from manuscripts from the 11th to 14th centuries. For example, the F rune's name was *får, kvæg* [sheep, cattle], the U rune's name was *urokse* [aurochs], the Th rune's name *trold*, [troll], the A rune's name *Asegud* [As god].

9 Cf. P. Meulengracht Sørensen 2001, p. 8.

10 Mogens Ørsnes and Jørgen Ilkjær write in their article 'Offerfund' [Sacrificial find], which deals with sacrificial finds from the Iron Age, that battles must have taken place between neighbouring areas where one party wanted control of the other's resources, commercial centres, roads and commodities. 'The sacrifices that for generations followed the same rituals at the same time-honoured sacred places helped confirm clan alliances, mutual military obligations, and mutual dependence on a chieftain and a warrior elite that surrounded him', Hvass and Storgaard 1993, p. 222.

11 In *Danmarks Oldtid. Ældre Jernalder 500 f.Kr. – 400 e.Kr.* [Denmark's early history. The Early Iron Age 500 BC – 400 AD] (2003) Jørgen Jensen examines the Torsbjerg find and gives an account of how life during this period was characterized by repeated clan battles, the aim and starting point of which changed over time. The Torsbjerg find indicates that all weapons were systematically destroyed in connection with the offering, cf. p. 508 ff.

12 The archaeologist and runologist Marie Stoklund writes about the find of a fine sword sheath in Nydam Engmose in 1995. The sword sheath dates from c. 300 AD and on one of its bronze belt straps a runic inscription was found which is extremely difficult to interpret. Stoklund mentions one proposed translation, as follows: '(You) destroy, attack!' – i.e. a magic invocation addressing the sword similar to the inscription on the Torsbjerg ferrule. See Stoklund 1996, p. 276. Lisbeth M. Imer is dismissive of the reading of runic inscriptions as magic invocations – including the inscription on the Torsbjerg ferrule. She allows that some of the inscriptions may have been conceived as auspicious (p. 148), but suggests – in contrast to Meulengracht Sørensen, for example – that the use of the runes in the written language was similar to the communicative use of written language undertaken by the Romans, cf. Imer 2007, p. 162 ff.

13 In the poem *Guldhornene* [The Golden Horns], Oehlenschläger refers to the horns as a 'gleaming pair from days of yore'. The horns gleam mysteriously across the ages and tell the story of a glorious national past, and by means of his poem Oehlenschläger wishes to create his own mythological reading of their history. This leads him to harsh criticism of his own age, particularly the insensitive academics who are incapable of experiencing the sacred mystery of the horns. For this reason, the gods take back the horns. The theft is the gods' punishment. At the end of his long poem, Oehlenschläger writes: 'Skies grow dark, the storms awaken!/Certain hour, your word is law./What they gave has been retaken./What was sacred is no more.' Translation by John Irons, included in *100 Danish poems. From the medieval period to the present day* (2010).

14 Finn Rasmussen supplies one of many interpretations of how to read the poem, *Guldhornenes tydning* [Interpreting the Gold Horns] (1990), see also Hans Bekker-Nielsens *Fra Runeskrift til trykte bogstaver* [From runic inscription to printed letters] (2002), p. 11 ff.

15 The actual find is described in Conrad Engelhardt's *Nydam mosefund, 1859-1863. Jernalderens våbenofferfund* [The Nydam bog find. Weapon offerings of the Iron Age, 1865, reissued 1969-70]. A more detailed account of the story of the find is be found in Peter Petersen's *Nydam offermose* [Nydam sacrificial bog] (1995), p. 102 ff., and in *Sejrens triumf. Norden i skyggen af det romerske imperium*, [The triump of victory. The North in the shadow of the Roman Empire], Lars Jørgensen et al., 2003, p. 66 ff.

16 Preben Meulengracht Sørensen advances this hypothesis about the runes in his *Kapitler af Nordens litteratur i oldtid og middelalder* [Chapters of Northern literature in the early and medieval periods], (2006). While Meulengracht Sørensen emphasizes here that runic writing was not primarily for communication, Gundhild Øeby Nielsen in her dissertation *Runesten*

og deres fundforhold [Runic stones and their find conditions], 2007, stresses the communicative aspect of the inscriptions on the runic stones. She does, however, point out that the runic inscriptions are not texts in the modern sense, but visual inscriptions in close contact with the medium – the stone (p. 98).

17 Cf. P. Meulengracht Sørensen 2006, p. 39.

18 Cf. M. Larsen 1943, vol. 1, p. 92.

19 Cf. Skautrup 1944–70, Vol. I., p. 81 ff. It is pointed out here that we have no knowledge of the spoken language before 800AD (cf. p. 80). In Nordic circles, everyone understood Danish around 1000AD, but by the mid-14th century, differentiation between the Nordic languages has become a reality.

20 It would seem that many women have raised runic stones: 'Over a score of the runic stones of the Viking period – and these are by no means the smallest – were raised by women [...].' This says something about women's independent position in Denmark in the Viking Age (women had the right to demand a divorce if they desired, noted the Hispano-Arabic, Sephardi Jewish merchant Ibrahim Ibn Ya 'qub who visited Hedeby c. 960AD. cf. Moltke 1976, pp. 253-54. The Arabic diplomat and traveler Ibn Fadlan also gave an account of his experiences on the vikings, jf. http://danmarkshistorien.dk/leksikon-og-kilder/vis/materiale/ibn-fadlan-om-vikingernes-ar-rus-skikke-ca-922/

21 In her PhD dissertation, *Runesten og deres fundforhold* [Rune stones and their find conditions], 2007, Gunhild Øeby Nielsen analyzes the positioning of the runic stones, concluding that they were originally placed in the landscape so that they could be seen by as many people as possible, p. 108.

22 Moltke 1976, p. 182.

23 Lis Jacobsen suggests the meaning 'outlawed dead man/corpse' in Jacobsen 1935, p. 61.

24 Concerning the composition of the text on the Glavendrup stone, see N.Å. Nielsen 1983, p. 78 ff.

25 Cf. Moltke 1976, p. 162 ff.

26 The new material objects and stylistic expressions were disseminated by travelling Nordic and European craftsmen and traders, Christian missionaries and the many Vikings who returned home after raids and voyages, says Iben Skibsted Klæsøe (2002), p. 15.

27 Cf. Gotfredsen 2002, p. 41.

28 Cf. Hvass 2000, pp. 10-11.

29 Adam of Bremen's Chronicle was published in Allan A. Lund's translation in 2000; see Adam of Bremen 2000.

30 Preben Meulengracht Sørensen discusses the Jelling stone as a communicative document in P. Meulengracht Sørensen 2006, p. 46 ff.

31 'It is misleading when the late acquisition of the cultural and social forms of the European Middle Ages are sometimes regarded as a late arrival, or Scandinavia as a peripheral area that only became civilized via a Christian culture at a late date. This view is the result of early Nordic culture being seen through the eyes of continental culture and not on the basis of its own prior conditions. This led to its being seen as backward or barbaric. But the late adoption by the North of European medieval culture should rather be thought of as the strength and high level of the early culture,' P. Meulengracht Sørensen 2001, p. 10.

32 In the article 'Grovhed og skjaldegave. Egils saga', *Læsninger i dansk litteratur* [Readings in Danish literature] (1998), Vol. I, p. 23 ff., Lise Præstgaard Andersen discusses why the Icelandic sagas have played such an important role in Danish literature, although their main subject is memorable Icelandic men and women. In her opinion, it is because the sagas were written in an ancestral Danish tongue, i.e. the language that was spoken and understood throughout the North in the 800AD to 1200AD period. She also emphasizes that the sagas have played an important role in Danish literary history from Oehlenschläger and Grundtvig to Martin A. Hansen because of their narrative strength and exiting plots.

33 Cf. P. Meulengracht Sørensen 2001, p. 7 ff.

34 The runologist Judith Jesch uses the concept of 'the power of poetry' in connection with the Viking runic inscriptions and oral skaldic poetry. She emphasizes that verse and poetry were not only instruments of political and military power that wanted to celebrate itself and ensure its posthumous reputation. Poetry also had a power in itself, by virtue of the fact that the skald and his listeners could remember and recognize it. That effect gave verse a special status in Viking society. See Jesch 2000, p. 21 ff.
It is also worth noting that the runologist Niels Åge Nielsen, in his dissertation *Danske runeindskrifter* [Danish runic inscriptions], 1983, lists a number of features that are characteristic of the runic verses, including the use of anaphora (repetition of the same words at the beginning of several lines) and epiphora (repetition of words at the end of several lines). There is moreover a highly conscious use of parallelism (sentences with the same word order, but different meaning) or synonymic variation (use of several different names for the same figure). These stylistic characteristics make it easier to interpret runic inscriptions – in cases of uncertainty, one can often still make a qualified guess.

35 Nielsen 1983, p. 58. Niels Åge Nielsen's hypothesis about the use of verse is not generally accepted in runic research.

36 Ibid., p. 56.

37 Cf. N.Å. Nielsen 1983, p. 153.

38 Preben Meulengracht Sørensen argues in *Kapitler af Norden litteratur i oldtid og middelalder* [Chapters of literature in the North in early and medieval history], 2006, that the inscription on the runic stone in Rök is an attempt to imitate writing in pictures, and that it is an experiment inspired by knowledge of foreign books with tales and poems (p. 51). Otto von Friesen analyzes the Rök stone in *Rökstenen i Bohuslän och runorna i Norden under folkvandringstiden* [The Rök stone in Bohuslän and runes in the North during the period of migration], (1924).

39 Cf. N.Å. Nielsen 1983, s. 182.

40 The manuscript was given as a present by the Icelandic bishop Brynjólfur to King Frederik III and was brought to Copenhagen. The bishop hoped that the poems could be published, though this did not occur until 1787. *Codex Regius* was returned to Iceland in 1971.

41 Cf. P. Meulengracht Sørensen 1977, p. 100 ff.

42 P. Meulengracht Sørensen and Steinsland explain it as follows: 'Present-day readers of the prophecy of the *Völuspá* encounter stanzas and sections that are difficult, if not impossible, to understand. The difficulty does not lie in the language. Apart from a few words, this is clear enough. The problem lies in the composition of the poem, and in the fact that we know too little about its basis, its inner cohesion and references to myths that are unknown to us, Sørensen and Steinsland 2001, p. 87.

43 Cf. E.O.G. Turville-Petre, who in *Myth and Religion of the North. The Religion of Ancient Scandinavia* (1964) concludes about the writer of the *Völuspá*: 'We could believe that he foresaw the decline and end of the pagan religion and hoped for a better one to take its place. He may also have been inspired by the widespread Christian apprehension that the world would come to an end in the year 1000 or 1300.' Turville-Petre 1975, p. 282.

44 V. Dranke 1997, Vol. II, p. 7.

45 In his reading of the poem, Vagn Steen suggests that when the vövla refers to Odin as Valfader, her reference also applies to the dead: 'I read this as the volva also invoking the dead. Without their being included in the utterance, one never gains the truth,' Steen 1994, p. 11.

46 Cf. Kress 1993, Vol. I, p. 22 ff.

47 Cf. Lönnroth 1978, p. 29 ff.

48 Cf. Bredsdorff 1998, Vol. I, p. 9 ff.

49 V. Dranke 1997, Vol. II, p. 19.

50 'It is the world of the word we see unrolled and perish in *Völuspá*, a world held together by words and dissolved by broken words,' Thomas Bredsdorff (1998), Vol. I., p. 18.
51 V. Dranke 1997, Vol. II, p. 14.
52 Ibid., p. 4.
53 Ibid., p. 24.
54 Cf. Steen 1994, p. 11.
55 Cf. P. Meulengracht Sørensen 2006, p. 121 ff.
56 Hans Henrik Lohfert Jørgensen, in his article 'Transhistorie. Om middelalderlige og moderne identiteter i forvandling' [Transhistory. On medieval and modern identities in transformation], Jørgensen 2005, p. 12, discusses how the medieval period has thinking in historical constituted a 'historical Otherness' in relation to the modern, unlike the Renaissance and Antiquity, in which later ages have found their own reflections.
57 Cf. Ingesman 1999, p. 12 ff. The historian Michael H. Gelting also emphasizes that, during the Middle Ages, Denmark was closer to Europe than in either the preceding or the succeeding period. He characterizes medieval culture as a rich mixture of regional variations on common themes such as urbanisation, legislation, the establishment of guilds of merchants and craftsmen, and the early use of the native tongue in official letters and papers. Another shared theme is the writing of history, where Saxo creates his variations in *Gesta Danorum*, a work that can bear comparison with the best at a European level. But with the Reformation, the cultural horizon is divided into North German, Central German and Scandinavian areas; cf. Gelting 1999, p. 334 ff.
58 The historian Kurt Villads Jensen, in his article 'Middelalderen i EU – centrum og periferi' [The Middle Ages in the EU – centre and periphery], Jensen 2005, p. 47, discusses how historians regard the medieval period as a common European cultural experience. The rising interest in the Middle Ages is connected to the contemporary phenomena of growing European cooperation. Jensen notes that the most important features of European culture have origins created in the Middle Ages, but also that people of the Middle Ages viewed themselves as linked to Antiquity.
59 For a more detailed account, see the chapter 'Akademiet', Mai 2010 I, p. 271 ff.
60 For a more detailed account of the Cistercian library, see the chapter 'Akademiet', Mai 2010 I, p. 266 ff.
61 Cf. Gregersen and Jensen 2003.
62 For more information about the rhymed chronicle, see the chapter 'Akademiet', Mai 2010 I, p. 271 ff.
63 Schmidt 2004, p. 72.
64 The Middle Ages compared manuscripts and sacred texts with Christ's own body. The page of a book is likened to Christ's skin, and the red chapter headings bleed as a sign of how the crown of thorns had pierced his head, cf. Liepe 2005, p. 120.
65 For a more detailed account of the ballads, see the chapter 'Herregård og Hof' (Manor and Court), Mai 2010 I, pp. 136-37.
66 Moltke 1976, p. 348.
67 Jacobsen 1931, pp. 6-7. As can be seen here, Lis Jacobsen has changed her reading so that it now agrees with that of Moltke, cf. also their shared reading in *Danmarks Runeindskrifter* [Denmark's runic inscriptions], 1941-42, Vol. II, pp. 203-204: 'Torsten Bre... carved these runes at Whitsuntide ... he had much pleasure of the notes in the morning there'.
68 Cf. Sunesen 1985, p. 283 ff.
69 Cf. Sunesen 1985, p. 68.
70 Ibid., p. 35 and p. 89.
71 Anders Sunesen's *Hexaëmeron* appeared in a complete Danish translation for the first time in 1985. The translator, H.D. Schepelern, together with the editor Jørgen Pedersen, give an account of the history of the work and its position in the European tradition in an afterword to the translation.

72 Sunesen 1985, p. 159.

73 Ibid., p. 267.

74 Saxo 2002, p. 4.

75 Minna Skafte Jensen analyzes this aspect of the work in her article 'Saxo: Gesta Danorum', Jensen 1998, p. 40 ff.

76 Cf.Inge Skovgaard-Petersen: *Da Tidernes Herre var nær. Studie i Saxos historiesyn* [When the Lord of the Ages was near. Study in Saxo's view of history, 1987].

77 Saxo 2002, p. 87.

78 Ibid., p. 452.

79 In his reading of Saxo on the website *Arkiv for dansk litteratur*, Peter Zeeberg emphasizes that Saxo wanted to show Denmark as a kingdom that could rival the Roman Empire. The references to Roman sources and literary works indicate this ambition: 'In Saxo's depiction, Denmark is a great, ancient European cultural nation, with roots stretching back as far as any other country. Or, to be quite specific: Denmark can bear comparison with the Roman Empire, both historically and culturally. And his work is itself proof of the fact that Denmark is still among the top nations,' see: www.adl. dk/

80 Cf. Saxo 2002, p. 269.

81 Cf. Ingesman 1999, p. 12 ff.

82 Riising 1969, p. 127 f.

83 Cf. the philosopher Dorthe Jørgensen, who gives an account of Plato's theories in *Skønhedens metamorfose. De æstetiske ideers historie* (The metamorphosis of beauty. The history of aesthetic ideas, 2001). My discussion is based on her analyzes.

84 Cf. ibid.

85 Song of Solomon V:1.

86 Early on, violent disagreement arose in the Catholic Church regarding the use of images. The so-called iconodules, supporters of images, thought that religious images could be holy. God could be present as a spiritual archetype in a man-made image, e.g. in images of Christ or the Virgin Mary. The beauty of the archetype could appear in a concrete image, which thereby became a divine manifestation and acquired supernatural powers. The iconoclasts rejected the use of images. They felt that the creation and worship of images was sheer idolatry. God could not be present within any human image, and there was absolutely no reason to attempt to locate him there. Particularly in the Eastern, Byzantine Church, where the art of making icons was greatly valued, there was a battle between supporters and opponents during the 8th and 9th centuries, one that also reached the Western, Roman Catholic Church. Here, the pope did not forbid the use of images, however, and in the present-day Catholic Church it is still possible to experience the veneration of figures of the Virgin Mary and images of Christ that are said to perform miracles or shed tears or blood. Concerning the history of images in the church, see, inter alia, Hans Jørgen Frederiksen: *Den katolske kirke i kunstens spejl* [The Catholic church in the mirror of art], 2001.

87 The perspective on finds in visual art in the medieval period was not a sign that medieval artists were not proficient enough to use linear perspective and collect all the lines of the picture into a vanishing point. Linear perspective simply did not interest medieval artists, because their way of viewing pictures was not linked to the personal approach each individual artist took in relation to his subject matter. One did not wish to see the motif of the picture from any one particular, subjective angle.

88 Cf. H.J. Frederiksen 1987, p. 23 ff.

89 Guild and Lent plays are dealt with in Lars Bisgaard and Leif Søndergaard's *Gilder, lav og broderskaber i middelalderens Danmark* [Guilds, companies and fraternities in medieval Denmark], 2002.

90 Jan Lindhardt has pointed out that the vulgar satire of the mass is difficult for a modern person to reconcile with a feeling of true piety. An ass is led into the church and mass is performed with the ass as main character, the Virgin Mary is called 'Porco Maria' (Pig Mary) and Joseph is derided with the idea that the Holy Spirit has cuckolded him. Saint Sebastian is also mocked, the saint who is meant to protect one against the plague, by saying that he himself has sent the plague. Lindhardt believes that the medieval scoffing and mocking makes the holy more familiar to ordinary people. This is done to such an extent that eventually one finds it difficult to connect the sacred with anything that goes beyond human existence; cf. Lindhardt 1993, p. 28 ff.

91 The art historian Ulla Kjær explains that the inscription on the golden altar in Sahl Church in West Jutland expresses precisely the medieval idea of art as a link between God and man. The inscription calls its reader to look behind the visible light emitted by the gold and discover how the divine light gleams in the story of Jesus that the altar relates. But if one is to see the invisible light behind the visible, one must purify one's mind through one's faith. Art thus links God and man; cf. Kjær 1999, p. 300 ff.

92 In their article 'Skulptur i spil' [Sculpture in plays, 2005]. Rikke Duve and Louise Langaa Pedersen analyze the liturgical plays and the role of sculptures in liturgical drama.

93 Concerning the allegoresis, see for example Lise Gotfredsen and Hans Jørgen Frederiksen: *Troens billeder* [The Images of Faith], 1987, Michael Ann Holly: *Past Looking. Historical Imagination and the Rhetoric of the Image* (1996), Umberto Eco: *The Limits of Interpretation* (1994), which discuss the interpretive system of the entire Middle Ages in more general terms, and Erik A. Nielsen: *Kristendommens retorik. Den kristne digtnings billedformer* [The rhetoric of Christianity. The imaging forms of Christian writing, 2009].

94 In his article 'Polysemi og den dynamiske tradisjon' [Polysemy and the dynamic tradition], 2005) Henning Laugerud discusses the medieval fascination with polysemantic interpretations and the search for traces of absolute truth, which mankind was cut off from during earthly existence. Polysemantics and contradictions are systematized, because one has an idea that there is an anchorage for such multiplicity of meanings in God, in the absolute (p. 97).

95 For more information, see the chapter 'Katedralen' (The Cathedral), Mai 2010 I, p. 72 ff.

96 Ibid, p. 79 ff.

97 Schmidt 2000: 'Guds faders magt kalder jeg på' [I call on the power of God the Father], p. 43.

98 The German-American art historian Erwin Panofsky has tried to show how a medieval *quaestio* takes place on the west facades of the cathedrals, cf. Panofsky 1957, p. 27 ff. He believes he is able to trace how the old circular rose window is discussed in the new architecture so as to be incorporated into and subjected to the Gothic idiom in the window of Saint Nicaise in Rheims, from the mid-13th century (p. 73 f. and pp. 142-43).

99 The writings of Boethius have been published in a translation by Niels Jørgen Green-Pedersen, cf. Boethius de Dacia 2001.

100 Norén 1993, p. 133.

101 The medieval historian Brian Patrick-McGuire notes that the late 13th century biography of Bishop Gunner describes the bishop's good deeds on the basis of examples from everyday life. The biography is purged of any accounts of miracles or references to the supernatural. It is here, in everyday life, that the spirit and morality are to be sought. The biography thus represents a break from the previous conventions of medieval hagiography. Cf. Patrick-McGuire 1976.

102 Concerning courtly culture and literature, see for example Valdemar Vedel: *Ridderromantikken i fransk og tysk middelalderdigtning* (Knightly romanticism in French and German medieval writing, 1906), or Nils Gunder Hansen: *Den høviske kærlighed* (Courtly love, 1985).

103 See the chapter 'Herregård og hof', [The Manor and Court], p. 146 ff.

104 See further analysis of the tradition of the ballads in Mai 2010 2, p. 51-72.

105 Bredsdorff, Mai and Irons 2011, p. 65

106 The literary historian Povl Schmidt has shown how the autobiography of the condemned Ole Kollerød from 1840 is profoundly influenced by the fixed literary turns of phrase of courtly culture. Kollerød knew this literary language from the chapbooks of his own age, which in the 18th and 19th centuries were regularly reprinted; cf. Schmidt 2003.

107 See the chapter 'Katedralen' [The Cathedral] Mai 2010 I, p. 92 ff.

108 The poem 'In Urania melegia autoris', De Nova Stella (1573), has been translated by Peter Zeeberg into Danish at: www.adl.dk, from Brahe 1913-29, Vol. I, pp. 65-70.

109 The most influential dissertation here is by the art and cultural historian Jacob Burckardt: *Die Cultur der Renaissance in Italien* (1860).

110 Danish Renaissance scholars have contributed with a number of sections in *Dansk litteraturs historie* [The history of Danish literature], 2006-09, vol. I. Here, the period from 1200 to 1800 is divided into three major phases: Middle Ages, Renaissance and Enlightenment. The literary-historical interest in the Renaissance has increased with the critique of the single-stringed Danish-national conception of literary history, which has often ignored Latin works written in Denmark. With the critique of the exclusive national construction, the Renaissance comes forward as a possible concept for periodisation.

In her discussion of the concept and theory of the Renaissance, Pil Dahlerup emphasizes that the Renaissance is important as a specifically literary period because here one can see the symbol being made independent: 'My own overall view is that in this entire rhetorical movement one can see the stamp of the Renaissance on the fundamental symbolic mode of thought that is the point of departure for all Christian periods. While the Middle Ages stressed the equality between the symbol and what is symbolized (the Gothic cathedrals are to be just as elevated as the God they represent), and while the Reformation sought to reduce the symbol to a neutral sign (it is a question of the word of the heart, said Luther, not of the mouth), the Renaissance in many ways brings about the independence of the symbol, i.e. a dissociation of the symbol from what it symbolized,' Dahlerup 1995, p. 37.

111 Montaigne 1993, Vol. I. p. 27.

112 See the chapter 'Herregård og hof' [The Manor and Court 3], Mai 2010, p. 132 ff.

113 Clara Priess translated *Memoirs of Leonora Christina, daughter of Christian IV of Denmark, written by Eleonora Christina Ulfeldt*, 1872. Further analysis of the memoirs from historians and literary scholars can be found in *Leonora Christina Ulfeldt. Historien om en heltinde* [Leonora Christina Ulfeldt. The story of a heroine, ed. Mai et al., 1983].

114 The concept of the Baroque is used, for example, in Mortensen and Schack's *Dansk litteraturs historie* [History of Danish Literature], 2007, vol. I. Here, it is a general period concept, cf. the section 'Orthodoxy, the Baroque and Absolutism', but it is also used in the subsection 'The Baroque – an upheaval' (p. 329 ff). Here, it describes a literary re-orientation, in which occasional verse and religious poetry express a new, special interpretation of a changing world with stark contrasts between chaos and order, perdition and salvation, dark and light. Also, the Baroque represents the emergence of a literary culture in Danish, which is said to culminate in Kingo, whose writing marks the climax of a stylistic tendency in which ideology and form fuse together. So the concept is used both as a designation for as well as a period and for a new literary interpretation of existence, to describe a particular style.

A mainly stylistic definition of Baroque literature is found in Ejnar Thomsen's standard work *Barokken i dansk digtning* [The Baroque in Danish writing], 1971, and Erik Sønderholm's *Dansk Barok 1630-1700* [Danish Baroque 1630-1700] 1979. Eira Storstein and Peer E. Sørensen also discuss the concept of the Baroque in *Den barokke tekst* [The Baroque text], 1999. Here, the Baroque is treated not as a period but as an artistic transit between the aesthetics of the Antiquity, the Middle Ages and the Renaissance, and particular attention is paid to the modern features of the Baroque: the first formulation of a modern authorial personality and the constant, allegorical thematization of the possibility for art to represent the eternal. The history of this Baroque modernity can be traced in the writing of such present-day authors as Simon Grotrian.

Torben Jelsbak deals with the Danish reception of the Baroque in the article 'Barokken i dansk digtning' [The Baroque in Danish writing], *Danske Studier* [Danish Studies], 1999.

115 Newton 2009.

116 Kingo 1975, p. 371

117 For more information about Povl Schmidt's reading of the petition, see *Læsninger i dansk litteratur* [Readings in Danish literature] 1998, Vol. I, p. 151 ff.

118 Niels Hemmingsen is part of the opening up of the European discussion of natural law, referring directly to St. Paul as his model: '[...] so that no one shall attack me and say that I am like the man in the proverb that harvests the field of another man, my defence is this. Last year, I was to give a lecture on Paul's Epistle to the Romans. In this, the apostle calls Natural Law Truth, and says that God's Law is known to the heathens, as they show by their deeds, while their conscience bears witness to it. I felt it most worth while to give an account of the power of this law,' Hemmingsen 1991-95, Vol. I. pp. x-xi.

The century of the Enlightenment 1700–1800

1 Staffeldt 2001: 'Ode. I den franske Ultrarevolutionsperiode' [Ode. In the period of the French Ultra-revolution], Vol. I, p. 123.

2 Baggesen 1965, p. 199.

3 Ibid., p. 313. In his analysis of *Labyrinten* [The Labyrinth] in *Oprørets æstetik* [The aesthetics of revolt], 2006 Svend Skriver rightly underlines the fact that Baggesen avoids an outright glorification of the Revolution and, broadly speaking, generalizes the political dimensions of his aesthetics of revolt, so that it is not narrowly linked to the actual events of the Revolution.

4 In the introduction to Max Horkheimer and Theodor W. Adorno's collection of texts, *Dialectic of Enlightenment* (1944/1997) it says: 'In the most general sense of progressive thought, the Enlightenment has always aimed at liberating men from fear and establishing their sovereignty. Yet the fully enlightened earth radiates disaster triumphant. The program of the Enlightenment was the disenchantment of the world; the dissolution of myths and the substitution of knowledge for fancy.' (p. 3) But when reason eliminates myths and gods, it ends up making itself its own meaningless goal; man becomes alienated and ends up as a phenomenon in a world of other phenomena and meaningless objects: 'Unlike its apologists, the black writers of the bourgeoisie have not tried to ward off the consequences of the Enlightenment by harmonizing theories. They have not postulated that formalistic reason is more closely allied to morality than to immorality. Whereas the optimistic writers merely disavowed and denied in order to protect the indissoluble union of reason and crime, civil society and domination, the dark chroniclers mercilessly declared the shocking truth' (p. 117-118). Horkheimer and Adorno analyze the pornographic work *Juliette* (1797) by the French 18th century author Marquis de Sade, which deals with sexual sadism. It is Horkheimer and Adorno's point that Juliette's sadism expresses the consequence of Enlightenment thinking, and that Sade attempts to make the Enlightenment afraid of itself.

5 Staffeldt 2001: 'Dommen. Ved Slutningen af det attende Aarhundred' [The judgement. At the end of the 18th century], Vol. I, p. 118.

6 Staffeldt 2001: 'Ode. I den franske Ultrarevolutionsperiode' [Ode. In the period of the French Ultra-revolution], Vol. I, p. 123.

7 Holberg 1969–71, Vol. I, p. 112.

8 Bording 1984–86: *Forhaabnings oc forhalings Griller paa mig selff och min Tynde Lyche Satyrisk viiss Jndvent Anno 1663*, [Hopeful and delaying fads on myself and my meager happyness. An invented satire] Vol. I, p. 91.

9 In Latin: 'Cogito ergo sum' and from the publication *Principia philosophiae*, Descartes 1644, Part I, § 7.

10 Cf. the British Enlightenment scholar Roy Porter, who in an article in The Guardian guardian.co.uk (12.6.2001) in connection with the publication of his thesis *Enlightenment. Britain and the Creation of the Modern World* says: 'For one thing, all historians now agree that the very labelling of the eighteenth century as an 'age of reason' is deeply misleading. Many of the century's leading intellectuals themselves dismissed the rationalist, system-building philosophers of the seventeenth century, notably Descartes (with his notion of 'clear and distinct ideas' self-evident to reason) and Leibniz. They repudiated them as fiercely as they rejected what they considered the verbal sophistries of rationalist, scholastic theology, developed first by St Thomas Aquinas in the Middle Ages (Thomism), and further elaborated in the

Counter-Reformation. In the light of the triumph of Newtonian science, the men of the Enlightenment argued that experience and experiment, not a priori reason, were the keys to true knowledge. Man himself was no less a feeling than a thinking animal. No doubt, as Goya observed, the 'sleep of reason produces monsters'. But divorced from experience and sensitivity, reason equally led to error and absurdity, as Voltaire delightfully demonstrated in his philosophical novel *Candide*, in which the stooge, Dr Pangloss, is so blinded by his Leibnizian metaphysical conviction that 'all is for the best in the best of all possible worlds', as to become utterly indifferent to the cruelty and suffering going on under his best of all possible noses.' See www.guardian.co.uk/education/2001/jun/12/artsandhumanities.highereducation

11 Svend Erik Larsen formulates this point in his analysis of Brorson's poem in the article 'Jordskælvet i Lissabon – et vendepunkt i oplysningstiden' ['The earthquake in Lisbon – a turning-point in the Enlightenment period'], 2007. Svend Erik Larsen claims that the earthquake helped to cause Enlightenment thinkers to believe that the possibility for human freedom is the aim of human life. This aim is in fact revealed by nature itself when man discovers how mighty and overwhelming nature is. Also Kant's concept of the sublime, according to Larsen, has its origin in this experience: 'The meeting with nature in this perspective converts Kant, without naming Lisbon, to his aesthetical concept of the sublime: the experience of the meeting with nature's superhuman power and dimensions' (p. 59).

12 Brorson III 1956, Vol. III, p. 192

13 Voltaire 2000, p. 27. http://archive.org/stream/candide19942gut/19942.txt The last sentence: 'It is almost more than I can bear' transl. by John Irons.

14 S.E. Larsen 2007, p. 59.

15 Holberg 1969–71: 'Naturens og Folke-Rettens Kundskab' [The knowledge of Nature and the Common law], Vol. I, p. 59.

16 Kant 195, p. 7 http://www.columbia.edu/acis/ets/CCREAD/etscc/kant.html

17 The historian Michael Böss sees the 18th century first and foremost as a innovative period: 'i.e. as an age when an upsurge of a diversity of new ideas took place, many of which were at variance if not on a collision course with each other,' cf. Böss 2007, p. 73. In the same presentation, Hans-Jørgen Schanz gives an account of the 'Enlightenmen'st horizon of ideas'. He stresses here that when we nowadays use a concept about Enlightenment's or the Age of the Enlightenment, we homogenize and create a phenomenon that 'if successful, is a fusion of a reconstruction and a construction. What we thereby create via this double manoeuvre is a phenomenon or image that probably not a single one of the protagonists would put their signature to as an adequate expression of what they actually meant and expressed' (p. 113). Schanz emphasizes that the historical framework for the Age of the Enlightenment is the earthquake in Lisbon in 1755 and Napoleon obtaining power in 1799. After the earthquake in Lisbon, philosophers had to abandon the idea of providence or theodicy regarding God's governing of the best of all possible worlds, and with the taking over of power by Napoleon the French Revolution came to an end.

18 Porter 2001, p. 3.

19 Israel 2006, p. 11.

20 Jonathan Israel discusses how Spinoza's point of view is still relevant to the present-day debate on tolerance and freedom of speech, cf. Freedom of Thought versus Freedom of Religion, *Kritik* 188, 2008, p. 20 ff. Israel's article is part of a theme on the importance of the Enlightenment for the present age and the present-day critique of Enlightenment thinking. The Enlightenment expert, professor of French John Pedersen, emphasizes in his article that the Enlightenment is a goal that is constantly changing: 'The period as a whole asked certain questions that cannot be answered once and for all, but which constantly have to be reformulated on the basis of new assumptions. How does one ensure equality (e.g. as regards education), how does one ensure (e.g. economic) freedom without introducing the law of

the jungle? How does one promote enlightenment in general without becoming addicted to paternalistic superciliousness?' (p. 58).

21 In his examination of the defence of the female sex by the Enlightenment thinkers, Israel particularly stresses François Poulain de la Barre as being an important philosopher, who in three works from the 1670s draws radical female-emancipatory conclusions from Descartes' thesis that the soul is without gender. But, according to Israel, Descartes is read in exactly the opposite way by other thinkers and with the aim of emphasizing women's necessary subjection to men. Nordic Enlightenment thinkers such as Holberg and Nordenflycht are to be taken into consideration here.

22 F.J. Billeskov Jansen uses the title 'The 18th century' for his description of the diverse authorships of the period in Politiken's *Dansk litteraturhistorie* [History of Danish Literature] 1976–77, Vol. II, p. 11 ff. In Gyldendal's history of literature, the literature of the 18th century is introduced under the overall heading 'Embedsmandskultur under enevælden' [Officialdom culture during Absolutism], *Dansk litteraturhistorie* 1983-85,Vol. III, p. 357 ff., and 'Patriotismens tid' [The Age of Patriotism], Vol. IV, p. 11 ff.

23 *Dansk litteraturs historie* [History of Danish literature] 2006–09, Vol. I, p. 429.

24 P.T. Andersen *Norsk litteraturhistorie* [History of Norwegian literature] 2001, p. 126 ff.

25 Cf. Frängsmyr 1993, p. 65.

26 Marianne Alenius' *Brev til eftertiden* [Letter to posterity] (1987) deals with Charlotta Dorothea Biehl and the new letter literature of the 18th century, placing Biehl's letters in a contemporary and historical European context.

Steffen Arndal's dissertation *'Den store hvide Flok vi see ...' H.A. Brorson og tysk pietistisk vækkelsessang* [The great white flock we see... H.A. Brorson and German pietist revivalist hymns] (1989) analyzes Brorson's hymns and his connection to German revivalist hymns and the pietist piety movements and their mysticism of faith. Arndal's point is that Brorson's hymns link Danish hymn-writing's closeness to reality with the psychological depth of the revivalist piety and the spirituality of the revivalist hymns.

Thomas Bredsdorff's dissertation on *Den brogede oplysning* [The diversifed Enlightenment] (2003) shows the broad, diversified composition of the Enlightenment. Bredsdorff includes new material about the Moravians, discusses lines of Nordic and international research on the Enlightenment and develops further the analysis of Brorson's hymns that he introduced in his thesis *Digternes natur* [The nature of poets] (1975).

Keld Zeruneith's *Soldigteren. En biografi om Johannes Ewald* [The sun poet. A biography of Johannes Ewald] (1985) makes use of a depth-psychologically organized biographical method and attempts to break through the familiar myths about Ewald in order to show how the poet lives through the internal contradictions in the bourgeois process of emancipation, as he ends by overcoming the distance that exists in his early poetry between word and action.

Erik A. Nielsen's *Solens fødsel. Seks tekster om kristendommens hemmeligheder* [The birth of the sun. Six texts about the secrets of Christianity] (1998) deals with, among others, Ewald and Mozart, depicting Ewald as a 'recalcitrant son of pietism' on the basis of a poetic theology. It attempts to get closer to a living, shaping spirit that is active in the texts via the poetic image that is at work despite the fossilization of the writing (p. 32). The core text here is Ewald's 'Ode til Sielen' [Ode to the Soul], the emblematic representation of which is analyzed and placed in a theological context. Ewald radicalizes pietism, is Erik A. Nielsen's interpretation, since he makes his super-ego a part of himself and thereby liberates himself from his life's guardians and mentors.

Peer E. Sørensen's dissertation *Håb og erindring. Johannes Ewald i oplysningen* [Hope and memory. Johannes Ewald in the Enlightenment] (1989) analyzes Ewald's oeuvre and argues against biographical interpretations of the core texts. Peer E. Sørensen is particularly interested in pointing out the break between the writing and the classicist aesthetic of pre-set rules and formulation of a modern aesthetics in which the work itself generates its own rules in the process of coming into existence, and the experience of the reader is emphasized in the formation of meaning. The beauty of the work is a quality that both the reader and writer produce.

Svend Skriver's dissertation *Oprørets æstetik* [The aesthetics of revolt] (2006) is an analysis of Jens Baggesen's *Labyrinten* [The Labyrinth], which exposes the political, erotic and aesthetic revolt of that work.

27 For more detail about Sneedorff's theories about the state, see *Hvor litteraturen finder sted*, Vol. I, 'Akademiet', [Where literature takes place] (2010) p. 335 ff.

28 Holberg 1969–71: 'Zille Hans Dotters Gynaicologia' (1722), Vol. II, pp. 412-13.

29 Holberg 1969–71: 'Første Brev til en højvelbaaren Herre, 1728' [First letter to an honourable gentleman], Vol. XII, p. 123.

30 Cf. Erik A. Nielsen 2007, p. 81 ff.

31 Holberg: *Jeppe of the Hill*, http://www.gutenberg.org/files/5749/5749.txt , act 1, scene 3.

32 Cf. The Danish educational canon. The canon is available on the website of the Ministry for Culture. *Jeppe of the Hill* is introduced here: https://kum.dk/uploads/tx_templavoila/KUM_kulturkanonen_uk_OK.pdf

33 Cf. Søren Kierkegaard Centret's webpublication of Søren Kierkgaard's Papers. See the quotation here: http://sks.dk/cc/txt.xml?hash=k17&zoom_highlight=montanus#k17

34 Holberg 1944: 'Domme over mine Komedier' [Opinions on my comedius], *Epistler* (nr. 249), Vol. III, p. 235

35 Holberg 1994: 'Jean de France', *Seks komedier* [Six Comedies], p. 51.

36 Ibid. p. 75

37 Ibid. p. 32.

38 Biehl (1986): *Mit ubetydelige Levnets Løb* [My Insignificant Life], p. 130

39 Voltaire 2004: Œuvres de 1771, Les Œuvres completes de Voltaire, Vol. 73, Voltaire Foundation, p. 424

Je me jette à tes pieds au neom du genre humain.
Il parle par ma voiz, il bénit ta clémence,
Tu rends ses droits à l'homme, et tu permet qu'on pense.
Sermon, romans, physique, ode, historie, opéra,
Chacun pet tout écrire: et siffle qui voudra.

40 For a more detailed presentation of early Danish identity formation, see Feldbæk 1991–93, Vol. I, p. 216 ff.

41 P.A. Heiberg 1884, p. 554.

42 P.A. Heiberg 1884, p. 578.

43 Clausen and P. Fr. Rist, 1906, p. 44.

44 Brorson 1951–56, Vol. III, p. 245.

45 Ewald 1969, Vol. III, p. 251.

46 Irons, Mai and Petersen 2018, p. 131

47 Ibid., p. 126

48 Ibid., p. 133.

49 In his 'Beobachtungen über das Gefühl des Schönen und Erhabenen' [Observations on the Feeling of the Beautiful and Sublime] (1764) Kant emphasizes: 'The fair sex has just as much understanding as the male, but it is a *beautiful understanding*, whereas ours should be a *deep understanding*, an expression that signifies identity with the sublime. [...] In history they will not fill their heads with battles, nor in geography with fortresses, for it becomes them just as little to reek of gunpowder as it does the males to reek of musk.' Kant 1975, Vol. I, p. 851 and p. 853. Here cited from Glente 1992, p. 33 & 34.

50 Else Viestad gives a brief comparison between Kant's and Rousseau's philosophy of the sexes in *Kjønn og ideologi. En studie af kvinnesynet hos Locke, Hume, Rousseau og Kant* (1989) [Gender and ideology. A study of the view of women in Locke, Hume, Rousseay and Kant] (1989).

51 K.E. Knudsen et al. 2002, p. 18.

52 Ibid., p. 18.

53 F.J. Billeskov Jansen gives a good introduction to classicism in *Danmarks Digtekunst* [Danish writings] (1944-58), Vol. II, where he deals precisely with the exchange between Danish and European literature.

54 Bredsdorff, Mai and Irons 2011, p. 103.

55 Stub 1972, Vol. I, p. 97.

56 Brief mention of reviews of Niels Klim can be found in R. Paulli's article 'Bedømmelsen af Niels Klim i udlandet' [The evaluation of Niels Klim abroad], in *Fund og Forskning*, Vol. II (1955), p. 144.

57 Court Chaplain J.B. Bluhme and Bishop Erik Pontoppidan had complained to the king about the travel account's barbed remarks about the church as an institution. Without actually naming names, Holberg writes in his last biographical letter: 'It is a common conception that the same gentlemen are the authors of the unjust and distorted criticism that took place in Göttingen. I am, however, unable to state this with certainty, and I do not think it is worth the trouble to carry out a great deal of detective work to find out who is behind it. There were some people who attempted to get me to repudiate their base calumnies. But when one is subjected to such abusive language, I do not feel one ought to return in kind. By doing so, one only places oneself on the same level as those attacking one. I am pleased that I managed to get the better of my passions. I only state that it would seem that all is lost in the world of learning when people of such sour dough not only write books but also act as critics. The judgment passed in other countries shows how favourable a reception this small work received; and since it shortly afterwards could be read in five different languages, one can easily deduce that it was just as popular abroad as it has become here at home.' Holberg 1969–71: 'Tredie Brev til en højvelbaaren Herre' (1743, Third letter to an honourable gentleman), Vol. XII., p. 197.

58 See how *Niels Klim* is presented in present-day international research in Søren Peter Hansen's paper 'Modern Thoughts Disguised as Ancient Genres – A Discussion on Ludvig Holberg's novel 'Niels Klim',' which was included in the conference Ancients and Moderns in the Eighteenth Century at the International Society for 18th Century Studies, 2008; cf. www.sdu.dk/Om_SDU/Institutter_centre/Ilkm/ Forskning/ AktuelForskning/2008 AF.aspx

59 Baggesen 1986: *Das Labyrinth oder Reise durch Deutschland und die Schweiz* (1789).

60 Ewald 1889, *The Death of Balder*.

61 Ewald 1998, p. 126.

62 Bredsdorff, Mai and Irons 2011, p. 119.

63 Ibid., p. 123.

64 Holberg 1969–71, Vol. II, p. 209.

65 Ewald 1998, p. 42.

66 Ibid., p. 43.

67 Baggesen 1965, p. 155.

68 Ibid., p. 160.

69 *Labyrinten* [The Labyrinth] is also discussed in Svend Skriver's PhD thesis *Europæere i 1800-tallets danske litteratur. Om Jens Baggesen, P.L. Møller og Georg Brandes* (2007, Europeans in 19th century Danish literature. On Jens Baggesen, P.L. Møller and Georg Brandes) and in his monograph *Oprørets æstetik. Om Jens Baggesens Labyrinten* (2006, The aesthetics of revolt. On Jens Baggesen's The Labyrinth), in which he further develops and compares readings of the work by Leif Ludwig Albertsen, Jette Lundbo Levy and Aage Henriksen. Ole Egeberg places Baggesen in a new line of literary history that stretches from Baggesen to Andersen and Højholt in *Labyrinter, latter & andre kunster. Et essay om tekster af Jens Baggesen, H.C. Andersen og Per Højholt*, [Labyrints, laughter & other arts. An essay on texts by Jens Bagegsen, Hans Christian Andersen and Per Højholt] (1997). The modernist and postmodern characteristics

of the work are precisely those that are discussed in recent readings. Susanne Willaing has carried out a particularly interesting philological investigation of a posthumously published travel account by Baggesen in her MA dissertation *Baggesen med og uden filter. En filologisk funderet, komparativ undersøgelse af Jens Baggesens rejsedagbog fra sommeren 1787 og sønnen August Baggesens gengivelse af den i 1843* (2007), [Baggesen with and without filter. A philologically grounded, comparative investigation of Jens Baggesen's travel diary from summer 1787 and his son August Baggesen's reproduction of it in 1843] (2007).

70 According to Leif Ludwig Albertsen, it is actually of quite secondary importance to Baggesen: '[...] he does not wish to devote himself to the surroundings but to his interpretation of them,' Albertsen 1969, p. 44.

71 Cf. Baggesen 1965, p. 13.

72 Eco's concept is inspired by the philosophers Gilles Deleuze and Felix Guattari's definitions of the rhizome. Eco briefly compares three types of labyrinth: the Theseus labyrinth at Knossos, with distinct entrance and exit, the modern labyrinth of the Baroque, with dead-ends and only one exit that is not easy to find, and finally the network labyrinth, which is potentially unending, cf. Eco 1983, p. 54ff.

73 Baggesen 1965, p. 13.

74 Mogens Davidsen formulates this point in his analysis 'Et svimmelmonument. Jens Baggesen: *Labyrinten'* [A dizzying monument. Jens Baggesen: The Labyrinth] (2001), p. 272.

75 Baggesen 1965, p. 269.

76 Ibid., p. 288.

77 Michael Rasmussen, in his analysis of *Labyrinten* [The Labyrinth], underlines in 'Det mystiske øjeblik hos Jens Baggesen' (2008, The mystical moment in Jens Baggesen, *Kritik* 187) that Baggesen's fascination with heights has to do with the fact that he shudderingly feels that there is something else, something much larger than the I itself. This love of heights is a protest against the fact that his age has replaced 'God' by 'I' and made the I quite self-autonomous. Baggesen does not express a modern but a pre-modern interpretation of existence in his praise of the high, which represents something metaphysical to which the I submits. The interpretation underlines that Baggesen is a transitional figure, but it connects somewhat heavy-handedly the modern with the self-autonomous I and therefore fails to grasp the modern, subjective experiencing of time and the modern condition, where the I seeks its reference in a 'nothingness': 'The spark that sprang out of Nothingness/my emergent I'; Baggesen 1965, p. 300. Baggesen does not perhaps fit the usual boxes used for the Enlightenment, but he expands our understanding of what modern subjectivity is.

78 Baggesen 1965, pp. 299-300.

79 Mogens Davidsen works on this comparison in his reading of *Labyrinten* [The Labyrinth], Davidsen 2001.

80 Goethe 1960–74, Vol. XII.

The ages of longing 1800–1900

1 H.C. Andersen 1971–77, Vol. IX, p. 299.

2 Jens Andersen deals with this theme in *Andersen. En biografi* [*Hans Christian Andersen. A Biography*, (2003), and the relation between biographical and fictional genres in Andersen is also dealt with in Jackie Wullschlager's biography *Hans Christian Andersen: the life of a storyteller* (2001).

3 See for example *Dansk litteratur historie* [History of Danish Literature], Vol. II (1976), edited by P.H. Traustedt et al. Here, Gustav Albeck depicts the breakthrough of Romanticism with Oehlenschläger's poetry, under the title 'A deity hovers over Copenhagen', p. 395 ff. In a much later presentation of literary history, *Hovedsporet* [The main track] (2005), edited by Jens Anker Jørgensen and Knud Wentzel, emphasis is placed on the emergence of the modern literary culture after 1770, although a decisive literary break is seen around 1800 with Steffens' lectures and influence on Oehlenschläger's debut: 'Denmark has the good fortune as regards literary history that Romanticism arrived almost dead on time. It took place in the summer of 1802, when the Danish-Norwegian natural scientist and philosopher Henrich Steffens (1773–1845) arrived in Copenhagen [...]', p. 300.

4 Asbjørn Aarseth discusses views of the concept of Romanticism in detail in his dissertation *Romantikken som konstruksjon* [Romanticism as a construction] (1985), emphasizing that the concept of Romantizism can at most function as a kind of searching concept and not as a clear periodisation concept. Aarseth does choose, however, to distinguish between several different subconcepts that can help the reader to trace aspects of the intellectual life of the Romantic period: 1) Sentimental Romanticism, which grasps the continuity between the 18th and 19th century cultivation of the emotional potential of the individual; 2) Universal Romanticism, which describes the Romantic fascination with untamed nature; 3) Vital Romanticism, which, based on the idea of a cosmic unity that includes and transcends the self, cultivates a vital sense thematically and metaphorically; 4) National Romanticism, which describes how the individual experiences a national community as the basis for his or her identity; 5) Liberal Romanticism, which comprises the Romantic cultivation of freedom and describes the social utopia that has its roots in the French Revolution and that also comes to include Marxism; 7) Regional Romanticism, which maintains the interest of Romanticism in popular life and the community of the village (cf. p. 251 ff.).

5 The idea of two diverging main tendencies in the 18th century and the concept of 'The Romanticism of the Enlightenment' are formulated by Martin Lamm in his thesis *Upplysningstidens romantik. Den mystiskt sentimentala strömningen i svensk litteratur*, [The Romanticism of the Enlightenment period. The mystically sentimental tendency in Swedish literature] Vols. I-II, 1918–20.

6 *Danmarks Digtekunst* [Danish Writing] 1944–58, Vol. II. Billeskov chooses the year 1784 as a benchmark, since this is the year of the powerful Deputy minister Ove Höeg Guldberg's fall, and also 1802, because it marks Oehlenschäger's debut. At the same time, he stresses that only a genre-historical presentation can shed light on the historical changes of literature. The problem with this genre-historical presentation, however, is that it is excellent for carrying out a literature-historical analysis of Classicism, but it becomes difficult to follow the genre-mixes of Romanticism and all of modern literature based on such a method of categorization. The genres break down and blend with each other in a way that is difficult to follow systematically.

7 A recent literature-historical presentation that argues in favour of using the concept of 'Preromanticism' in the history of European literature is Marshall Brown's *Preromanticism* from 1991. The term is brought forward here and analyzed to show how it can shed light on characteristics in a number of works from the end of the 18th century that point forwards towards European 'Romanticism'. At the centre of the dissertation is an analysis of Oliver Goldsmith's novel *The Vicar of Wakefield* (1766), which is categorized as being preromantic, since in the text a conflict is developed between the narrator, the old vicar and *pater familias*, and the dramatic narration itself. The narrator becomes simply overpowered by his own narrative, loses overview and insight, and the narrative is freed of all moral anchorage. There is also a tradition in British literary research of working with a concept of the 'long' 18th century, 1688–1815 or even 1848, e.g. Marianna D'Ezio's *Literary and Cultural Intersections during the Long Eighteenth Century* (2009). The discussion of the relation between Romanticism and Enlightenment is carried out with great energy in the Anglo-Saxon context, particularly since Arthur O. Lovejoy declared in his essay 'On the Discrimination of Romanticism' (1924, reprinted 1975) that the concept of 'Romanticism' could not be defined. In his opinion, the concept had become so over-simplified and diluted as a the term for a period that it had ended up completely overshadowing the dynamism of the history of art and thought. Marshall Brown follows in Lovejoy's footsteps in his critique of the concept of Romanticism in the essay 'Romanticists and Enlightenments' (1997). Here, it is emphasized that it is completely impossible to define the two periods clearly, but that it can be useful to study the relation between the end of the 18th century and beginning of the 19th century and here discover breaks, turning points and connections. For example, neo-Classicism in order to from this point of view is seen as being a strong tendency that links the 18th and 19th centuries (p. 197), while it is stressed that the Romantic feeling for nature is already very much in evidence at the end of the 18th century (p. 198).

8 In Gyldendal's *Litteratur-historier. Perspektiver på dansk teksthistorie fra 1620 til nutiden* [Literary histories. Perspectives on Danish textual history from 1620 to the present day] (1994), Jette Lundbo Levy uses the concept of 'præromantik/førromantik' (preromanticism) as a term for writing that, from a historical perspective, anticipates important features of Romanticism, cf. p. 71 ff. The concept of 'sentimentalism' is also employed.

9 See also the writer and literary figure H.W. Gerstenberg, who mediates Ossian and Norse mythology in publications in the 1760s, especially in his letters about the distinctive features of the literature *Briefe über Merkwürdigkeiten der Literatur* (1766–67, 1770), in *Dansk litteraturhistorie* [History of Danish Literature] 1983–85, Vol. IV, p. 310 ff.

10 Harold Bloom uses the concept of *anxiety of influence* and the concept of *misreading* in his dissertation *The Anxiety of Influence* (1973), in which he describes precisely the struggle of the English Romantics to try to excel the 17th century writer Milton.

11 John Chr. Jørgensen's *Den sande kunst. Studier i dansk 1800-talsrealisme* [The true art. Studies in Danish 19th century realism] (1980) deals with works by Poul Martin Møller, Hans Egede Schack, Herman Bang and Georg Brandes. John Chr. Jørgensen places emphasis on indicating a modern tradition for realism prior to the modern breakthrough. A literature-historical method which employs as its main contrast that between 'Romanticism' and 'the modern breakthrough' will find it hard to catch sight of realism prior to Romanticism. Conversely, it will find it hard to catch sight of the renewal of Romanticism in the modern breakthrough. One can provide literature-historical analysis with a better perspective if one avoids viewing Romanticism and the modern breakthrough as literary '-isms'. They are eras in a literary culture in which various literary tendencies and schools come into being.

12 For a closer look at the relation between Biedermeier and Romanticism, see Lunding 1968 and K.P. Mortensen 1993.

13 Andersen 1829. The first verse in translation reads: 'At the bend made by the road/Lies a lovely old abode./All its walls are slightly skew/Window panes are small and few,/Door

that's now begun to sag,/Dog that barks, the scallywag,/'Neath the eaves are chirping swallows,/Setting sun – you know what follows. (Translation by John Irons, 2014). The poem can be accessed at: http://johnirons.blogspot.dk/2014/08/a-famous-hans-christian-andersen-poem.html

14 See, for example, the division of Romanticism into Universal Romanticism and National Romanticism in *Litteraturens veje* [The paths of literature] 1996, p. 520.

15 In the feature article 'Aandslivet og Vrængbilledet' [Intellectual life and distorted image] *Politiken*, 8.12.1946, Jørgen Bukdahl discusses Grundtvig and the national, based on the concept of *folkelighed* (≈ popular character). Grundtvig is an anti-nationalist: 'The popular is that which punctures the national in all its self-sufficiency – and so Grundtvig is the great anti-nationalist. As is known, it would never occur to him to write a history of Denmark. He wrote two large histories of the world, and his 'Living Memory' is an overview of the main tendencies in European history in the final age of Man. The struggle he and his disciples waged against National Liberalism was one against a now locally constricted culture of *Bildung* that took the state church, and especially the university, as its authority in spiritual matters – the Copenhagen home-spun philosophy that despite everything was found in the heroes of National Liberalism, the narrow-minded and bigoted, their mistaken, religious-coloured humanism. Brandes attacked the same thing from his own angle. Where the Grundtvig supporters said (although not with emphasis) Universalism, he said (although with emphasis) Europeanism.'

16 Grundtvig 1810, p. 166 ff.

17 Grundtvig 1875, pp. III-VIII.

18 'I am Danish by birth and mentality, but I would never say anything against Sweden, if only Danishness could urge me to do so, for I am a Christian. God has so ordered things that all the families of mankind dwell on the face of the earth as beings of one blood, and it cannot be otherwise than that whoever has communion with God must lovingly open up his heart to all peoples, who, speaking all sorts of different tongues, cover the face of the earth.' 'Til Fædrenelandet' [To the Homeland], Grundtvig 1904–09, Vol. II, p. 711. This statement dates from 1813 and was written under the influence of the loss of Norway and the state bankruptcy – and the union between Sweden and Norway.

19 Flemming Lundgreen-Nielsen lists these three nuclei of Danishness and popular character in *Dansk Identitetshistorie* 1991-93 [The history of Danish identity], Vol. III, p. 9 ff. He concludes that many of Grundtvig's formulations concerning Danishness – the special 'God's calling' etc. – may grate on present-day ears, especially when taken out of context. Lundgreen-Nielsen stresses that Grundtvig's view of language and nation was taken from German philosophy as formulated by Herder, Fichte and Steffens, but according to Lundgreen-Nielsen, the interesting thing in the history of Danish identity is that 'everything that in Germany leads from Herder and Fichte to the catastrophes under Wilhelm II and Hitler leads in Denmark to the folk high school, the cooperative movement and parliamentary and popular culture based on conversation and compromise [...]', p. 173.

20 Maria Davidsen's dissertation *Havde man ikke vor Herre, saa havde man Ingenting! Om episk opløsning i H.C. Andersens eventyr og historier* [If one did not have the Lord God, one would have nothing! On epic disintegration in the fairytales and stories of Hans Christian Andersen] (2000) contributes to the discussion of various modern features in Andersen's prose. She links Andersen's prose to a concept of impressionism.

21 H.C. Andersen, 1963–90, Vol. V, p. 89.

22 Ibid., p. 90.

23 Baudelaire 1996, p. 108. Translation by James McGowan: (http://www.baudelaire.cz/works.html?aID=200&artID=82). The original title is 'Le goût du néant'. It was printed on 20 January 1859 in *Revue Française* and included in the 1861 edition of *Les Fleurs du Mal*.

24 In his monograph *Andersen* [*Hans Christian Andersen. A New Life*] from 2003, Jens Andersen draws much attention to the fact that Andersen avoids sexual contact with the prostitutes in order to preserve the innocence that makes him productive as an artist.
25 https://www.futurelearn.com/courses/hans-christian-andersens-fairy-tales/1, translated by John Irons.
26 Ibid.
27 Nowadays, Staffeldt's poem 'Indvielsen' (*Initiation*) from his *Digte* [Poems] (1804) probably overshadows Oehlenschläger's poem. This shift also possibly has to do with the fact that it is to a greater extent Staffeldt's themes of personal fragmentation and loss that interest present-day readers, rather than Oehlenschläger's images of a mythical period and Golden Age. An English translation is available in *100 Danish Poems* (2011), ed. by Bredsdorff, Mai and Irons.
28 Oehlenschläger 1803, p. 82.
29 In his memoirs, Steffens describes how he experienced the French Revolution in 1789. In his chronology, a new age begins at this point: 'It was a marvellous time; it was not only a French but a European revolution; it was there, it put down roots in millions of minds; clear-sighted greatness recognized the common power, even honoured it; a sentence was passed on the passing age, a decisive victory over miserable, wretched conditions had been won. The revolution was already there in all the free minds of Europe, even where no revolution broke out. The first moment of enthusiasm in history, even when it unfortunately develops a frightful future, has something pure, even holy, about it that must never be forgotten.' Steffens 1840, Vol. I, p. 319.
30 In the work *Formationer i europæisk romantik* [Formations in European Romanticism] (2003), Marie-Louise Svane discusses the view of time in Romantic art. In her opinion, time emerges as a field between two poles: 'finitude' and 'infinity'. The Romantics dream of the infinite, and they show how they experience infinity – in nature, in love or in art – that suddenly breaks through to something divine. But the paradoxical thing is that the one who reaches out for infinity also comes to experience finitude. An alternation arises between infinite and finite in which the physical and tangible and the popular and naive is irradiated by infinity and thereby emerges as an expression of a higher meaning. Conversely, however, infinity can also turn around and point towards finitude, towards death and disappearance or the possibility of only experiencing and enjoying nature immediately. Blicher is named as a Danish example.
31 Oehlenschläger later used his periodical *Prometheus* (1832–34) to publish chapters of a dissertation on aesthetics. Here, among other things, he discusses the use of historical material in writing. Can one as a writer freely make use of historical material, or must one seek a historical truth? '[...] Poetry neither lies nor deceives; for it admits straight away that it is a fiction, a self-invention, that does not seek its value in an imitation of real truth but in a presentation of a real beauty' (Vol. IV, p. 117). The writer is not a historian, but uses history in his 'artistic purpose' (ibid.) so that through his fiction he can give the reader visions of times and of beauty. Time becomes the subject of artistic creation.
32 Oehlenschläger 1803, p. 81.
33 H.C. Ørsted, who became the great scientific innovator of Romanticism, was definitely not impressed by Steffens' knowledge of natural science, although he was well aware that his importance as an inspirer and conveyor of new ideas, 'Lightning flashes for guidance' (Ørsted 1870, Vol. I, p. 227) were Steffens' strongest asset. Ørsted travelled to Berlin and Jena in 1801, where he met Fichte, Schlegel and Schelling. In Jena, he became highly interested in a work by a Hungarian chemist, Jacob Joseph Winterl from 1800. Winterl presented a dualistic chemical system based on the principle of acids and alkalis and on the idea that all of nature's forces have one and the same source – the hypothesis that Schelling also advanced.
34 Oehlenschläger 1803: 'Harpespilleren ved Posthuset' [The Harpist at the Post Office], p. 114.
35 George Brandes wrote a characterization of Staffeldt for the F.L. Liebenberg 1832 edition of

his *Digte* [Poems]. The following year it was published in Brandes' own *Mennesker og Værker i nyere evropæisk Literatur* [People and works in contemporary European literature].

36 Staffeldt 1804, pp. 3-4.

37 Staffeldt 1804, pp. 398-99.

38 Grundtvig 1811, pp. 56-57.

39 Grundtvig 1904-09, Vol. IX, p. 46.

40 Jørn Erslev Andersen, in his account of *Idealistic Romanticism in Fichte and Hölderlin* (Andersen, J. E. 1997), emphasizes the feeling of freedom that Fichte gave the young students in Jena when in his lectures in 1794 he attempted to think beyond the boundary of cognition and surmount the problems Kant had raised in philosophy. Erslev Andersen stresses in particular that Fichte radically asks about the very phenomenon of thinking when he says that we cannot prove or define any first principle of human knowledge. We can look for such a principle, and we can formulate it, but we cannot prove it. For that reason, we both can and must rethink the earlier philosophical ideas and hypotheses.

41 In his introduction to the publication of Steffens' lectures, Johnny Kondrup emphasizes the connection between Steffens and Schelling. At the same time, though, Steffens does turn against some of Schelling's ideas. Johnny Kondrup points out that: 'Instead of the mythical relaxe in the unity of the universe, which was the aim of Schelling's striving, Steffens sought an understanding of the coherence of nature that did not lose sight of the individual phenomena. He constantly maintained a boundary line between God and nature, which was considered to be an emanation of the divine being. – But Steffens could also nurture more comprehensive ideas; he was the first person to have declared that the free personality is the final point of all existence and thereby the hidden reason for all development in nature.' Steffens 1996, p. 172.

42 H.C. Ørsted collected his articles and dissertations in the two-volume work *Aanden i Naturen* [The Spirit in Nature], which he published in 1850, the 50th anniversary of his career as a university teacher. He emphasized the dissemination of the new natural science, which he viewed as the central comprehensive culture innovation of his age and was also extremely interested in language and language development. He created such Danish words as *ilt* (oxygen), *brint* (hydrogen), *rumfang* (volume), *vægtfylde* (specific gravity) and *varmefylde* (specific heat) as a direct result of his understanding of the alternation and connection between the study of nature and 'formation of the spirit'. Ørsted was also particularly interested in music and wrote about musical sound images that it was 'Nature's deep, infinite, incomprehensible reason that speaks to us via the stream of notes'. A greeting to Hans Christian Andersen in a small volume of verse that Andersen took with him on his journey to Italy in 1833 was: 'Reason in Reason = the True; Reason in Will = the Good; Reason in Phantasy = the Beautiful' (cf. H.C. Andersen 1951, Vol. I, p. 128).

43 Steffens 1996, p. 18.

44 Ibid., p. 23.

45 F. Schlegel 2000, p. 106. Published in Athenaäum, Vol. I, 2nd section, 1798. Translation by Jonathan Skolnik: http://germanhistorydocs.ghi-dc.org/sub_document.cfm?document_id=368

46 A different critical practice from the genre system of J.L. Heiberg could be found in P.L. Møller. He realized the qualities of Blicher, Goldschmidt and Aarestrup early on, but made a scathing attack on Kierkegaard's *Enten – Eller* (*Either / Or*), starting a literary feud that was to cost both of them dearly. Kierkegaard became the subject of caricatural articles and drawings in the satirical periodical *Corsaren*, while Kierkegaard criticized P.L. Møller so harshly that the latter chose to leave the country. Jon Helt Haarder, in his dissertation *Portrættets moment. Forfatterportrættet hos Sainte-Beuve, P.L. Møller, Georg Brandes og Herman Bang* [The moment of the portrait. The portrait of the writer in Sainte-Beuve, P.L. Møller, Georg Brandes and Herman Bang] (2003) provides an interesting and entlightening account of P.L. Møller's

literary criticism. He rehabilitates P.L. Møller, whose modern literary criticism has not previously been the subject of so detailed an analysis. He underlines that P.L. Møller imports Sainte-Beuve's literary portrait to Denmark and is an important transitional figure between an idealistically slanted genre-aesthetics and a psychological-biographical literary criticism.

47 J.L. Heiberg 1990, p. 130.

48 The idea of the spark of the soul and *imago dei* finds a special formulation in the medieval theologian Meister Eckhart. For more information, see C.F. Kelley's *Meister Eckhardt on Divine Knowledge* (1977).

49 A more detailed presentation of the history of the concept of *Bildung* can be found in Harry Haue's thesis *Almendannelse som ledestjerne. En undersøgelse af almendannelsens funktion i dansk gymnasieundervisning 1775-2000* [General Education as leading star. An investigation of the function of general education in Danish upper secondary education] (2003).

50 Goethe 1917: 'Natur und Kunst' [c. 1800]. English translation by John Irons, with brief commentary, at: http://johnirons.blogspot.dk/2011/09/work-in-progress-translation-of-goethes.html

51 Schiller 1962, Vol. XX, p. 288. The essay *Über Anmuth und Würde* was first published in *Die neue Thalia*, 1793. English translation: 'On Grace and Dignity' Friedrich Schiller. Translated by Jane V. Curran', in: *Schiller's 'On Grace and Dignity' in Its Cultural Context. Essays and a New Translation*. Eds. Jane V. Curran and Christophe Fricker., p. 153.

52 J.L. Heiberg 1990, p. 129 and p. 130.

53 Oehlenschläger 1854. 'Om Ewald som lyrisk Digter' [About Ewald as a lyrical poet], Vol. I, p. 51.

54 Lise Præstgaard Andersen, as do other Oehlenschläger researchers, describes the development of the authorship as a moving away from an extreme Romanticism in *Poetiske Skrifter I-II* [Poetic Writings I-II] 1805: 'It has to do here with the exceptional individual, the genius, the born artist, but also with the harmonious individual who is capable of living in the world, not with the Romantic who transcends all boundaries, the one who insists on embracing everything at one go in a constant intensity, and who is willing in this embracing gesture to let both physical boundaries and personal identity be obliterated. [...] In the new works [i.e. after *Poetiske Skrifter*] the divine is present as a matter of course in the selected individual, who nevertheless is able to find a place in earthly existence. Oehlenschläger, with *Nordiske Digte* [Nordic poems], was turning away from extreme Romanticism with its possibly amoral implications – a development we have also seen the first signs of in *Poetiske Skrifter*', cf. Arkiv for dansk litteratur [Archive of Danish Literature], www.adl.dk/

55 Oehlenschläger 1926–30, Vol. II, p. 66.

56 Jens Kr. Andersen views Schack's *Phantasterne* [The Phantasts] as the first consistently liberalist work in Danish literature, cf. Arkiv for dansk litteratur [Archive of Danish Literature], www.adl.dk/

57 Goldschmidt 1999, Vol. II, p. 85.

58 Ibid., p. 317.

59 Ibid., p. 327.

60 Ibid., p. 320.

61 Kierkegaard 1997–2008, Vol. XIX:I, p. 102. Translation of the quotation by K. Brian Söderquist in Joakim Garff: 'Andersen, Kierkegaard – and the Deconstructed *Bildungsroman*', in: *Kierkegaard Studies*, 2006, p. 91-92.

62 In his work *SAK. Søren Aaby Kierkegaard (Søren Kierkegaard. A Biography)* (2000/2005) Joakim Garff analyzes Kierkegaard's relation to J.L. Heiberg and relates how Kierkegaard sent his books to Heiberg without receiving any reply. Not until Kierkegaard mentions Thomasine Gyllembourg's novella *To Tidsaldre* [Two Ages] in 1846 does Heiberg come up with a friendly reply. But by that time, Kierkegaard's critique of Heiberg's ideas about *Bildung*, according to Garff, have come together, and, unlike Heiberg, he insists on being sharp and primitive

in his thought. Primitive thought holds onto the primitive relation to God, in which man is simply obliged to believe or not believe unconditionally; cf. Garff 2000, p. 317 ff.

63 Grundtvig 1904–09, Vol. II, p. 327.

64 H.C. Andersen 1986, p. 90.

65 Ibid., p. 141.

66 H.C. Andersen 2001, p. 143.

67 Ibid., p. 190.

68 H.C. Andersen 1971–77, Vol. V, p. 419.

69 Maria Davidsen examines Kierkegaard's critique of Andersen in the article 'Poesie er Seier over Verden. Om Søren Kierkegaards H.C. Andersen-kritik' [Poetry is a victory over the world. On SK's critique of HCA], *Nordica*, Vol. XII, 1995.

70 Kierkegaard 1997–2008, Vol. XVIII:1, p. 172.

71 Grundtvig 1904–09, Vol. I, p. 111.

72 Kierkegaard *The Concept of Dread*, Translated by Walter Lowrie, p. 135.

73 Kierkegaard 1997–2008, Vol. XX, p. 281.

74 Kierkegaard 1997–2008, Vol. XVIII:1, pp. 170-171.

75 H.C. Andersen 1963-1990, Vol. 7, p. 222, translated by John Irons: http://johnirons.blogspot.com/2017/04/andersens-auntie-toothache.html

76 Grundtvig; N.F.S: 'Now Gleams the Sun in All its Splendour', *Fashioners of Faith*, ed. Anne-Marie Mai et. al., p. 221.

77 Kierkegaard: 'The Concept of Anxiety', translated by Reidar Thomte p. 43–44.

78 Kierkegaard: *Either/Or*, Vol. I, translated by David F. Swenson and Lillian M. Swenson, p. 363.

79 Klaus P. Mortensen deals with this problem area in the dissertation *Thomasines oprør* [Thomasine's revolt]' (1986).

80 In Fredrika Bremer's novel, Hertha is presented as a *belle âme* who is no longer willing to let her emotions and longing for freedom be constrained by her oppressive father: '"Father," Hertha resumed, for seven years I have waited for the freedom which you once promised me, and which I regard as being my right – that to decide over my own person and my future; I have waited for your consent, I have submitted to your will. I am unable to do so any longer. It has to do with another person's life. Yngve is my intended, my husband before God. Before God I am responsible for his life at this time. My mind is made up. Do not drive me to extremities. You can deny me my freedom, deny me the right to become Yngve's wife, but nothing in the world except manifest violence shall prevent me from hereafter following Yngve and becoming his nurse, even if I as a result were to lose my reputation! ...', 'Are you threatening me? Defying me? Would you coerce me?' the director exclaimed, beside himself. 'You are perhaps contemplating summoning me before a judge, dragging your father to court?!...' Bremer 1856, Vol. I, pp. 426-27.

81 In the dissertation *Fredrika Bremer och den borgerliga romanens födelse* [Fredrika Bremer and the birth of the bourgeois novel] (1981), Birgitta Holm has analyzed the relation between Romanticism and Realism in Bremer's novel-writing. Holm views it as an extremely important characteristic of Bremer's work that she combines the depiction of the longing of the female, Romantic *belle âme* for passion and inner liberation with the realistic depiction of an external outside world and woman's position in society. The studies carried out by Birgitta Holm and others in the 1970s and 1980s of 19th century female novel writing re-discover the importance of the woman writers in the history of the novel and realism. See also *Nordisk kvindelitteraturhistorie* (*The history of Nordic Women's Literature*) (1993-98), http://nordicwomensliterature.net/writer/bremer-fredrika, and Lise Busk-Jensen's dissertation *Romantikkens forfatterinder* [Female writers of Romanticism] (2010).

82 *Nordisk kvindelitteraturhistorie* (*The History of Nordic Women's Literature*), (1993–98), http://nordicwomensliterature.net/ mediates and collects this new research.

83 Thomasine Gyllembourg 1986, p. 9.

84 *Dansk Litteratur-Tidende* 1833, p. 145 ff.

85 St. St. Blicher 1945, p. 220.

86 In *St. St. Blicher. Digter og samfundsborger* [St. St. Blicher. Writer and citizen], (1984) the author Knud Sørensen underlines that Blicher's special importance is that he is the first person to take the Danish peasant population seriously and to tell these people in their own language that they have strength and human values. He creates a common people with self-awareness and a belief in itself.

87 M. Hansen 1870, p. 68.

88 The literary scholar Dan Ringgaard stress precisely the poem as the autonomous art of words in his presentation of the authorship in *Udvalgte digte* [Selected poems] (1998): 'As shown, it has always been a striking feature of Aarestrup's poetry that the language makes itself autonomous, and it is this characteristic that projects him beyond his time and place and links him to aestheticism. One realizes that language and verse make a difference, that the poem does not only reflect or purify nature but that it also creates it. But one also understands that the poem, like nature, takes place in time and can be for pleasure.' (p. 275).

89 Aarestrup 1998, p. 9.

90 Aarestrup's poems have been analyzed and his life and work described by a number of literary figures in the 20th century. Dan Ringgaard gathers together the discussion and in his analysis of Aarestrup's poetry he stresses in a afterword to *Udvalgte digte* [Selected poems] (1998) that Aarestrup in a melancholy fashion cultivates the artistic form and beauty in art as a quality in itself, as a reaction against the impoverished belief of modernity in progress. He emphasizes that Aarestrup positions himself in relation to an international aestheticism, in which art withdraws in relation to modern society in an insistence on its own autonomy and beauty. Ringgaard is of the opinion that language becomes a self-valid material in Aarestrup's poetry. Are the poems enamelled and too artificial? Ringgaard, at any rate, views Aarestrup's eroticism as being unoriginal, a mere product of ingenious rhetoric.

91 Aarestrup 1998, p. 238 and 166.

92 Aarestrup 1998, p. 245.

93 Borup 1947-49, Vol. III, p. 197.

94 P.M. Møller 1930, Vol. I, p. 106.

95 G. Brandes 1877.

96 Jacobsen 2006, p. 187, translated by Tiina Nunnally.

97 In his dissertation, *J. P. Jacobsens digtning* [J.P. Jacobsen's writing] 1984, Jørn Vosmar does not think that Jacobsen uses the concept of dying death in accordance with Kierkegaard's concept. In his attempt to escape from belief, Niels has precisely experienced dying death during large sections of his adult life. Now he finally actually dies. One could, however, claim that Niels does not really experience the despair involved in getting rid of and escaping from belief until he is on his deathbed. Only in his moment of death does he die death.

98 In his article 'Det moderne gennembrud og romantikken' [The modern breakthrough and Romanticism] (2004), Sune Auken discusses the relation between the modern breakthrough and Romanticism and emphasizes that Sven Møller Kristensen's idea of the dualism of Romanticism in *Den dobbelte eros* [The double Eros] 1966 confuses the concepts. Auken rightly stresses that Romanticism is not dualistic but on the contrary monistic, seen from a history of ideas perspective. Møller Kristensen's dualism makes it difficult to see the real differences and similarities between Romanticism and the modern breakthrough.

99 G. Brandes 1899–1910, Vol. IV, p. 5.

100 H. Bang 1965, p. 20.

101 For a considerable number of years, Georg Brandes was to many people 'the most detested and hated figure, the personification of the undermining of old values, respect, tradition, morality, Christianity and fatherland that seeped in everywhere, at the same time as the country was being transformed into a modern, conflict-ridden industrial society, an undermining

that it seemed possible to combat by combatting and condemning him as a person. For a small but active group of supporters, comprising angry young men and infatuated women, he was the hope of deliverance from all suppressive norms, rigid authorities and stupid hypocrisy, an inspiring ideal with his unflagging zeal, his intransigence, his zest for constant renewal, his legendary and indefatigable capacity for work. To most people, he was a known name, a vague threat from modern life', cf. Jørgen Knudsen's portrayal of Georg Brandes: www.adl.dk/ Jørgen Knudsen's large, eight-volume biographical work on Brandes' life and work *Georg Brandes* was published 1985–2004.

102 G. Brandes 1890 s. 5, 1900, Vol.V, p. 304.

103 Zola 1959, p. 73.

104 Zola 1992/1998, p.2

105 Zola 1992/1998, p. 6

106 G.Brandes, 1901, Vol.VII, p. 204-222.

107 The relationship between Henrik Pontoppidan and Georg Brandes was and remained complex, as is also apparent from a later poem that Pontoppidan published in 1912 in *Politiken*. The occasion was the 70th birthday of Georg Brandes on 4 February. The poem is definitely not in the form of a traditional tribute. Pontoppidan chose to confront both the man and his supporters with the realities:
We have stood here with torches, banners, orchestra/
to celebrate a friend, pay tribute to a master./
But he had disappeared, had smilingly fled/
from the thanks of friends and the well-meant festivities./
One has asked, one has grumbled. Myself, I know not the reason,/
but a little bird's told me in no uncertain terms,/
a night bird, an owl. I listened to the screech/
an anxious minute between waking and dozing./
What became – it shrieked – of the kingdom he created?/
It has crumbled away! And silence and desolation/
now grazes on the plot with the outlawed dead./
The sun of truth he set in the heavens -/
To whom did it bring happiness? To whom did it give strength?/
He cried 'Let there be light!' – and darkness grew./
The spring storm he raised in the mind of youth,/
the flowers that teemed out of the earth where he trod,/
now drift in the air like frowsty wind./
The tree of knowledge he has planted in the land, that embraced so wide across fjords and bays,/
now poisons the people with worm-eaten fruit./
And Adam, the new one, became as stupid as the old one./
And Eve made free with the gift of love and ate with every lustful gorilla in the garden./
But no one has mourned, and no one will complain./
What a miracle, he retreated from the festive gathering/
and turned away despondently from his work. –/
My guess is he's celebrating his day with the dead.

108 Drachmann 1872.

109 Bang *Katinka*, 1990 p. 26

110 Nietzsche 2005, p. 112.

111 Nietzsche1995, pp.101-103

112 At the time of the European unrest in 1848 and the prospect of war, Hans Christian Andersen sent open letters with calls for peace to his European contacts and wrote songs for the Danish soldiers. In 1864, he involved himself in collections and bazaars in favour of the

soldiers, their families and surviving widows and children and wrote verses for the collection boxes. On 12 December 1863, he wrote in his diary: 'It is as if the last time has come to Denmark, all my thoughts are taken up with war or rebellion, my mind is subdued; one hears only empty political speeches. I see my paltry savings vanish, see [myself] as a beggar in my old age [...],' cf. H.C. Andersen 1971–77, Vol. V, p. 442.

113 Peer E. Sørensen, in *Vor tids temperament* [The temperament of our time] (2009) deals with the exile as a theme in Bang's life and work.

114 Interview with Strindberg i *Politiken* 2 April 1905. Also printed in Strindberg 1912–20, Vol. LIV, pp. 443-45.

115 Claussen 1990, p. 79.

116 Ibid., p. 87. The poem, which was written in 1894, was published in *Antonius i Paris* [Antonius in Paris] i 1896. This sonnet rhymes in the original Danish.

References

FUTHER WORKS ON DANISH LITERARY HISTORY AND BIOGRAPHY

Anskuelsesformer. Træk af dansk litteraturhistorie (1991), Vol. 1, by Johan de Mylius, Odense Universitetsforlag.
Bidrag til den danske Literaturs Historie (1867-71), Vols. 1-5, by N.M. Petersen, 2. ed. by C.E. Secher, Kjøbenhavn: Fr. Wøldikes Forlag.
Danmarks Digtekunst (1944-58), Vols. 1-3, by F.J. Billeskov Jansen, Kbh.: Munksgaard.
Danmarks litteratur (1963), by Mogens Brøndsted and Sven Møller Kristensen, Kbh.: Gyldendal.
Dansk biografisk leksikon (1979-84), Vols. 1-16, started 1887 by C.F. Bricka and continued 1933-44 by Povl Engelstoft and Svend Dahl, 3rd. ed., ed. Sv. Cedergreen Bech, Kbh.: Gyldendal.
Dansk kvindebiografisk leksikon (2000-01), Vols. 1-4, ed. Jytte Larsen, Kbh.: Rosinante.
Dansk litteratur. Middelalder (1998), Vols. 1-2, by Pil Dahlerup, Kbh.: Gyldendal.
Dansk litteraturhistorie (1976-1977), Vols. 1-6, ed. P.H. Traustedt, Kbh.: Politikens Forlag.
Dansk litteraturhistorie (1983-85), Vols. 1-9, ed. Johan Fjord Jensen et al., Kbh.: Gyldendal.
Dansk litteraturs historie (2006-09), Vols. 1-5, ed. Klaus P. Mortensen and May Schack, Kbh.: Gyldendal.
Danske digtere i det 20. århundrede (2000-2001) Vols. 1-3, ed. Anne-Marie Mai, Kbh.: Gads Forlag.
Danske kvindelige forfattere (1982), by Stig Dalager and Anne-Marie Mai, Kbh.: Gyldendal.
Den Danske Litteraturs Historie (1945-77), Vols. 1-2, by Oluf Friis, Kbh.: H. Hirschsprungs Forlag.
Den store danske encyklopædi (1994-2006), Vols. 1-24, ed. Jørn Lund, Kbh.: Danmarks Nationalleksikon.
Digteren og Samfundet (1942-45/1970), Vols. 1-2, 1st and 2nd Sven Møller Kristensen, Kbh.: Athenæum/Munksgaard.
Galleri 66. En historie om nyere dansk litteratur (2016), by Anne-Marie Mai, Kbh.: Gyldendal.
Hovedsporet. Dansk litteraturs historie (2005), ed. Jens Anker Jørgensen et al., Kbh.: Gyldendal.
Hvor litteraturen finder sted (2010-2011), Vols. 1-2, by Anne-Marie Mai, Kbh.: Gyldendal
Illustrerad svensk litteraturhistoria (1985), Vols. 1-6, 3. ed. Henrik Schück and Karl Warburg, Stockholm: Gidlunds.
Illustreret Dansk Litteraturhistorie (1924-34), Vols. 1-4, ed. Vilhelm Andersen and Carl S. Petersen, Kbh.: Gyldendalske Boghandel, Nordisk Forlag.
Litteraturens veje (1996/2003), 1st og 2nd ed. Johannes Fibiger and Gerd Lütken, Kbh.: Gads Forlag.
LitteraturDK (2009), ed. Brian Andreasen et al., Kbh.: Lindhardt & Ringhof.
Litteraturhistorie for folkeskolen (1993), by Jørgen Aabenhus, Kbh.: Dansklærerforeningen.
Litteratur-Historier (1994), ed. Jette Lundbo Levy, Klaus P. Mortensen and Erik A. Nielsen, Kbh.: Danmarks Radio Forlaget.
Litterær reformation (2016) by Pil Dahlerup, København: U-Press.
Læsninger i dansk litteratur (1997-99/2001), Vols. 1-5, 1st and 2nd ed. Povl Schmidt et al., Odense: Odense Universitetsforlag.
Nordens litteratur (1972), Vols. 1-2, ed. Mogens Brøndsted, Kbh.: Gyldendal.
Nordisk kvindelitteraturhistorie (1993-98), Vols. 1-5, ed. Elisabeth Møller Jensen et al., Kbh.: Rosinante.
Ordbog over det danske sprog (1981), Vols. 1-28, 4th ed., Kbh.: DSL/Gyldendal.

Saxo & Co. Dansk litteraturhistorie og tekstanalyze (2003), ed. Søren Graversen and Steen Hvorslev Mogensen, Kbh.: Gads Forlag.
Sanselig middelalder (2010) by Pil Dahlerup, Aarhus: Aarhus Universitetsforlag.
Verdens litteraturhistorie (1994-95), Vols. 1-7, 2. ed. Hans Hertel, Kbh.: Gyldendal.

WORKS REFERENCED IN THE NOTES/ESPECIALLY RELEVANT WORKS

Adam af Bremen (2000): *Adam af Bremens krønike*, translated by Allan A. Lund, Højbjerg: Wormianum.
Adorno, Theodor W. and Horkheimer, Max (1944/1997): *Dialectic of Enlightenment*. UK/USA: Verso.
Albertsen, Leif Ludwig (1969): *Odins mjød. Et studie i Baggesens mytiske poetik*, Århus: Akademisk Boghandel.
Alenius, Marianne (1987): *Brev til eftertiden. Om Charlotta Dorothea Biehls selvbiografi og andre breve*, Kbh.: Museum Tusculanums Forlag.
Alenius, Marianne (1993): '... med den ene fod i graven ville jeg fortsat læse. Om Birgitte Thott', *Nordisk kvindelitteraturhistorie*, Vols. 1, ed. Elisabeth Møller Jensen, Kbh.: Rosinante/ Munksgaard.
Andersen, H.C. (1837): *Kun en Spillemand*, Kbh.: C.A. Reitzels Forlag.
Andersen, H.C. (1951): *Mit Livs Eventyr*, Vols. 1-2, ed. H. Topsøe-Jensen, Kbh.: Gyldendal. [*The Fairy Tale of My Life*, Cooper Square Press, New York: 2000].
Andersen, H.C. (1963-90): *H.C. Andersens Eventyr*, Vols. 1-7, Kbh.: Hans Reitzels Forlag.
Andersen, H. C. (1971-77): *H.C. Andersens Dagbøger 1825-1875*, Vols. 1-12, ed. Kåre Olsen and H.
Topsøe-Jensen, Kbh.: Gad.
Andersen, H.C. (1986): *Skyggebilleder* [1831], by Johan de Mylius, DSL, Kbh.: Gyldendal.
Andersen, H.C. (2001): *At være eller ikke være* [1857], DSL, Kbh.: Borgen.
Andersen, Jens (2003): *Andersen. En biografi*, Vols. 1-2. (*Hans Christian Andersen. A New Life*, 2006), Kbh.: Gyldendal.
Andersen, Jens Kr. (1992): *Handling og moral. En strukturel studie i elleve Holberg-komedier*, Kbh.: Akademisk Forlag.
Andersen, Jens Kr. (1993): *Professor Holbergs komedier. En strukturel og historisk undersøgelse*, Kbh.: Akademisk Forlag.
Andersen, Jørn Erslev (1997): 'Grundens forvitring – idealistisk romantik hos fichte og Hölderlin', *At gå til grunde. Sider af romantikkens litteratur og tænkning*, ed. Anne-Marie Mai og Bo Kampmann Walther, Odense: Syddansk Universitetsforlag.
Andersen, Lise Præstgaard (1998): 'Grovhed og skjaldegave. Egils saga', *Læsninger i dansk litteratur*, Vol. 1, ed. Povl Schmidt et al., Odense Universitetsforlag.
Andersen, Niels Knud (1980): 'Aleneste Gud i Himmerrig. Bidrag til reformationstidens salmehistorie', Kirkehistoriske samlinger, Kbh.: Akademisk Forlag.
Andersen, Per Thomas (2001): *Norsk litteraturhistorie*, Oslo: Universitetsforlaget.
Anne Krabbes visebog: Kallske Saml., Det Kongelige Biblioteks håndskriftsamling, nr. 393.4.
Appel, Charlotte and Fink-Jensen, Morten (2009): *Når det regner på præsten. En kulturhistorie om sognepræster og sognefolk 1550-1750*, Højbjerg: Hovedland.
Appel, Charlotte (2006): 'Den gemene mand og bogstavernes verden', *Danmark og renæssancen 1500-1650*, ed. Carsten Bach-Nielsen et al., Kbh.: Gads Forlag.
Arenfeldt, Pernille (1999): 'Frederik II's hof', *Svøbt i mår. Dansk folkevisekultur 1550-1700*, Vol. 1, ed. Flemming Lundgreen-Nielsen and Hanne Ruus, Kbh.: C.A. Reitzel.
Arnheim, Louise (1999): *Registrant over Johan von Bülows manuskriptsamling i Sorø Akademis bibliotek*, Sorø Lokalhistoriske Selskab.

Aristoteles (2007): *Physics*, translated by R.P Hardie and R.K. Gaye, The University of Adelaide Library, University of Adelaide, South Australia: eBooks@Adelaide, http://ebooks.adelaide.edu.au/a/aristotle/physics/

Arndal, Steffen (1989): 'Den store hvide Flok vi see...'. *H. A. Brorson og tysk pietistisk vækkelsessang*, Odense: Odense Universitetsforlag.

Arrebo, Anders (1965-1983): *Samlede Skrifter* I-V, ed. Vagn Lundgaard Simonsen et al. Kbh: Det Danske Sprog- og Litteraturselskab.

Auken, Sune (1998): *Eftermæle. En studie i den danske dødedigtning fra Anders Arrebo til Søren Ulrik Thomsen*, Kbh. Museum Tusculanums Forlag.

Auken, Sune (2004): 'Det moderne gennembrud og romantikken', *Det stadig moderne gennembrud*, red. Hans Hertel, Kbh.: Gyldendal.

Auken, Sune (2005): *Sagas Spejl: Mytologi, historie og kristendom hos N.F.S. Grundtvig*, Kbh.: Gyldendal.

Aurelius, Eva Hättner (1996): *Inför lagen. Kvinnliga svenska självbiografier från Agneta Horn till Fredrika Bremer*, Lund: Lund University Press.

Bach-Nielsen, Carsten et al., ed. (2006): *Danmark og renæssancen 1500-1650*, Kbh.: Gads Forlag.

Baggesen, Jens (1889-1903): *Poetiske Skrifter*, Vols. 1-5, by A. Arlaud, Kbh.: Det Schubotheske Forlag.

Baggesen, Jens (1965): *Labyrinten* [1792-1793], Kbh.: Gyldendal.

Baggesen, Jens (1986): *Das Labyrinth oder Reise durch Deutschland in die Schweiz 1789*, translated by Gisela Perlet, Leipzig and Weimar: Beck.

Baggesen, Jens (2016): *Labyrinten*, Vols. I-II, ed. Henrik Blicher. Kbh.: Det danske Sprog- og Litteraturselskab.

Bakhtin, Mikhail (2006): *Rum, tid & historie. Kronotopens former i europæisk litteratur*, translated by Harald Hartvig Jepsen, Århus: Forlaget Klim.

Bang, Herman (1965): *Haabløse Slægter* [1880], Kbh.: Gyldendal.

Bang, Herman (1990): *Katinka* [1886], Seattle: Fjord Press. Translated by Tina Nunally.

Banning, Knud, ed. (1984): *Biblia Pauperum – billedbibelen fra middelalderen*, Kbh.: Gads Forlag

Bech, Sven Cedergreen (1975): *Brev fra Dorothea*, Kbh.: Politikens Forlag.

Bekker-Nielsen, Hans (2002): *Fra runeskrift til trykte bogstaver. Et festskrift udgivet i anledning af OAB-Tryks 75 års jubilæum i 2001*, Odense: OAB-Tryk.

Bertelsen, Lise Gjedssø, ed. (2002): *Vikingetidens kunst. En udstilling om kunsten i vikingernes verden og efterverden ca. 800-1250*, Jelling: Fonden Kongernes Jelling.

Biehl, Charlotta Dorothea (1778): *Til den 29. Januarii 1778*, Kbh.

Biehl, Charlotta Dorothea (1783): *Brevvexling imellem fortrolige Venner*, Vols. 1-3, Kbh.: Bogtrykker Peder Horrebow.

Biehl, Charlotta Dorothea (1865-66): 'Charlotte Dorothea Biehls historiske Breve (meddelte af J.H. Bang efter originalerne i Sorø Akademis Manuskriptsamling Nr. 71, 20)'. *Historisk Tidsskrift*, 3. rk., Vol. 4, ed. by Den danske historiske Forening, Kbh.

Biehl, Charlotta Dorothea (1986): *Mit ubetydelige Levnets Løb* [1787], Kbh.: Museum Tusculanums Forlag.

Bisgaard, Lars; Nyberg, Tore og Søndergaard, Leif, ed. (1999): *Billeder i middelalderen. Kalkmalerier og altertavler*, Odense: Odense Universitetsforlag.

Bisgaard, Lars and Søndergaard, Leif, ed. (2002): *Gilder, lav og broderskaber i middelalderens Danmark*, Odense: Syddansk Universitetsforlag.

Bjørn, Hans (2001): 'Adlens skrivekløe', *Riget, magten og æren. Den Danske Adel 1350-1660*, ed. Per Ingesman og Jens Villiam Jensen, Århus: Århus Universitetsforlag.

Bjørn, Hans (2010): 'Anne Krabbe, salig Jakob Bjørns til Stenalt', *Stenalt*, ed. Palle Kirk, Randers Amts Historiske Samfund.

Blicher, St. St. (1945): 'The Hosier and his Daughter', *Twelve Stories by Steen Steensen Blicher*, translated by Hanne Astrup Larsen, Princeton: Princeton University Press.

Blicher, St. St. (1982-83): *Udvalgte værker*, Vols. 1-4, udg. af Blicher-Selskabet, Kbh.: Gyldendal.
Blicher, St. St. (1991): *Noveller*, ved Esther Kielberg, Kbh.: Borgen.
Bloom, Harold (1973): *The Anxiety of Influence*, New York: Oxford University Press.
Boethius de Dacia (2001): *Verdens evighed. Det højeste gode. Drømme*, ed. and translation by Niels Jørgen Green-Pedersen, Frederiksberg: Det lille Forlag.
Bond, Donald F., ed. (1965): *The Spectator*, Vols. 1-5, Oxford: Oxford University Press.
Bording, Anders (1984-86): *Samlede Skrifter*, Vols. 1-3, ed. Erik Sønderholm and Paul Ries, Kbh.: DSL/C.A. Reitzels Forlag.
Bourdieu, Pierre (1992): *Les Règles de l'art: genèse et structure du champ littéraire*, Paris: Seuil. English edition 1996: *The Rules of Art. Genesis and Structure of the Literary Field*, Cambridge: Polity Press. Translated by Susan Emanuel.
Brahe, Tycho (1913-29): *Opera Omnia*, Vols. 1-12, Kbh.: DSL/Gyldendal.
Brandes, Georg (1877): *Søren Kierkegaard. En kritisk Fremstilling i Grundrids*, Kbh.: Gyldendal.
Brandes, Georg (1905-08): *Levned*, Vols. 1-3, Kbh.: Gyldendal.
Brandes, Georg (1899-1910): *Samlede skrifter*, Vols. I-XVII, Kbh.: Gyldendal.
Brandt, C. J., ed. (1860-62): *Ældre Danske Digtere. Et Udvalg*, Vols. 1-8, Kbh.: Th. Michaelsen & Tillges Forlag.
Bredsdorff, Thomas (1975): *Digternes natur. En idés historie i 1700-tallets danske poesi*, Kbh.: Gyldendal.
Bredsdorff, Thomas (1998): 'Det gode med det onde. 'Vølvens spådom'', *Læsninger i dansk litteratur*, Vol. 1, ed. Povl Schmidt et al., Odense: Odense Universitetsforlag.
Bredsdorff, Thomas (2003): *Den brogede oplysning. Om følelsernes fornuft og fornuftens følelse i 1700-tallets nordiske litteratur*, Kbh.: Gyldendal.
Bredsdorff, Thomas, Mai, Anne-Marie, Irons, John (eds.) (2011): *100 Danish Poems*, Copenhagen: Museum Tusculanum and Washington University Press.
Bregnsbo, Michael (2007): *Caroline Mathilde. Magt og skæbne. En biografi*, Kbh.: Aschehoug.
Bremer, Fredrika (1856): *Hertha eller En själs historia. Teckning ur det verkliga lifvet*, Vols. 1-2, Stockholm: Bonniers.
Bricka, C.F. og Gjellerup, S.M. (1874-75): *Den danske Adel i det 16de og 17de Aarhundrede*, Vol. 1, Kbh.: Rudolph Klein.
Bricka, C.F. og Gjellerup, S.M. (1913): *Den danske Adel i det 16de og 17de Aarhundrede*, Vol. 2, Kbh.: Vilhelm Trydes Boghandel.
Brorson, H.A. (1951-56): *Samlede skrifter*, Vols. 1-3, ed. J.L. Koch, Kbh.: DSL/O. Lohses Forlag.
Brorson, H.A. (1994): *Udvalgte salmer og digte*, by Steffen Arndal, Kbh.: Borgen.
Brown, Marshall (1991): *Preromanticism*, Stanford California, Stanford University Press.
Brown, Marshall (1997): 'Romanticists and enlightenments', *Turning Points. Essays in the History of Cultural Expressions*, California: Stanford University Press.
Brøgger, Suzanne (2015): *Vølvens Spådom*, Kbh: Gyldendal.
Burckhardt, Jacob (1860): *Die Cultur der Renaissance in Italien*, Basel: Der Schweighauser'schen Verlagsbuchhandlung.
Bukdahl, Jørgen (1946): 'Aandslivet og Vrængbilledet', *Politiken*, 8th december 1946.
Busk-Jensen, Lise (2010): *Romantikkens forfatterinder*, Vols. 1-3, Kbh.: Gyldendal.
Butler, Judith (1990): *Gender Trouble. Feminism and the Subversion of Identity*, New York, London: Routledge.
Böss, Michael (2007): 'Den britiske oplysning og det moderne nationsbegreb', *Oplysningens verden. Idé, historie, videnskab og kunst*, ed. Ole Højris and Thomas Ledet, Aarhus: Aarhus Universitetsforlag.
Bülow, Johan (1899): *Johan Bülows Selvbiografi. Meddelt ved Aage Friis*, I-II, *Dansk Tidsskrift*, Kbh.: Vilhelm Trydes Forlag, p. 406-428, 475-493.
Casey, Edward S. (1993): *Getting Back into Place. Toward a Renewed Understanding of the Place-*

World, Bloomington & Indianapolis: Indiana University Press.
Casey, Edward S. (1997): *The Fate of Place. A Philosophical History*, Berkeley Calif.: University of California Press.
Christensen, Anemette S. (2000): 'Herremandsliv i Danmark 1500-1660', *Svøbt i mår. Dansk folkevisekultur 1550-1700*, Vol. 2, ed. Flemming Lundgreen-Nielsen and Hanne Ruus, Kbh.: C.A. Reitzel.
Christiansen, C.P.O. (1926): *Bernard af Clairvaux. Hans Liv fortalt af Samtidige og et Udvalg af hans Værker og Breve*, Kbh.: Det Schønbergske Forlag.
Clausen, Julius and Rist, P. Fr. (1906): *Fra Hoffet og Byen. Stemminger og Tilstande 1793-1822 i Breve til Johan Bülow til Sanderumgaard*, Kbh.: Gyldendal.
Claussen, Sophus (1990): *Antonius i Paris* [1896], ed. Jørgen Hunosøe, Kbh.: Gyldendal.
Colbert, David W. (1999): 'Når folkeviser finder sted', *Svøbt i mår. Dansk folkevisekultur 1550-1700*, Vol. 1, ed. Flemming Lundgreen-Nielsen and Hanne Ruus, Kbh.: C.A. Reitzel.
Dahlerup, Pil (1993): 'Om danske Mariaviser', *Nordisk kvindelitteraturhistorie*, Vol. 1, ed. Eva Hættner Aurelius and Anne-Marie Mai, Kbh.: Rosinante/Munksgaard.
Dahlerup, Pil (1995): 'Renæssanceteori og renæssancetekst', *Hindsgavl Rapport. Litteraturteori i praksis*, ed. Thomas Bredsdorff and Finn Hauberg Mortensen, Odense Universitetsforlag.
Dal, Erik (1968): *Ballader – danske og fremmede*, Kbh.: Gyldendal.
Dansk Litteratur-Tidende (1833), 'Samlede Noveller af S.S. Blicher. Første Deel', Kbh.: Andreas Seidelin.
Dante Alighieri (2003): *The Divine Comedy*, New York: New American Library.
Davidsen, Maria (1995): 'Poesie er Seier over verden. Om Søren Kierkegaards H.C. Andersen-kritik', *Nordica*, Vol. 12, Odense: Odense Universitetsforlag.
Davidsen, Maria (2000): *Havde man ikke vor Herre, saa havde man Ingenting! Om episk opløsning i H.C. Andersens eventyr og historier*, Odense: Syddansk Universitetsforlag.
Davidsen, Mogens (2001): 'Et svimmelmonument. Jens Baggesen: *Labyrinten*', *Læsninger i dansk litteratur*, Vol. 1, ed. Povl Schmidt et al., Odense: Odense Universitetsforlag.
Degn, Ole (1971): *Livet i Ribe 1560-1700 i samtidiges optegnelser*, Århus: Universitetsforlaget.
Descartes, Renati (1644): *Principia philosophiae*, Amsterodami: Apud Ludovicum Elzevirium.
D'ezio, Marianna (2009): *Literary and Cultural Intersections during the Long Eighteenth Century*, Cambridge Scholars Publishing.
Diderichsen, Paul (1963-65): *Dansk Prosahistorie*, Vols. 1-3, Kbh.: Københavns Universitets Fond til Tilvejebringelse af Læremidler.
Doctor, Jens Aage (1970): 'Sandhedens rolle – Om Leonora Christinas Jammers Minde', *Kritik* nr. 16.
Drachmann, Holger (1872): *Digte*, Kbh.: Andr. Schous forlag.
Dranke, Urusla (1997): *The Poetic Edda*, Vols. I-II, Oxford: Clarendon Press.
Dreyer, Kirsten (1997-98): *H.C. Andersens brevveksling med Lucie og B.S. Ingemann*, Vols. 1-3, Kbh.: Museum Tusculanums Forlag.
Duve, Rikke and Pedersen, Louise Lungen (2005): 'Skulptur i spil', *Passepartout*, 25, Aarhus: Aarhus Universitet.
Duncker, Dorthe (1999): 'Visernes vej. Sammenhæng mellem visebøger?', *Svøbt i mår. Dansk folkevisekultur 1550-1700*, Vol. 1, eds. Flemming Lundgreen-Nielsen and Hanne Ruus, Kbh.: C.A. Reitzel.
Ebbesen, Sten and Koch, Carl Henrik (2003): *Dansk filosofi i Renæssancen 1537-1700, Den danske filosofis historie*, Vol. 2, Kbh.: Gyldendal.
Eco, Umberto (1983): *The name of The Rose*. London: Secker & Warburg (*Il nome della rosa* 1980),
Eco, Umberto (1994): *The limits of interpretation*, Bloomington: Indiana University Press.
Eco, Umberto (2002): *Art and Beauty in The Middle Ages*. Yale: Nota Bene.
Egebjerg, Ole (1997): *Labyrinter, latter & andre kunster. Et essay om tekster af Jens Baggesen, H. C. Andersen og Per Højholt*, Århus: Forlaget Modtryk.

Eilschov, Friderich Christian (1749): *Forsøg til en Fruentimmer-Philosophie eller Alvorlige og lystige Samtaler med et Fruentimmer om det der er nyttigt og fornøyeligt i alle Philosophiens Parter*, Kbh.: Ernst Henrich Berling.
Elizabeth-Charlotte, Duchesse d'Orleans (1899): *Memoirs of the Court of Louis XIV and of the Regency*, Boston: L.C. Page and Company, based on German edition from Strasburg 1789, www.gutenberg.org/dirs/3/8/5/3859/3859-h/3859-h.htm
Elverskov, Anne and Jørgensen, Jens Anker, ed. (1996): *Den hellige jomfru i Esrum*, Frederiksborg Amt.
Engelhardt, Conrad (1865/1970): *Nydam mosefund 1859-1863. Jernalderens våbenofferfund*, Kbh.: Gads Forlag.
Enquist, Per Olov (1997/2002): *The Visit of the Royal Physician*, Washington: Washington Square Press.
Erichsen, John and Pedersen, Mikkel Venborg, eds. (2005): *Herregården. Menneske, samfund, landskab og bygninger*, Vol. 2, Kbh.: Nationalmuseet.
Ewald, Johannes (1969): *Samlede skrifter*, Vols. 1-6, ed. Hans Brix et al., Kbh.: Gyldendal.
Ewald, Johannes (1998): *Udvalgte digte 1765-1781*, ed. Esther Kielberg et al., Kbh.: Borgen.
Ewald, Johannes (1889/2004): *The Death of Balder*, translated by G. Borrow, London: Kessinger Publishing.
Falster, Christian (1982): *Satirer* [1720-42], Vols. 1-2, Kbh.: DSL/C.A. Reitzels Forlag.
Feldbæk, Ole, ed. (1991-93): *Dansk Identitetshistorie*, Vols. 1-5, Kbh.: C.A. Reitzel
Felski, Rita (1995): *The Gender of Modernity*, London: Harvard University Press.
Felski, Rita (2015): *Limits of Critique*, Chicago: Chicago University Press.
Felski, Rita (2020): 'On the Ambiguities of the Modern', *Nonmodern Practices: Latour and Literary Studies,* ed. Elisabeth Arnould-Bloomfield and Claire Chi-Ah Lyu. London: Bloomsbury Academic.
Fibiger, Johannes et al. (2001): *Litteraturens tilgange*, Kbh.: G.E.C. Gads Forlag.
Fo, Dario (2015): *Der er en gal konge i Danmark*, Kbh.: Multivers.
Foucault, Michel (1976): *La volonté de savoir*, Paris: Éditions Gallimard.
Foucault, Michel (1984): 'What Is Enlightenment?' *The Foucault Reader*, ed. P. Rabinow, Harmondsworth: Penguin Books.
Foucault, Michel (1966): *Let mots et les choses*, Paris: Éditions Gallimard.
Foucault, Michel (1969): *L'archéologie du savoir*, Paris: Édition Gallimard.
France, James (2000): 'Cistercienserne under Jomfru Marias kappe', in Jørgensen, Jens Anker et al., eds.: *Fjernt fra menneskers færden. Sider af Esrum Klosters 850-årige historie*, Kbh.: C.A. Reitzels Forlag.
Frederiksen, Hans Jørgen (1987): 'Liturgi og kirkebygning', *Troens billeder*, eds. Lise Gotfredsen and Hans Jørgen Frederiksen, Herning: Systime.
Frederiksen, Hans Jørgen (2001): *Den katolske kirke – i kunstens spejl*, Herning: Systime.
Frederiksen, Niels Werner (2000): 'En adelsdame ved arbejdsbordet. Studier i Anne Krabbes visebog', *Svøbt i mår. Dansk folkevisekultur 1550-1700*, Vol. 2, ed. Flemming Lundgreen-Nielsen and Hanne Ruus, Kbh.: C.A. Reitzel.
Friesen, Otto von (1924): *Rökstenen i Bohuslän och runorna i Norden under folkvandringstiden*, Uppsala: Lundquist.
Frängsmyr, Tore (1993): *Sökandet efter Upplysningen. En essä om 1700-talets svenska kulturdebatt*, Höganäs: Wiken.
Galster, Kjeld (1935): *Carsten Hauchs Manddom og Alderdom (1827-1872)*, Kolding: Konrad Jørgensens Bogtrykkeri.
Garff, Joakim (2005): *Søren Kierkegaard. A Biography*. Translated by Bruce H. Kirmmse. Princeton/Oxford: Princeton University Press.
Garff, Joakim (2006): 'Andersen, Kierkegaard – and the Deconstructed *Bildungsroman*', in: *Kierkegaard Studies*. Edited on behalf of the Søren Kierkegaard Research Center by Niels Jørgen Cappelørn and Herman Deuser / Yearbook 2006 Berlin, New York: Walter de Gruyter.

Gelting, Michael H. (1999): 'Danmark – en del af Europa', *Middelalderens Danmark. Kultur og samfund fra trosskifte til reformation*, ed. Per Ingesman et al. Kbh.: Gads Forlag.

Genette, Gerard (1997): *Paratexts. Thresholds of interpretation*, Cambridge: Cambridge University Press.

Glahn, Alfred (1925): *Sorø Akademi og Holberg*. Ed. af Holbergsamfundet af 3. December 1922.

Glahn, Torben (1975): *Soraner-Biografier 1747-1800*, Sorø: Soransk Samfund.

Glente, Karen (1992): *Mennesket og kvinden. Om oplysningen, dannelsen og kønnet*, Kbh.: C.A. Reitzel.

Godtfredsen, Lise (2002): 'Den romanske kunst og vikingetidens efterliv', *Vikingetidens kunst. En udstilling om kunsten i vikingernes verden og efterverden ca. 800-1250*, ed. Lise Gjedssø Bertelsen, Jelling: Fonden Kongernes Jelling.

Godtfredsen, Lise and Frederiksen, Hans Jørgen, eds. (1987): *Troens billeder*, Herning: Systime.

Goethe, Johan Wolfgang von (1960-74): *Von Deutscher Baukunst* [1773], *Goethes Werke*, Vols. 1-14, Hamburg: Beck/Wegner.

Goethe, J.W. (1774/2001): *Die Leiden des Jungen Werthers*, Berlin: Reclam.

Goldschmidt, M.A. (1999): *Hjemløs*, Vols. 1-2, ed. Mogens Brøndsted, Kbh.: Borgen.

Grady, Hugh (2000): 'Shakespeare's Links to Machiavelli and Montaigne: Constructing Intellectual Modernity in Early Modern Europe', *Comparative Literature* 52:2, University of Oregon, Eugene.

Grave, Erich Mogenssøn (1683): *Et godt Skifte …*, Kbh.

Greenblatt, Stephen (1980): *Renaissance of Self-Fashioning. From More to Shakespeare*, Chicago, Ill.: University of Chicago Press.

Gregersen, Bo and Jensen, Carsten Selch, eds. (2003): *Øm Kloster. Kapitler af et middelalderligt cistercienserabbedis historie*, Øm Kloster Museum: Syddansk Universitetsforlag.

Gress, Elsa (1979): 'Holberg i samtale med den fraværende Dorothea Biehl', *Fanden til forskel*, Kbh.: Gyldendal.

Grinder-Hansen, Keld (2006): 'Den danske adels frie skole', *Danmark og renæssancen 1500*-1650, ed. Carsten Bach-Nielsen et al., Kbh.: Gads Forlag.

Grundtvig, N.F.S. (1810): *Danske og Norske Mindesange*, ed. Knud lyne Rahbek, Kbh.: Thoring & Colding.

Grundtvig, N.F.S. (1811): *Saga. Nytaarsgave for 1812*, Kbh.: Andreas Seidelin.

Grundtvig, N.F.S. (1875): *Danske kæmpeviser til skolebrug* [1847], Kbh.: Karl Schönbergs forlag.

Grundtvig, N.F.S (1904-09): *Udvalgte Skrifter*, Vols. 1-10, ved Holger Begtrup, Kbh.: Gyldendal.

Grundtvig, N.F.S. (1968): 'Skolen for Livet og Academiet i Soer' [1838], *Grundtvigs skoleverden i tekster og udkast*, Vol. 2, ed. Knud Eyvin Bugge, Institut for Dansk Kirkehistorie, Kbh.: G.E.C. Gads Forlag.

Grundtvig, Svend et al. (1966-76): *Danmarks gamle Folkeviser*, Vols. 1-12, Kbh.: Universitets-Jubilæets Danske Samfund.

Grundtvig, Svend (1854/1970): *Gamle danske Minder i Folkemunde*, Kbh.: Akademisk Forlag.

Grüner-Nielsen, Hakon (1912-31): *Danske Viser fra Adelsvisebøger og Flyveblade 1530-1630*, Vols. 1-7, Kbh.: Gyldendal.

Gyllembourg, Thomasine (1986): *Drøm og Virkelighed. To Tidsaldre*, Kbh.: Det Danske Sprog- og Litteraturselskab.

Hansen, Mads (1870): *Sange. Anden Samling*, Kbh.: C.G. Iversens Boghandel.

Hansen, Martin A. (1952): *Orm og Tyr*, Kbh.: Wivel. 6. edition 1963. With illustrations by Sven Havsteen-Mikkelsen, Kbh.: Gyldendal.

Hansen, Nils Gunder (1985): *Den høviske kærlighed*, Kbh.: Forlaget Basilisk.

Hansen, Søren Peter (2008): 'Modern Thoughts Disguised as Ancient Genres – A Discussion on Ludvig Holberg's novel 'Niels Klim',Konferencepaper om 'Ancients and Modern in the Eighteenth Century'', *International Society for 18th Century Studies 2008*, www.sdu.dk/

Om_SDU/Institutter_centre/Ilkm/Forskning/AktuelForskning/2008AF.aspx
Hansen, S. (1909): 'Et mærkeligt Syn i Aarslev Enge', *Aarbog*, Randers Amts Historiske Samfund.
Harbsmeier, Michael et al., ed. (2005): *Hviids Evropa*, Kbh.: Forlaget Vandkunsten.
Harrits, Flemming (2001): 'Indfoldets lykke. Trylleviser', *Læsninger i dansk litteratur*, Vol. 1, 2. ed. Povl Schmidt et al., Odense: Odense Universitetsforlag.
Hauch, Carsten (1846): 'Nogle Bemærkninger med Hensyn til Digteren H. C. Andersens Poesie', *Dansk Ugeskrift*. Anden Række. Ottende Bind. Nr. 182-208, ed. Schouw, J.F., Kbh.: Udgiverens Forlag i det Schulziske Bogtrykkeri.
Hauch, Carsten (1926): 'En polsk Familie', *Udvalgte Skrifter*, Vol. 1, Kbh.: Holbergselskabet af 23. September.
Hauch, Carsten (1988): *Digte af Carsten Hauch*, ed. Asger Schnack, LyrikBiblioteket, Kbh.: Hans Reitzels Forlag.
Haue, Harry (2003): *Almendannelse som ledestjerne. En undersøgelse af almendannelsens funktion i dansk gymnasieundervisning 1775-2000*, Odense: Syddansk Universitetsforlag.
Heede, Dag (1992): *Det tomme menneske. Introduktion til Michel Foucault*, Kbh.: Museum Tusculanum.
Hegelund, Peder (1578/1888-90): *Susanna og Calumnia*, ed. S. Birket-Smith, Kbh.: Universitets-Jubilæets Danske Samfund.
Hegelund, Peder (1976): *Almanakoptegnelser*, Vols. 1-2, ed. Bue Kaae, Historisk Samfund for Ribe Amt.
Heiberg, Johan Ludvig (1990): *Nye Digte 1841*, ed. by Klaus P. Mortensen, Kbh.: Borgen.
Heiberg, P.A. (1884): *Udvalgte Skrifter*, ed. Otto Borchsenius and Fr. Winkel Horn. Kbh.: Otto B. Wroblewskys Forlag.
Helgesen, Poul (1932-37): *Skrifter af Paulus Helie*, Vols. 1- 6, Kbh.: DSL/Gyldendal.
Helleberg, Maria (1991): *Mathilde, magt og maske*, Kbh.: Gyldendal.
Hemmingsen, Niels (1991-95): *Om Naturens Lov 1562*, Vols. 1-4, Virum: Forlaget Øresund.
Henriksen, Aage (1961): *Den rejsende. Otte kapitler om Baggesen og hans tid.* Kbh.: Gyldendal.
Hertel, Hans (1999): *Litteraturens vaneforbrydere. Kritikere, forlæggere og lystlæsere – det litterære liv i Danmark gennem 200 år*, 2nd rev. ed., Kbh.: Gyldendal.
Holberg, Ludvig (1749): *Dannemarks og Norges Geistlige og Verdslige Staat.* 2nd Edition. *Trykt paa Autors egen Bekostning*, Kjøbenhavn.
Holberg, Ludvig (1913-63): *Samlede Skrifter*, Vols. 1-18, Kbh.: Gyldendal.
Holberg, Ludvig (1944-54): *Epistler*, Vols. 1-8, Kbh.: H. Hagerup.
Holberg, Ludvig (1969-71): *Værker i tolv Bind. Digteren • Historikeren • Juristen • Vismanden*, Vols. 1-12, ed. F.J. Billeskov Jansen, Kbh.: Rosenkilde & Bagger.
Holberg, Ludvig (1992): *Moralske Tanker*, Kbh.: DSL/Borgen.
Holberg, Ludvig (1994): *Seks komedier*, Kbh.: DSL/Borgen.
Holberg, Ludvig (2005): *Niels Klims underjordiske Reise*, ed. Thomas Bredsdorff, Kbh.: Gyldendal
Holden, Helge and Overskaug, Kristian (2012): *Høydepunkter i Skrifter og Forhandlinger: et utvalg artikler fra perioden 1761-2011* (Det Norske Selskab). Oslo: Tapir Akademisk Forlag.
Holly, Michael Ann (1996): *Past Looking. Historical Imagination and the Rhetoric of the Image*, New York: Cornell University Press.
Holm, Birgitta (1981): *Fredrika Bremer och den borgerliga romanens födelse*, Stockholm: Nordstedt.
Holst, Elisabet (1999): 'Kvindedyd og kvindedød i danske ligprædikener 1570-1700', *Svøbt i mår. Dansk folkevisekultur 1550-1700*, Vol. 1, ed. Flemming Lundgreen-Nielsen and Hanne Ruus, Kbh.: C.A. Reitzel.
Holst, Elisabet (2000): 'Elskovs dyd', *Svøbt i mår. Dansk folkevisekultur 1550-1700*, Vol. 2, ed. Hanne Ruus and Flemming Lundgreen-Nielsen, Kbh.: C.A. Reitzel.
Holst, Lisbeth (1993): 'Djævlens mælkedejer', *Nordisk kvindelitteraturhistorie*, Vol. 1, eds. Elisabeth Møller Jensen et al., Kbh.: Rosinante/Munksgaard.
Hvass, Steen (2000): *De kongelige monumenter i Jelling. Deres historie, forvaltning og formidling*, Jelling:

Fonden Kongernes Jelling.
Hvass, Steen og Storgaard, Birger, eds. (1993): *Da klinger i muld … 25 års arkæologi i Danmark*, Aarhus: Aarhus Universitetsforlag.
Høiris, Ole and Ledet, Thomas, eds. (2007): *Oplysningens verden. Idé, historie, videnskab og kunst*, Aarhus: Aarhus Universitetsforlag.
Høiris, Ole and Vellev, Jens, eds. (2006): *Renæssancens verden. Tænkning, kulturliv, dagligliv og efterliv*, Aarhus: Aarhus Universitetsforlag.
Haaning, Aksel (1999): *Den kristne mystik – fra middelalderens verden*, 2nd ed., Kbh.: Reitzel.
Haarder, Jon Helt (2004): 'Litteraturvidenskab i den performative biografismes tidsalder', *Kritik* 167, Kbh.: Gyldendal.
Haarder, Jon Helt (2003): *Portrættets moment. Forfatterportrættet hos Sainte-Beuve, P.L. Møller, Georg Brandes og Herman Bang*, Odense: Syddansk Universitetsforlag.
Ilsøe, Harald (1999): *Det kongelige Bibliotek i støbeskeen. Studier og samlinger til bestandens historie indtil ca. 1780*, Vols. 1-2, Kbh.: Det kongelige Bibliotek, Museum Tusculanums Forlag.
Imer, Lisbeth Mogensen (2007): *Runer og runeindskrifter. Kronologi, kontekst og funktion i Skandinaviens jernalder og vikingetid*, ph.d.-dissertation, Københavns Universitet: Det Humanistiske Fakultet.
Ingemann, B.S. (1816): 'Kong Valdemars Jagt. (Et sjællandsk folkesagn)', *Julegave, en Samling Digte*, Kbh.: Boas Brünnich.
Ingemann, B.S. (1842): *Folkedands-Viser og Blandede Digte*, Kbh.: Forfatterens Forlag.
Ingemann, B.S. (1853-62): *Samlede Skrifter*, vols. 1-43, in 18 vol., 2nd ed., Kbh.: C.A. Reitzels Forlag.
Ingemann, B.S. (1987): *Valdemar Seier*, 1826, Kbh.: DSL/Borgen.
Ingemann, B.S. (1998): *Levnetsbog. Tilbageblik*, Kbh.: DSL/Reitzel.
Ingemann, Lucie (1996): *Et lille Levnetsløb til Bernhard*, Kbh.: C.A. Reitzel.
Ingesman, Per, ed. (1999): 'Middelalderen – en introduktion', *Middelalderens Danmark. Kultur og samfund fra trosskifte til reformation*, Kbh.: Gads Forlag.
Irons, John, Mai, Anne-Marie, Petersen and Jørn Henrik, eds. (2018): *Fashioners of Faith*, Odense. University Press of Southern Denmark.
Irigaray, Luce (1993): *An Ethics of Sexual Difference*, London: Athlone Press.
Israel, Jonathan (2001): *Radical Enlightenment. Philosophy and the Making of Modernity 1650-1750*, Oxford: Oxford University Press.
Israel, Jonathan (2006): *Enlightenment Contested. Philosophy, Modernity, and the Emancipation of Man 1670-1752*, Oxford: Oxford University Press.
Israel, Jonathan (2008): 'Tankefrihed versus religionsfrihed. Et dilemma fra det 18. århundrede, nu også det 21. århundrede', *Kritik* 188, Kbh.: Gyldendal.
Jacobsen, Jens Peter (1880/1986): Niels Lyhne, DSL, Kbh.: Borgen.
Jacobsen, Jens Peter (2006): *Niels Lyhne*. Translated by Tiina Nunnally. New York: Penguin Books.
Jacobsen, Lis (1931): *Nye Runeforskninger*, Kbh.: Levin og Munksgaards Forlag.
Jacobsen, Lis (1935): *Forbandelsesformularer i nordiske runeindskrifter*, Stockholm: Akademiens Förlag.
Jacobsen, Lis and Moltke, Erik (1941-42): *Danmarks runeindskrifter*, Vols. 1-3, Kbh.: Munksgaard.
Jansen, F.J. Billeskov (1949): 'Et hjørne af Holbergs Bibliotek og af mit', *Soranerbladet*, March 1949.
Jansen, F.J. Billeskov (1992): *Efterskrift til Ludvig Holberg: Moralske Tanker*, Kbh.: DSL/Borgen.
Jelsbak, Torben (1999): 'Barokken i dansk digtning', *Danske studier*, Vol. 94, Kbh.: C.A. Reitzel.
Jensen, Janus Møller, ed. (2006): *Broderliste Broderskab Korstog Bidrag til opklaringen af en gåde fra dansk middelalder*, Odense: Syddansk Universitetsforlag.
Jensen, Jørgen (2003): *Danmarks oldtid. Ældre jernalder 500 f.Kr. – 400 e.Kr.*, vol.3, Kbh.: Gyldendal.
Jensen, Kurt Villads (2005): 'Middelalderen i EU – centrum og periferi', *Passepartout årg. 13, nr.*

25, Aarhus Universitet: Institut for Æstetiske Fag, Afdelingen for Kunsthistorie.
Jensen, Minna Skafte (1998): 'Saxo: Gesta Danorum' *Læsninger i dansk litteratur*, Vol. 1, ed. Povl Schmidt et al., Odense: Odense Universitetsforlag.
Jensen, Minna Skafte (2006): 'Dansk renæssancelitteratur', *Danmark og renæssancen 1500-1600*, ed. Carsten Bach-Nielsen et al., Kbh.: Gads Forlag.
Jensen, Vivi (2006): 'Guds vilje og dronningens', *Danmark og renæssancen 1500-1600*, ed. Carsten Bach-Nielsen et al., Kbh.: Gads Forlag.
Jensen, Vivi (2007): *Dorothea. Guds vilje – og dronningens*, Kbh.: Gads Forlag.
Jesch, Judith (2000): 'The Power of Poetry', *Beretning fra Nittende Tværfaglige Vikingesymposium*, Aarhus Universitet, eds. Else Roesdahl and Preben Meulengracht Sørensen, Højbjerg: Forlaget Hikuin.
Johannsen, Birgitte Bøggild and Johannsen, Hugo (2005): 'Adelsvælde og renæssance', *Herregården. Menneske, samfund, landskab og bygninger*, Vol. 2, eds. John Erichsen and Mikkel Venborg Pedersen, Kbh.: Nationalmuseet.
Jónsson, Fínnur (1932): *De gamle Eddadigte*, Kbh.: Gad.
Jorn, Asger et al. (1999-2005): *10.000 års nordisk folkekunst*, Vols. 1-7, Kbh.: Borgen and Silkeborg Kunstmuseum.
Jørgensen, Dorthe (2001): *Skønhedens metamorfose. De æstetiske idéers historie*, Odense: Odense Universitetsforlag.
Jørgensen, Hans Henrik Lohfert (2005): 'Transhistorie. Om middelalderlige og moderne identiteter i forhandling', *Passepartout,* Vol.13, no. 25, Aarhus Universitet: Institut for Æstetiske Fag, Afdelingen for Kunsthistorie.
Jørgensen, Jens Anker et al., ed. (2000): *Fjernt fra menneskers færden. Sider af Esrum Klosters 850-årige historie*, Kbh.: C.A. Reitzels Forlag.
Jørgensen, John Chr. (1980): *Den sande kunst. Studier i dansk 1800-talsrealisme*, Kbh.: Borgen.
Jørgensen, Lars et al., ed. (2003): *Sejrens triumf. Norden i skyggen af det romerske imperium*, Kbh.: Nationalmuseet.
Kallestrup, Louise Nyholm (2009): *I pagt med djævelen. Trolddomsforestillinger og trolddomsforfølgelser i Italien og Danmark efter reformationen*, Frederiksberg: Forlaget Anis.
Kant, Immanuel (1975): 'Beobachtungen über das Gefühl des Schönen und Erhabenen', *Vorkritische Schriften bis 1768, Werke in sechs Bänden*, Vol. 1, ed. Wilhelm Weischedel, Wissenschaftliche Buchgesellschaft Darmstadt.
Kelley, C.F. (1977): *Meister Eckhardt on Divine Knowledge*, New Haven and London: Yale University Press.
Kierkegaard, Søren (1846): 'En omreisende Æsthetikers Virksomhed, og hvorledes han dog kom til at betale Gjæstebudet', *Fædrelandet,* no. 2078, 27 december 1846.
Kierkegaard, Søren (1944): *Either – Or*, Vol 1, Translated by David F. Swenson and Lillian M. Swenson. Oxford: Oxford University Press.
Søren Kierkegaard, (1980): 'The Concept of Anxiety: A Simple Psychologically Orienting Deliberation on the Dogmatic Issue of Hereditary Sin June 17, 1844 Vigilius Haufniensis', ed. and trans. Reidar Thomte, in *Kierkegaard's Writings*, Vol. VIII, Princeton: Princeton University Press.
Kierkegaard, Søren (1844/1991): *Begrebet Angest*, Kbh.: DSl/Borgen.
Kierkegaard, Søren (1991): *Samlede værker*, Vols. 1-20, Kbh.: Gyldendal.
Kierkegaard, Søren (1997-2008): *Søren Kierkegaards Skrifter*, Vols. 1-25:2, Kbh.: Gad
Kingo, Thomas (1939-1974/1975: *Samlede Skrifter*, Vols. I-VII ed. Hans Brix, Paul Diderichsen and F.J. Billeskov Jansen. Kbh: C.A. Reizel.
Kjær, Ulla (1999): 'Kunst og kunsthåndværk', *Middelalderens Danmark. Kultur og samfund fra trosskifte til reformation*, ed. Per Ingesman et al., Kbh.: Gads Forlag.
Klæsøe, Iben Skibsted (2002): 'Den tidlige vikingetids kunst', *Vikingetidens kunst. En udstilling*

om kunsten i vikingernes verden og efterverden ca. 800-1250, ed. Lise Gjedssø Bertelsen, Jelling: Fonden Kongernes Jelling.

Knudsen, Gunnar, ed. (1921-32): *Sydrak*, Kbh.: H.H. Thieles Bogtrykkeri.

Knudsen, Jørgen (1985-2004): *Georg Brandes*, Vols. 1-8, Kbh.: Gyldendal.

Knudsen, Karin Esmann et al. ed. (2002): *Danske litterære tekster fra 1700-tallet*, Odense: Syddansk Universitetsforlag.

Knudsen, Rasmus H. (1926): 'Anne Krabbe', *Aarbog*. Randers Amts Historiske Samfund.

Korsgaard, Ove (1997): *Kampen om lyset. Dansk voksenoplysning gennem 500 år*, Kbh.: Gyldendal.

Krabbe, Anne (1612): *Sal. Jac. Biørns Til Stenalt, En liden nyttig Bøne-bog, indholdende nogle korte trøstelige Bøner; med nogle vdlæsne Sententzer, vdtagen aff Bibelen*, Kbh.

Kress, Helga (1993): 'Hvad en kvinde kvæder. Kultur og køn på Island i den norrøne middelalder', *Nordisk kvindelitteraturhistorie*, Vol. 1, ed. Elisabeth Møller Jensen et al., Kbh.: Rosinante.

Kristensen, Sven Møller (1966): *Den dobbelte Eros*, Kbh.: Gyldendal.

Kroman, Erik (1924): 'Hvem har skrevet Hjertebogen', *Edda* XXI.

Kuhlmann, Annelis (2006): 'Teatralitet i dansk dramatik fra renæssancen', *Renæssancens verden. Tænkning, kulturliv, dagligliv og efterliv*, ed. Ole Høiris and Jens Vellev, Århus, Aarhus Universitetsforlag.

Kværndrup, Sigurd (2006): *Den østnordiske ballade – oral teori og tekstanalyze*, Kbh.: Museum Tusculanums Forlag.

Lafayette, Marie-Madeleine de (1994): *The Princess of Cleves* (*La Princesse de Clèves*, 1678), New York: W.W. Norton & Company.

Lamm, Martin (1918-1920): *Upplysningstidens romantik. Den mystiskt sentimentala strömningen i svensk litteratur*, Vols. I-II, Stoch. : Hugo Geber.

Lange, Eline (1991): 'På tæt hold af Ingemanns', *I felten med spade og båndoptager. Sorø Amts Museum 1916-1991*, ed. Helge Torm, Sorø Amts Museum.

Larsen, Finn Stein (1973): 'En impressionist fra baroktiden? En tekstlæsning i Leonora Christinas Jammersminde', *Kritik* 25, Kbh.: Gyldendal.

Larsen, Martin, ed. (1943): *Den ældre Edda og Eddica minora*, Kbh.: Munksgaard.

Larsen, Svend Erik (2007): 'Jordskælvet i Lissabon – et vendepunkt i oplysningstiden', *Oplysningens verden. Idé, historie, videnskab og kunst*, eds. Ole Højris and Thomas Ledet, Århus, Aarhus Universitetsforlag.

Larsen, Thøger (ed, transl.) (1926-1928/2019): *Eddamyterne*, Kbh.:Imprimatur.

Lasson, Anna Margrethe (1723): *Den beklædte Sandhed*, printed in Odense, Fyn.

Latour, Bruno (2005): *Reassembling the Social. An Introduction to Actor-Network Theory*, Oxford: Oxford University Press.

Laugerud, Henning (2005): 'Polysemi og den dynamiske tradisjon', *Passepartout*, Vol. 13, no. 25, Aarhus Universitet: Institut for Æstetiske Fag, Afdelingen for Kunsthistorie.

Leonora Christina (1949): *Jammers Minde og andre selvbiografiske Skildringer*, eds. Johs. Brøndum-Nielsen and C.O. Bøggild-Andersen, Kbh.: DSL/Rosenkilde & Bagger.

Leonora Christina (1958): *Leonora Christina Grevinde Ulfeldts Franske Levnedsskildring* 1673, ed. C.O. Bøggild-Andersen, Kbh.: Forening for Boghaandværk.

Leonora Christina (1977): *Hæltinners Pryd*, ed. Christopher Maaløe, Kbh.: DSL/C.A. Reitzels boghandel.

Levy, Jette Lundbo (1997): 'Det talende skrammel. Bevægelser rundt i Baggesens labyrint', *Digternes Paryk – Studier i 1700-tallet*, eds. Marianne Alenius, Kbh.: Museum Tusculanums Forlag.

Levy, Jette Lundbo (2002): 'Kvinden i Labyrinten. Baggesen og Erotismen', *Mere lys! Indblik i oplysningstiden i dansk litteratur og kultur*, ed. Mads Julius Elf and Lasse Horne Kjældgaard, Hellerup: Forlaget Spring.

Liepe, Lena (2005): 'Medeltiden 'hands-on'', *Passepartout* Vol. 13, no. 25, Aarhus Universitet:

Institut for Æstetiske Fag, Afdelingen for Kunsthistorie.
Lindhardt, Jan (1993): *Frem mod middelalderen. TV – det levende billede i det åbne rum*, Kbh.: Gads Forlag.
Lorenzen, Jørgen, ed. (1974): *Danske folkeviser*, Kbh.: Gad.
Lovejoy, Arthur O. (1975): 'On the Discrimination of Romanticisms', *English Romantic Poets. Modern Essays in Criticism*, ed. M.H. Abrahams, New York: Oxford University Press.
Lundgreen-Nielsen, Flemming (1992): 'Grundtvig og danskhed', *Dansk Identitetshistorie*, Vol. 3, ed. Ole Feldbæk, Kbh.: C.A. Reitzels forlag.
Lönnroth, Lars et al. (1997): Den svenska litteraturen, Vols. I-VII, Stockholm: Bonniers Forlag.
Lundgreen-Nielsen, Flemming (2006): 'Dansksproget digtning under Frederik II', *Renæssance-forum* 2, https://www.njrs.dk/2_2006/renaessanceforum_2_2006_7_lundgreen.pdf.
Lunding, EErik (1968): 'Biedermeier og romantismen', *Kritik* 7, Kbh.: Gyldendal.
Lyschander, Claus Christoffersen (1989): *C.C. Lyschander's Digtning 1579-1623*, Vols. 1-2, Kbh.: DSL/C.A. Reitzels Forlag.
Mai, Anne-Marie (1994): *Moralske Fortællinger 1761-1805*, Kbh.: DSL/Borgen.
Mai, Anne-Marie (1995): 'Forsøg til en fruentimmerfilosofi', *Lys og Blade. Festskrift til Povl Schmidt*, ed. Johs. Nørregaard Frandsen et al., Odense: Odense Universitetsforlag.
Mai, Anne-Marie (1996): 'Patrioterne, fruentimmerne, deres dyd and samfund', Svante Nordin and Rebekka Lettevall (eds.): *Dygd och medborgarskap i 1700-tallets politiska tänkande, Ugglan* nr. 6, Lunds Universitet.
Mai, Anne-Marie (1997): 'Overvættes læselyst. Om nogle kvindelige læsere i det danske 1700-tal', *Digternes Paryk. Festskrift til Thomas Bredsdorff*, ed. Marianne Alenius et al., Kbh.: Museum Tusculanum.
Mai, Anne-Marie (2010-2011): *Hvor litteraturen finder sted*, Vol.I-II, Kbh: Gyldendal.
Mai, Anne-Marie and Bramming, Torben (2009): *Litteraturhistorier fra Ribe*, Odense: Syddansk Universitetsforlag.
Mai, Anne-Marie and Bredsdorff, Thomas (2011): *100 Danish Poems*, translated by John Irons, Kbh. Museum Tusculanum.
Mai, Anne-Marie and Bredsdorff, Thomas (2000): *1000 danske digte*, Kbh.: Rosinante.
Mai, Anne-Marie et al. ed. (1983): *Leonora Christina. Historien om en heltinde*, Aarhus: Arkona.
Malling, Ove (1777/1992): *Store og gode Handlinger af Danske, Norske og Holstenere*, Kbh.: DSL/Gyldendal.
Manguel, Alberto (2003): *Af læsningens historie*, Kbh.: Gyldendal.
Malling, Anders (1962-78): *Dansk salmehistorie*, Vols. 1-8, Kbh.: J. H. Schultz Forlag.
Molbech, Christian (1836): *Præsten i Odense. Herr Michaels tre danske Rimværker fra Aar 1496*, Kbh.: Andreas Seidelin.
Moltke, Erik (1960): 'Runepindene fra Ribe', *Fra Nationalmuseets arbejdsmark 1960*, Kbh.: Nationalmuseet.
Moltke, Erik (1976): *Runerne i Danmark og deres oprindelse*, Kbh.: Forum.
Montaigne, Michel de (1580/1993): *The Complete Essays*, London: Penguin Classics.
Mortensen, Birgit (2001): 'Et gammelt Barn', *Læsninger i dansk litteratur*, ed. Povl Schmidt et al., Vol. 1, Odense: Odense Universitetsforlag.
Mortensen, Klaus P. (1986): *Thomasines oprør*, Kbh.: Gad.
Mortensen, Klaus P. (1993): *Himmelstormerne. En linje i dansk naturdigtning*, Kbh.: Gyldendal.
Motteville, Françoise de (1615-1689/1824): *Mémoires*, Paris: Foucault, http://gallica.bnf.fr/ark:/12148/bpt6k308970/f125.item
Møller, P.L., ed. (1845-47): *Gæa, æsthetisk Aarbog, årg. 1-3*, Kbh.: Udgiverens forlag.
Møller, Poul Martin (1930): 'Kunstneren mellem Oprørerne', *Skrifter i Udvalg*, Vols. 1-2, ed Vilhelm Andersen, Kbh.: Gad.
Nedergaard, Leif (1979): 'Erasmus Montanus. Kætterske betragtninger over Holberg's stykke

som komedie og som universitetssatire samt dets plads i striden om verdensbilledet', *Danske Studier*, Kbh.: Akademisk Forlag.
Newton, Isaac (2009): *Theoretical Notebook* (part 2: materials from the front of the notebook), *2009 The Newton Project*, University of Sussex; http://www.newtonproject.sussex.ac.uk
Nielsen, Erik A. (1998): *Solens fødsel. Seks tekster om kristendommens hemmeligheder*, Frederiksberg: Forlaget ANIS.
Nielsen, Erik A. (2009): *Kristendommens retorik. Den kristne digtnings billedformer*, Kbh.: Gyldendal.
Nielsen, Gunhild Øeby (2007): *Runesten og deres fundforhold. Magt og mentalitet, kontinuitet og brud i tiden for religions- og kulturskiftet ca. 950-1200*, ph.d.-dissertation, Afdelingen for Middelalder- og Renæssancearkæologi, Aarhus Universitet.
Nielsen, Niels Åge (1983): *Danske runeindskrifter. Et udvalg med kommentarer*, Kbh.: Hernov.
Nietzsche, Friedrich (1995): 'Om sandhed og løgn i udenommoralsk betydning', *Den unge Nietzsches lidelser. Tre tidlige skrifter*, ed. Niels Henningsen, Højbjerg: Hovedland.
Nietzsche, Friedrich (2005): *Antikrist. Forbandelse over kristendommen*, Frederiksberg: Det lille forlag.
Norén, Kjerstin (1993): 'Sjælen er af langt bedre natur end kroppen. Om Birgitta af Vadstena', *Nordisk kvindelitteraturhistorie*, Vol. 1, ed. Elisabeth Møller Jensen et al., Kbh.: Rosinante.
Oehlenschläger, Adam (1803): *Digte af Adam Øhlenslæger*, Kbh.: Fr. Brummers Forlag.
Oehlenschläger, Adam (1805): *Poetiske Skrifter*, Vols. 1-2, Kbh.: Schubothe.
Oehlenschläger, Adam (1832-34): *Prometheus. Tidsskrift for Poesie,* Æsthetik *og Kritik*, Vols. 1-6, Kbh.: Trykt, paa Udgiverens forlag.
Oehlenschläger, Adam (1854): *Om Evald og Schiller. Forelæsninger holdte ved Kjøbenhavns Universitet i Aarene 1810 og 11*, Vols. 1-2, Kbh.: Lose & Delbanco.
Oehlenschlæger, Adam (1926-30): *Poetiske Skrifter*, Vols. 1-5, ed. by H. Topsøe-Jensen, Kbh.: Holbergselskabet af 23. september.
Oehlenschläger, Adam (1974): *Levnet. Fortalt af ham selv*, Vols. 1-2, Kbh.: Oehlenschläger Selskabet.
Pade, Marianne and Jensen, Minna Skafte, eds. (1988): *Renæssanen: dansk, europæisk, globalt*, Kbh.: Museum Tusculanums Forlag.
Palladius, Peder (1925): *Peder Palladius' Visitatsbog*, ed. by Lis Jacobsen, Kbh.: Gyldendalske Boghandel.
Palladius, Peder (2003): *En Visitatsbog*, ed. by Martin Schwarz Laustsen, Kbh.: Anis.
Panofsky, Erwin (1951/1957): *Gothic Architecture and Scholasticism*, New York: Meridian Books.
Patrick-McGuire, Brian (1976): *Conflict and continuity at Øm Abbey. A Cistercian experience in medieval Denmark*, Kbh.: Museum Tusculanums Forlag.
Paulli, R. (1955): 'Bedømmelsen af Niels Klim i udlandet', *Fund og Forskning*, Vol. 2, Kbh.: Det Kongelige Bibliotek.
Pedersen, John (2008): 'En mørk periode', *Kritik* 188, Kbh.: Gyldendal.
Pedersen, Vibeke A. (1999): 'Dronning Sophias visebog', *Svøbt i mår. Dansk folkevisekultur 1550-1700*, Vol. 1, ed. Flemming Lundgreen-Nielsen and Hanne Ruus, Kbh.: C.A. Reitzel.
Pedersen, Vibeke A. (2006): 'Anne Krabbe og Vibeke Bild', *Danmark og renæssancen 1500-1650*, ed. Carsten Bach-Nielsen et al., Kbh.: Gads Forlag.
Petersen, Carl S. (1949): *Afhandlinger til Dansk Bog- og Biblioteks Historie*, Kbh.: Gyldendal.
Petersen, Peter (1995): *Nydam offermose. Mosefund i Danmark gennem 2000 år*, Kbh.: Dansk Historisk Håndbogsforlag.
Platon (1932-41): *Platons Skrifter*, Vols. 1-10, eds. Carsten Høeg and Hans Ræder, Kbh.: C.A. Reitzels Forlag.
Pontoppidan, Henrik (1912): 'Vi har staaet med fakler, med faner', *Politiken,* 4 February 1912.
Pontoppidan, Henrik (1968): *Lykke-Per* [1898], Vols. 1-2, 1. ed. by Esther and Thorkild Skjerbæk, Kbh.: Gyldendal.

Porter, Roy (2001): *Enlightenment. Britain and the Creation of the Modern World*, London: Penguin Books.

Poulsen, Bjørn (2002): 'Fromhed og magt i senmiddelalderen', *Gilder, lav og broderskaber i middelalderens Danmark,* eds. Lars Bisgaard and Leif Søndergaard, Odense: Syddansk Universitetsforlag.

Rasmussen, Finn (1990): *Guldhornenes tydning. Forhistoriske billedsymboler, runerne og den gamle nordiske religion*, Lyngby: Dansk Historisk Håndbogsforlag.

Rasmussen, Michael (2008): 'Det mystiske øjeblik hos Jens Baggesen', Kritik, Kbh.: Gyldendal.

Riis, Jacob A. (2007): *Den gamle by*, translated by Søren Mulvad, Ribe: Taarnborg

Riising, Anne (1969): *Danmarks middelalderlige Prædiken*, Kbh.: Gads Forlag.

Ruus, Hanne (1999): 'Dansk Folkevisekultur 1550-1700', *Svøbt i mår. Dansk folkevisekultur 1550-1700*, Vol. 1, eds. Flemming Lundgreen-Nielsen and Hanne Ruus, Kbh.: C.A. Reitzel.

Salling, Per (1990): *Fra tugtens tid. Erindringer fra Sorø Akademis Skole. 1822-1962*, Kbh.: Borgen.

Saxo Grammaticus (2000): *Saxos Danmarks historie*, Vols. 1-2, translated by Peter Zeeberg, Kbh.: DSL/Gads Forlag.

Saxo Grammaticus (2002): *The History of the Danes*. Book I-IX, ed. H.E. Davidson, translated by Peter Fisher, Cambridge: D.S. Brewer.

Schiller, Friedrich (1793/2005): '"On Grace and Dignity', translated by Jane V. Curran', in: *Schiller's 'On Grace and Dignity' in Its Cultural Context. Essays and a New Translation*, eds. Jane V. Curran and Christophe Fricker. London: Camden House.

Schanz, Hans-Jørgen (2007): 'Oplysningens idéhorisont', *Oplysningens verden. Idé, historie, videnskab og kunst*, eds. Ole Højris and Thomas Ledet, Aarhus: Aarhus Universitetsforlag.

Schmidt, Povl (1998): 'Thomas Kingo. Sange og digte' *Læsninger i dansk litteratur*, Vol. 1, Odense: Odense Universitetsforlag.

Schmidt, Povl (2000): *Danske litterære tekster fra yngre middelalder*, 2nd ed., Odense: Syddansk Universitetsforlag.

Schmidt, Povl, ed. (2001): *Danske litterære tekster fra 1500- og 1600-tallet*, Odense: Syddansk Universitetsforlag.

Schmidt, Povl (2003): 'Den levende skrift', *Synsvinkler. Særnummer*, Odense: Center for Nordiske Studier: Syddansk Universitet.

Schmidt, Povl (2004): *Danske litterære tekster 1100-1500*, 2nd ed., Odense: Syddansk Universitetsforlag.

Seppä, Anita (2004): 'Foucault, Enlightenment and the Aesthetics of the Self', *Contemporary Aesthetics*, Vol. 2, www.contempaesthetics.org/index.html

Shaftesbury, Anthony Asley Coeper (1981-2007): *Complete Works*, Vols. I-X, Stuttgart-Bad Cannstatt: Friedrich Frommann Verlag.

Shakespeare, William (1897-1900): *Dramatiske Værker*, Vols. 1-9, translated by Edv. Lembcke, 3rd ed., Kbh.: Det Schubotheske Forlag.

Simonsen, Karen-Margrethe et al., ed. (2007): *Lov og litteratur*, Aarhus: Aarhus Universitetsforlag.

Skautrup, Peter (1944-70): *Det danske Sprogs Historie*, Vols. 1-5, Kbh.: Gyldendal.

Skovgaard-Petersen, Inge (1987): *Da Tidernes Herre var nær. Studier i Saxos historiesyn*, Kbh.: Den Danske Historiske Forening.

Skovgaard-Petersen, Karen (1991): 'Non scholea sed vitæ – en programerklæring for latinundervisningen ved Sorø Akademi', *Uddannelseshistorie 1991*, ed. Harry Haue et al., Odense: Odense Universitetsforlag.

Skriver, Svend (2006): *Oprørets æstetik. Om Jens Baggesens Labyrinten*, Herlev: Spring.

Skriver, Svend (2007): *Europæere i 1800-tallets danske litteratur. Om Jens Baggesen, P. L. Møller og Georg Brandes*, ph.d-dissertation, Kbh.: Det Humanistiske Fakultet: Københavns Universitet.

Skyum-Nielsen, Niels et al. ed. (1957-90): *Danmarks riges breve*, 1. række, Vols. 1-7, ed. Franz Blatt, Kbh.: DSL/C.A. Reitzels Boghandel.

Sneedorff, Jens Schielderup (1757): *Om Den Borgerlige Regiering*, Kbh.: Johann Benjamin Ackermann.

Sneedorff, Jens Schielderup (1759): *Breve*, printed by Jonas Lindgren, det Ridderlige Akademies Bogtrykker, Soröe.

Sneedorff, Jens Schielderup (1767): *Fruentimmer-Tidenden og Fredags-Selskabet i Kiøbenhavn*, Første Aargang, published by Kongl. privilegerede Adresse-Contoir, u. n.

Sneedorff, Jens Schielderup (1761-63): *Den patriotiske Tilskuer*, Vols. 1-6, Sorøe: Jonas Lindgren, det Ridderlige Akademies Bogtrykker.

Sneedorff, Jens Schielderup (1775-77): *Sneedorffs samtlige Skrivter*, Vols. 1-9, København: Gyldendal.

Sneedorff, Jens Schielderup (1994): 'Coelis Historie' [1762], *Moralske Fortællinger 1761-1805*, ed. Anne-Marie Mai, Kbh.: Borgen.

Spang-Hanssen, Ebbe (1965): *Erasmus Montanus og naturvidenskaben*, Kbh.: Gad/Holberg-samfundet af 3. December 1922.

Sperling, Otto (1885): *Dr.med. Otto Sperlings Selvbiografi (1602-1673)*, ed. S. Birket Smith, Kbh.: Andr. Fed. Høst & Søns Forlag.

Staffeldt, Schack A.W. von (1804): *Digte*, Kbh.: Fr. Brummers Forlag.

Staffeldt, Schack A.W. von (2001): *Samlede digte*, Vols. 1-3, Kbh.: Det danske Sprog- og Litteraturselskab, C.A. Reitzel.

Steen, Vagn (1994): 'flygr Vol. yfir – den flyver højt', *Weekendavisen*, 16. september.

Steffens, Henrich (1840-45): *Hvad jeg oplevede. Nedskrevet efter Hukommelsen*, Translated by Frederik Schaldemose. Vols. 1-10, Kbh.: Steens forlag.

Steffens, Henrich (1996): *Indledning til philosophiske Forelæsninger* [1803], ed. Johnny Kondrup, DSl, Kbh.: C.A. Reitzels forlag.

Stjernfelt, Karoline (2017-2020): *I Morgen Bliver Bedre*, Vols. 1-2 Kbh.: Nota.

Stoklund, Maria (1996): 'Runer 1995', *Arkæologiske udgravninger i Danmark 1995*, ed. Rigsantikvarens Arkæologiske Sekretariat, Kbh.: Det Arkæologiske Nævn.

Storstein, Eira and Peer E. Sørensen (1999): *Den barokke tekst*, Frederiksberg: Dansklærerforeningen.

Strindberg, August (1912-20): *Samlade skrifter*, Vol. LIV, Efterslåtter, Stockholm: Bonnier.

Stub, Ambrosius (1972): *Ambrosius Stubs Digte*, Vols. 1-2, ed. Erik Kroman, Gentofte: Rosenkilde & Bagger.

Sunesen, Anders (1985): *Hexaëmeron*, translated by H.D. Schepelern, ed. Jørgen Pedersen, Kbh.: DSL/Gads Forlag.

Svane, Marie-Louise (2003): *Formationer i europæisk romantik*, Kbh.: Museum Tusculanums forlag.

Søndergaard, Leif (1989): *Fastelavnsspillet i Danmarks senmiddelalder – om Den utro hustru og fastelavnsspillets tradition*, Odense: Odense Universitetsforlag.

Søndergaard, Leif (1999): 'Magiske tegn, figurer og formler i senmiddelalderlige kalkmalerier', *Billeder i middelalderen. Kalkmalerier og altertavler*, ed. Lars Bisgaard, Tore Nyberg and Leif Søndergaard, Odense: Odense Universitetsforlag.

Søndergaard, Leif (2002): 'Kulturelle aktiviteter i gilder og lav', *Gilder, lav og broderskaber i middelalderens Danmark,* ed. Lars Bisgaard and Leif Søndergaard, Odense: Syddansk Universitetsforlag.

Sønderholm, Erik (1974): *Dansk Barok 1630-1700*, Kbh.: Gyldendal.

Sørensen, Knud (1984): *St. St. Blicher. Digter og samfundsborger*, Kbh.: Gyldendal.

Søndergaard, Leif (2006): 'Talen og den trykte tekst', *Danmark og renæssancen 1500-1650*, ed. Carsten Bach-Nielsen et al., Kbh.: Gads Forlag.

Sørensen, Peer E. (1989): *Håb og erindring. Johannes Ewald i oplysningen*, Kbh.: Gyldendal.

Sørensen, Peer E. (2009): *Vor Tids Temperament. Studier i Herman Bangs forfatterskab,* Kbh.: Gyldendal.

Sørensen, Preben Meulengracht (1977): *Saga og samfund. En indføring i oldislandsk litteratur*, Kbh.: Berlingske Forlag.

Sørensen, Preben Meulengracht (2001): *Kort oversigt over Nordens litteratur i oldtid og middelalder*, Frederiksberg: Dansklærerforeningen.

Sørensen, Preben Meulengracht (2006): *Kapitler af Nordens litteratur i oldtid og middelalder*, ed. Judith Jesch and Jørgen Højgaard Jørgensen, Aarhus: Aarhus Universitetsforlag.

Sørensen, Preben Meulengracht and Steinsland, Gro, eds. (2001): *Vølvens spådom*, Kbh.: Høst.

Thomsen, Ejnar (1935/1971): *Barokken i dansk digtning*, Kbh.: Munksgaard.

Trap, J.P. (1901): *Kongeriget Danmark*, 3rd ed., Vol. 4, Kbh.: G.E.C. Gad.

Turville-Petre, E.O.G. (1964/1975): *Myth and Religion of the North. The Religion of Ancient Scandinavia,* Westport, Connecticut: Greenwood Press, Publishers.

Ulfeldt, Leonora Christina: see Leonora Christina.

Vedel, Anders Sørensen, ed. (1588): *En sørgelig Ligpredicken. Salig och høylofflig Ihukommelse: Høybaarne Første oc Herre, Herr Frederich den Anden, Danmarckis ... Konning... til en Christsalig amindelse* (...). Kbh.

Vedel, Anders Sørensen (1926-27): *Folkevisebog*, Vols. 1-2, ed. Paul V. Rubow, Kbh.: Holbergselskabet af 23. September.

Vedel, Anders Sørensen (1993): *Anders Sørensen Vedels Hundredvisebog*, ed. Karen Thuesen, Kbh.: C.A. Reitzels Forlag.

Vedel, Valdemar (1906): *Ridderromantikken i fransk og tysk Middelalder*, Kbh.: Gyldendal.

Viestad, Else (1989): *Kjønn og ideologi. En studie av kvinnesynet hos Locke, Hume, Rosseau og Kant*, Oslo: Solum.

Voltaire, François (2000): *Candide*, ed. Karen Nyrop Christensen, Frederiksberg: Dansklærerforeningen.

Voltaire, Jean François Marie Arouet de (2004): *Writings of 1771* [Œuvres *de 1771*], *Les* Œuvres *completes de Voltaire*, Vol. 73, Oxford: Voltaire Foundation.

Voragine, Jacobus de (1988): *Helgonlegender. Valda Stycken ur Legenda Aurea*, translated by Johannes Gabrelsson, Stockholm: Artos.

Vosmar, Jørn (1984): *J. P. Jacobsens digning*, Kbh.: Gyldendal.

Walde, O. (1917): 'Stephanii bibliotek och dess historia', *Nordisk Tidskrift för Bok- och Biblioteksväsen*, nr. 1 and nr. 4, Uppsala & Stockholm.

White, James Boyd (2007): 'Retorik og ret', *Lov og litteratur*, ed. Karen-Margrethe Simonsen et al., Aarhus: Aarhus Universitetsforlag.

Willaing, Susanne (2007): *Baggesen med og uden filter. En filosofisk, komparativ undersøgelse af Jens Baggesens rejsedagbog fra sommeren 1787 og sønnen August Baggesens gengivelse af den i 1843*, Magisterkonferens, Nordisk Filologi, Københavns Universitet.

Wilster, Christian (1990): 'Nogle Breve fra Sorø 1826-1827', *Fra tugtens tid. Erindringer fra Sorø Akademis Skole. 1822-1962*, ed. Per Salling, Kbh.: Borgen.

Wittendorff, Alex (1994): *Tyge Brahe*, Kbh.: Gad.

Worm, Ole (1643): *Danicorum Monumentorum Libri Sex eruti*. Det Kongelige Bibliotek.

Worsøe-Schmidt, Lisbeth (1994): *Forfatter i Danmark 1894/1994*, Kbh.: Dansk Forfatterforening.

Worsøe-Schmidt, Lisbeth (1999): *1700-tallets danske forfattere og deres offentlighed, forbundet med en komplementær kulturteori*, ph.d.-afhandling, Kbh.: Institut for Nordisk Filologi.

Worsøe-Schmidt, Lisbeth (2004): 'Spectators in Denmark', *Enlightened Networking*, eds. Thomas Bredsdorff and Anne-Marie Mai, Odense: University Press of Southern Denmark.

Zeeberg, Peter (1994): *Tycho Brahes 'Urania Titania' – et digt om Sophie Brahe*, Kbh.: Museum Tusculanums Forlag.

Wullschlager, Jackie (2001): *Hans Christian Andersen: the life of a storyteller*. New York: A.A. Knopf.

Zeruneith, Keld (1985): *Soldigteren. En biografi om Johannes Ewald*, Kbh.: Gyldendal.

Zola, Émile (1959): 'Les Réalistes du Salon' [11. May 1866], *Salons*, Paris: Librairie Minard.

Zola, Émile (1970): *Thérèse Raquin* [1867], Paris: Garnier-Flammarion.

Zola, Émile (1992/1998): *Thérèse Raquin*, translated by Andrew Rothwell. Oxford: Oxford University Press

Ørsnes, Mogens and Ilkjær, Jørgen (1993): 'Offerfund', *Da klinger i muld... 25 års arkæologi i*

Danmark, eds. Birger Storgaard and Steen Hvass, Aarhus: Aarhus Universitetsforlag.
Ørsted, H.C. (1850-51): *Aanden i Naturen*, Vols. 1-2, Kbh.: Andr. Fred. Høst.
Ørsted, H.C. (1870): *Breve fra og til Hans Christian Ørsted*, ed. Mathilde Ørsted, Vols. 1-2, Kbh.: Linds Forlag.
Aarestrup, Emil (1998): *Udvalgte digte*, ed. by Dan Ringgaard, Kbh.: Borgen.
Aarseth, Asbjørn (1985): *Romantikken som konstruksjon*, Bergen: Universitetsforlaget.

WEBSITES

http://archive.org/stream/candide19942gut/19942.txt (Voltaire: Candide)
https://archive.org/stream/TheConceptOfDread/TheConceptOfDread_djvu.txt (Kierkegaard: The Concept of Dread)
http://www.columbia.edu/acis/ets/CCREAD/etscc/kant.html (Kant: What is Enlightenment?) (http://www.baudelaire.cz/works.html?aID=200&artID=82) (Baudelaire: The taste of nothingness)
https://contempaesthetics.org/newvolume/pages/journal.php?search=true (Anita Seppä on Foucault)
https://dsl.dk/projekter/latinsk-hyrdedigtning/projektbeskrivelse (A project on Pastoral Poetry translated from Latin)
http://gallica.bnf.fr/ark:/12148/bpt6k308970/f125.item (Mémoires de madame de Motteville)
http://germanhistorydocs.ghi-dc.org/sub_document.cfm?document_id=368 (Schlegel)
http://holbergsskrifter.dk/holberg-public/view?docId=adm/main.xml&lang.set=dk (Holberg: Collected Writings in Danish)
http://johnirons.blogspot.com/2017/04/andersens-auntie-toothache.html (H. C. Andersen)
https://nordicwomensliterature.net/ (History of Nordic Women's Literature)
http://ordnet.dk/ods/index_html (Dictionary of the Danish Language)
http://pub.uvm.dk/2004/kanon (The Literary Canon of the Ministry for Education)
http://sks.dk/cc/txt.xml?hash=k17&zoom_highlight=montanus#k17 (Søren Kierkegaard: Collected works, on Erasmus Montanus)
https://kum.dk/uploads/tx_templavoila/KUM_kulturkanonen_uk_OK.pdf (The Cultural Canon of the Ministry for Culture: On Jeppe on the Hill)
http://www.gutenberg.org/files/1150/1150-h/1150-h.htm (The Danish History of Saxo Grammaticus)
http://www.gutenberg.org/files/5749/5749.txt (Ludvig Holberg: Jeppe of the Hill, The Political Thinker and Erasmus Montanus)
www.adl.dk/(Arkiv for dansk litteratur)
www.dlb.dansklf.dk
www.fortidensjelling.dk/kongernes_jelling.htm (The Jelling Monuments)
www.renaessanceforum.dk/rf_2_2006.htm (Flemming Lundgreen-Nielsen on poetry in Danish language during the reign of Frederik II):
www2.kb.dk/elib/mss/skatte/mss/thott_1510.htm (On the ballad-book, The Book of the Heart)

Cronological overview

Danish history	Danish literature	Benchmarks
0-400 The Roman Iron Age Import of Roman goods	**0-1100 The Antiquity**	**40s and 50s** Paul the Apostle writes his letters to Christian congregations
	200-750 The age of Old Norse	**70-100** The gospels are written down
400-700 Germanic Iron Age Urbanization in Ribe	**200-250** Offering of war booty, for instance in Tornsbjerg. Inscriptions in elder Futhark	**300-500** The fall of the Roman Empire. A period of Migration
	c. 400 The Gallehus Horn. More than 150 inscriptions in elder Futhark have been found. More are still found.	**500** Franks and Anglo-Saxons establish Christian kingdoms. The migrations cut off Old Norse from other German languages
		c. 400 Saint Augustine, the bishop, writes his confessions
800-1100 The viking Age Raids of Hamburg, Paris, England Settlement in England	**800-1100 The age of the old Danish Language**. Old Norse is divided into an East Scandinavian branch, consisting of old Danish and Swedish, and, secondly, a West Scandinavian branch, consisting of Norwegian, Faroese and Icelandic and, thirdly, an Old Gutnish branch	**451** The abbey institution becomes an official part of the church
737 The construction of the defence entrenchment Dannevirke		**400-1500 The European Middle Ages**
826 The baptism of Harald Klak at the court of the Frankish King, Louis the Pious		**610** Muhammed the Prophet preaches in Mekka
	c. 800-1150 Runestones with inscriptions in younger Futhark are present all over Denmark. 150 runestones have been found, more are still found	**622** Year 0 of the Islamic chronology
850 The monk Ansgar tries to have churches built in Hedeby and Schleswig		**7-800** Handwritten bibles, church histories, legends in many areas of Europe
958 Gorm the Old is buried in Jelling	**The second half of 900s.** The runestones in Jelling are set up	**800** Charlemagne is crowned in Rome as German-Roman emperor
1019-1042 Denmark and England are united by Knud the Great and Hardeknud.		**900-1100** Heroic poetry is known in many areas of Europe
1100 The start of the The Middle Ages	**1000-1100** Icelandic bards visit Nordic and English courts	**c. 1000** The Swedish runestone, Rökstenen which has a literary inscription is set up. 3000 inscriptions have been found in Sweden on stones and cliffs
1103 The first archbishop of Lund	**900-1100** The transition from the Viking Age to the The Middle Ages	
1157-1241 The Age of the Valdemar-kings	**1100-1500** The Middle Ages	**1100** Troubadour poetry and novels in verses are known in many areas of Europe
		1075 Adam of Bremen writes his chronicle
		1150 The University of Paris is opened
		The 1200s A Nordic branch of the Renaissance. The Islandic sagas are written down. The German Empire is weakened.

Danish history

1100-1536 The Middle Ages

1013 Svend Tveskæg conquers England

1016 Knud II conquers England

1086 Knud the Holy is murdered and is sanctified 1101 as the first Danish saint.

1169 The Vendic city of Arkona is conquered

1219 Estonia is conquered

1241 The Jutlandic law is implemented

1340 The plague rages. The Danish kingdom is in a state of disintegration

1400-1536 The late Middle Ages

1397-1523 The Kalmar Union between Norway, Denmark and for periods Sweden.

1460 Chr. I is nominated Duke of Schleswig and Count of Holstein after an agreement with the Schleswig-Holstein knighthood

1479 The University of Copenhagen is opened

1520 The bloodbath of Stockholm. The Kalmar Union with Sweden is destroyed

1534-1536 The count's feud. A civil war that starts with a feud over the nomination of a new king and ends with the Reformation

1536-1660 The old nobility rules together with elected kings

1563-1570 The Nordic Seven Years war. Frd. II tries to resurrect the Kalmar Union

1625-1629 Chr. IV engages Denmark in the Thirty Years' War. Denmark is weakened. Sweden is the new superpower of the Baltic Sea

1657-1600 War against Sweden

1658 The peace treaty of Roskilde. Denmark surrenders Skåne, Halland and Blekinge to Sweden

1660 Frd. III becomes the first absolute king

Danish literature

1100-1536 The Middle Ages

1060 The Dalby-book

Late 1100s The laws of Sealand and Skåne are written in Danish

The early 1200s Saxo writes his Danish history, *Gesta Danorum*. Anders Sunesen writes *Hexaëmeron*

1200-1300s Cronicles, legends, law books and medical books

c. 1270 Boethis de Dacia lectures in Paris

1329 Elegy in Latin on the state of the kingdom of Denmark

Early 1400s Peder Laale's collection of proverbs is used in the teaching of Latin

Late 1400s the oldest preserved Danish copy of *Lucidarius*

1495 Printing of *Den danske Rimkrønike*

1515 The parish priest Michael Nielsen's Maria ballads are printed

1536-1660 The Renaissance

1515/1518 Christiern Pedersen publishes *Jærntegnspostillen*

1550 *The Danish Bible* of Chr. III

1562 Niels Hemmingsen's dissertation on the natural law

1579 *The Danish hymn book* by Hans Thomissøn

1591 *Hundredvisebog* by Anders Sørensen Vedel

1648 Søren Therkelsen: *Astree-Sjunge Choor*

1660-1720 The Age of the Baroque

1661 Anders Arrebo: *Hexaëmeron*

1673 Leonora Christiana writes her *French autobiography* and starts her *Memoirs*

1678 Dorothe Engelbrechtsdatter. *Siælens Sang-Offer*

1699 Kingo's *Hymn book* is officially implemented.

Benchmarks

1054 The East-West Schism of the church

1100 The age of the courtly culture of knights in France. The writing down of the *Roland Epos*

1096-1099 The first crusade. Jerusalem is conquered

1100-1200s The first European universities are founded

1220-1300 The Icelandic sagas are written down

1200-1300 The realm of the Aztecs

1300s Printing of books in China. The middle eastern folk tales, *One Thousand and one Nights*

1320 Dante: *The Divine Comedy*

1350 Boccacio: *Decameron*

The mid-1300s The revelations of the holy Birgitta

1368-1644 The Ming Dynasty

1400-1500s The beginning of the Renaissance in several European countries

1454 *The Gutenberg Bible*

1492 Columbus travels to America

1517 Luther's thesis in Wittenberg

1532-1564 Rabelais: *Gargantua and Pantaguel*

1543 Copernicus questions Prolemæus' understanding of the universe

1500-1600s The age of the Baroque begins in European countries

1605-15 Cervantes: *Don Quijote*

!635 The French Academy is founded

1651 Hobbes: *Leviathan*

1653 Moliere's first comedies

1687 Newton: *Principia*

1696-97 Bayle: *Encyclopedia*

1600-1700s The age of Classicism

Danish history	Danish literature	Benchmarks
1720-1800 The Enlightenment	**1720-1800** The Enlightenment	**1700-1720** The Great Northern War
The Danish Enlightenment begins in the long peace period after the Great Nordic War.	**1720-1800** Classicism	**1710** Leibniz: *Essai de théodicée*
1721 Frd. III establishes the first public schools for children, the abbre-viation cavalry schools, at the estate of the crown	**1720** *Kjøbenhavnske Lærde Efterret-ninger* starts publication	**1710** Berkeley: *A Treatise concerning the principles of human knowledge*
1721 Hans Egede arrives in Green-land to missionize and colonize Greenland	**1722** The opening of the first Danish speaking theatre	**1711** Pope: *Winsor Forrest*
1728 Copenhagen burns	**1730-1770** The Rococo	**1719** Defoe: *Robinson Cruseo*
1730 Chr.VI is crowned	**1738** Theatre performances are prohibited	**1721** Montesquieu: *Persian Letters*
1732 The Danish Asia Company is established	**1747** The founding of Sorø Academy	**1722** The first division of Poland
1733 Serfdom is implemented for the benefit of estate owners	**1748** The new theatre building in Copenhagen is opened	**1726** Swift: *Gulliver's Travels*
1733 The Moravian Brethern arrive in Greenland	**1749** The newpaper Berlingske Tidende is published	**1739** Hume: *A Treatise on Human Nature*
1735 The Trade Office is founded in order to strengthen trade and finances	**1759** The founding of 'Det Sma-gende Selskab', an influential literary society	**1740** Richardson: *Pamela*
1736 Mandatory confirmation	**1760 ff.** Literary prose works are published	**1742-1745** Young: *Night-Thoughts*
1737 The Church Inspection office is opened. State Pietism rules	**1761-1763** *Den Patriotiske Tilskuer* is published	**1748-1773** Klopstock: *Der Messias*
1741 Regulation of religious meet-ings	**1770** The founding of Det norske Selskab. The opening of The Royal Theatre	**1751-1765** *The French Encyclopedia*
1757 The agriculture commission is established	**1770 ff.** Neoclassicism	**1755** Earthquake in Lisbon
1766 Chr.VII is crowned	**1775** The founding of Det danske litteraturselskab, the founding of Drejer's club	**1759** Voltaire: *Candide*
1767 New agriculture commission	**1785** The journal *Minerva* is pub-lished	**1759-1767** Sterne: *Tristam Shandy*
1770-1772 The reform reign of Struensee	**1799** Peter Andreas Heiberg is ex-pelled	**1762** Rousseau: *Emile*
1772 Guldberg's coup against Stru-ensee		**1770ff.** 'Sturm und Drang'
1773 The founding of a state union of Denmark after a treaty between Denmark and Russia		**1771** Herder: *Über die Ursprung der Sprache*
1776 Danish citizenship is imple-mented		**1774** Goethe: *Die Leiden des jungen Werther*
1784 A. P. Bernsdorff deposes Guld-berg.		**1776** The American War of Inde-pendence
1786 The major agricultural com-mission is established		**1781** Kant: *Kritik der reinen Vernuft*
1788 Serfdom is abolished		**1786** The Swedish Academy is founded
1792 Slave trade is prohibited		**1788** Colonization of Australia
		1789 The French Revolution
		1790 Kant: *Kritik der Urteilskraft*
		1791-1792 Karamzin: *Letters of a Russian traveler*
		1792 Wollstonecraft: *A Vindication of the Rights of Women*
		1793 Hölderlin: *Hyperion*
		1793-1794 The terror reign of the French Revolution

Danish history	Danish literature	Benchmarks
1801-1814 Danish participation in the Napoleonic Wars	**1800-1870** Romanticism: Universal romanticism, Biedermeier, critical romanticism	**1800-1815** The Napoleonic Wars
1801 The Battle of Copenhagen	**1802** Steffens lectures in Copenhagen. The Rahbeks move to the Bakkehus	**1800** Schelling: *System des Transcendentalen Idealismus*
1807 The bombardment of Copenhagen	**1810** Friederike Brun moves to Sophienholm	**1800** Schlegel: *Gespräch über die Poesie*
1813 Bankruptcy of the Danish State	**1813-1817** Molbech publishes the journal *Athene*	**1807** Hegel: *Phänomenologie des Geistes*
1814 The cession of Norway. Economic crisis. Public teaching of children	**1813-1819** Baggesen's critique of Oehlenschläger starts a fight between Danish authors	**1807** Stäel: *Coninna*
1815 The first meetings of classes of society	**1816-1819** Grundtvig publishes the journal *Danne-Virke*	**1808-1832** Goethe: *Faust I-II*
1844 The opening of the first folk high school in Rødding	**1827-1837** Heiberg publishes the journal *Kjøbenhavns flyvende Post*	**1809-1811** Byron: *Child Harold*
1848 The absolute monarchy is abolished. The First Schleswig War begins	**1827-1829** Blicher publishes the journal *Nordlyset*	**1812** Grimm: *Märchen*
1849 The new constitution is implemented	**1832-1834** Oehlenschläger publishes the journal *Prometeus*	**1813** Austen: *Pride and Prejdudice*
1851 The State union of 1773 between Denmark, Schleswig and Holsteins is renewed	**1840-1846** Goldschmidt publishes the journal *Corsaren*	**1818-1819** Schopenhauer: *Die Welt als Wille und Vorstellung*
1855 United constitution	**1844-1846** Heiberg publishes the yearbook *Urania*	**1819** Scott: *Ivanhoe*
1857 Law on freedom of trade	**1845-1847** P. L. Møller publishes the yearbook *Gæa*	**1820** Keats: 'Ode on a Grecian Urn'
1863 The November constitution. Schleswig and Denmark are attached. Holstein is not included	**1851** Literary quarrel on Mathilde Fibiger's novel, *Clara Raphael. Twelve letters*	**1820** Shelley: *Prometheus Unbound*
1864 The Second Schleswig War. Preussen and Austria attack Denmark because of the November constitution. Denmark loses Schleswig and Holstein	**1855** Kierkegaard publishes the journal *Øieblikket*	**1821-1829** The Greek War of Indepence
After 1864 More high schools are founded, growth of the cooperative movement	**1859** The weekly magazine *Illustreret Tidende* is published	**1829-1854** Balzac: *La Comédie Humaine*
1866 The constitution is revised	**1870 ff.** The modern breakthrough: Realism, naturalism, impressionism	**1830** The French July revolution. Stendhal: *Le rouge et le noir*
1870 The united left demands a return to the constitution of 1849	**1871** Georg Brandes lectures in Copenhagen	**1832-1840** Comte: *Course on Positive Philosophy*
1871 The Danish section of the international labour movement and Danish women's movement start	**1874-1877** Georg and Edvard Brandes publish the journal *Det 19. Aarhundrede*	**1836-1842** Gogol's most famous short stories
1885-1894 The government rules by provisional laws	**1884** The newspaper *Politiken* is founded	**1841** Feurbach: *Das Wesen des Christentums*
1898 The united union movement of workers is founded	**1893-1894** Johannes Jørgensen publishes the journal *Taarnet*	**1844** Heine: *Deutschland. Ein Wintermärchen*
1901 Parliamentarism is implemented		**1847** Brontë: *Wuthering Heights*
		1848 Marx and Engels: *The Communist Manifesto*
		1848 The March revolution in France and Germany
		1849 Dickens: *David Copperfield*
		1855 Whitman: *Leaves of Grass*
		1856 Flaubert: *Madame Bovary*
		1859 Darwin: *The Origin of Species*
		1865-1869 Tolstoy: *War and Peace*
		1871 The Paris Commune

Index

Absalon of Lund 43-45, 64
Adam of Bremen 25
Adorno, Theodor W. 93
Alexander the Great 65*, 65-66
Andersen, Hans Christian 141, 142*, 143-144, 147-149, 151-154, 156, 171, 178-184, 188, 192, 197, 202, 204, 215-216
Andersen, Thomas 102
Ansgar(missionary) 22
Aquinas, Thomas 59-60
Aristotle 55, 60
Arrebo, Anders 43, 77, 80, 84, 96*
Augier, Emile 208
Austen, Jane 192

Baggesen, Jens 91, 95, 127, 129-130, 132, 134-137, 137*, 138-139, 145, 157
Balslev, Birgitte 83*
Bang, Arne 217*
Bang, Herman 149, 207*, 208-212, 215-216
Baudelaire, Charles 152, 153
Bernard of Clairvaux 49, 51
Biehl, Charlotta Dorothea 95, 108, 112-115, 127-129, 139
Bille, Beate 66, 73
Birgitta of Vadstena 62
Birket-Smith, Sophus 78
Bissen, H.V. 138*, 157*, 203*
Bjørnson, Bjørnstjerne 143, 179, 210
Blicher, Steen Steensen 143, 147-149, 188, 193-194, 194*, 195, 196-198, 202
Blixen, Karen 134*
Bloom, Harold 145
Bluetooth, Harald 21-22, 25
Boileau-Despréaux, Nicolas 124
Bording, Anders 96*, 97, 124
Brahe, Tycho 66, 73, 81
Brandes, Edvard 210-211
Brandes, Georg 145, 149-150, 143, 154, 163, 176, 198, 206-207, 209-211, 213-215, 218
Brede, Torsten 40
Bredsdorff, Thomas 103
Bremer, Fredrika 192-193
Brontë, Emily 192
Brorson, Hans Adolph 95, 98, 119-122, 125
Brun, Frederike 139, 188, 189*
Brøgger, Suzanne 30
Brøndsted, Mogens 177
Burke, Edmund 127
Bülow, Johan 113-114, 118
Bødtcher, Ludvig 147, 149, 202

Capion, Etienne 109
Carl Alexander 215
Caroline Mathilde 114-115
Cassirer, Ernst 100
Charlemagne 37, 48, 65*, 66, 70*
Christian II 71
Christian III 71
Christian IV 75, 78, 103
Christian V 86
Christian VI 119
Christian VII 113-115
Claussen, Sophus 216, 217*, 218, 219
Collett, Camilla 192, 193
Comte, Auguste 211
Corneille, Pierre 124
Cæsar, Julius 65*, 66

D'Alembert, Jean 100
D'Holbach, Paul-Henri 100
Darwin, Charles 210
David, Christian 120
De Dacia, Boethius 60
De Montaigne, Michel 74-75
De Montaigu, René Magnon 109
De Montesquieu, Charles 127
De Mylius, Johan 179
De Sévigné, Madame 124
De Staël, Madame 192
De Troyes, Chrétien 64
De Voragine, Jacobus 57
Defoe, Daniel 126-127
Descartes, René 97
Destouches, Philippe 112
Diderot, Denis 100
Dionysius of Areopagite 47-48
Drachmann, Holger 149, 210
Du Bartas, Guillaume 43
Dyggve, Ejnar 79*

Eco, Umberto 135
Ehrensvärd, Carl Fredrik Gyllembourg 191
Engelbretsdatter, Dorothe 80
Engelhardt, Conrad 16
Enquist, Per Olov 114-115
Eric I 25
Eriksen, Edvard 154
Eskild 35
Evens, Otto 146*
Ewald, Johannes 95, 96*, 108, 113, 120, 127-132, 138*, 139, 144-145, 146*, 147-148, 174, 181

Felski, Rita 10-12, 156
Feuerbach, Ludwig 205
Fibiger, Mathilde 191
Fichte, Johann Gottlieb 160, 166, 169, 171, 178
Fo, Dario 115
Frederik II 66
Frederik III 78
Frederik IV 95, 109, 113, 118
Frederik V 103-104
Frederik VII 196*
Freud, Sigmund 186
Frängsmyr, Tore 103

Garnass, Jørgen Christensen 116*
Goldoni, Carlo 112
Goldschmidt, M. A. 147, 149, 176-177, 177*
Gorm the Old 21-22, 45
Gotfred of Ghemen 35
Gotfredsen, Lise 23
Grammaticus, Saxo 18, 29, 39, 43
Greenblatt, Stephen 8
Gregory of Tours 45
Grotius, Hugo 89, 94
Grund, Johan Gottfried 116*
Grundtvig, Nikolai Frederik Severin 144-145, 147-149, 167-169, 178-180, 180*, 181-182, 184, 186, 188, 196, 204
Gunner63
Gustav III 191
Gutenberg, Johannes 34
Gyllembourg, Thomasine 117, 147-149, 172, 174, 188, 190*, 191-193, 195

Habermas, Jürgen 102
Hansdotter, Zille 106
Hansen, Mads 197
Hauch, Carsten 147, 149, 202, 203*
Hegel, Georg Wilhelm Friedrich 9, 147, 170-172, 184, 205-206
Heiberg, Johan Ludvig 147, 171-172, 174, 177-179, 191-192, 200
Heiberg, Johanne Louise 172, 191, 195
Heiberg, Peter Andreas 95, 115-118, 191
Heine, Heinrich 204
Helleberg, Maria 114-115
Hemmingsen, Niels 89
Herder, Johann von Gottfried 144, 172
Hetsch, Gustav Friedrich 177*
Hieronymus 45
Hitler, Adolf 25
Hobbes, Thomas 89
Holberg, Ludvig 94-95, 99, 101-104, 106-107, 107*, 109-112, 118-119, 123-125, 127, 129, 131-132, 139, 164*, 188
Homer 27
Horkheimer, Max 93
Hugo, Victor 204, 205
Hus, Jan 120
Høegh-Guldberg, Ove 115
Haarder, Jon Helt 7

Ibsen, Henrik 156, 206, 210, 216
Ingemann, B. S. 147, 149, 193, 196
Israel, Jonathan 100-101

Jacobsen, J. P. 149, 206, 210-211
Jacobsen, Lis 40
Jansen, F. J. Billeskov 125, 144
Jarlsberg, Wedel 118
Jens(abbot) 36
Jensen, Johannes V. 216
Johansen, Helga 213
Juliane Marie(queen dowager) 115

Kant, Immanuel 99, 100, 123, 127, 166, 169, 172
Kierkegaard, Søren 110, 139, 148-149, 172, 177-181, 183-184, 185*, 186-188, 192-193, 202, 204-206, 208
Kingo, Thomas 78, 80, 82-83, 83*, 84, 86, 95-96, 96*, 121
Klak, Harald 22
Klopstock, Friedrich Gottlieb 93, 108, 127, 145
Kollerød, Ole 70-71
Krabbe, Anne 66, 67*
Kuma, Kengo 150*

Larsen, Thøger 30
Lasson, Anne Margrethe 69
Latour, Bruno 10-11
Lavard, Knud 50
Leibniz, Gottfried Wilhelm 98-99
Lepage, Robert 153
Levy, Jette Lundbo 144
Locke, John 94, 97
Lombard, Peter 41
Lord Byron 204, 209
Louis the Pious 22, 48
Luckow-Nielsen, Henrik 142*
Luther, Martin 34, 76, 120

Macpherson, James 144
Madsen, Peder 47
Malling, Ove 113, 117-118
Marmontel, Jean-François 112
Martha of Karise 57
Marx, Karl 206
Melanchthon, Philip 76
Merthe of Sorø 57
Mill, John Stuart 208, 210
Milton, John 43
Molbech, Christian 195
Moliere, Jean-Baptiste 109, 124-125
Moltke, Erik 14, 40
Montrose, Louis 8
Mortensen, Klaus P. 102, 144
Mussolini, Benito 215
Møller, Poul Martin 147, 188, 192, 204-205

Newton, Issac 81-82
Nielsen, Anton 197
Nielsen, Erik A. 144
Nielsen, Niels Åge 28
Nietzsche, Friedrich 206, 213-215, 219
Nordenflycht, Hedvig Charlotta 101

Oehlenschläger, Adam 16, 139, 144-145, 147-148, 157*, 157-160, 161*, 162-164, 166, 171, 174-175, 178-179, 181-182, 188, 199
Olav the Holy 33
Otto the Great 22

Palladius, Peder 71
Pasteur, Louis 11
Paul the Apostle 59
Pedersen, Christiern 46, 76
Petrarch 73
Philo of Alexandria 41
Plato 47-48, 54, 166, 172
Plotinus 47-48, 166
Pontoppidan, Henrik 210
Porter, Roy 100, 103
Pram, Christen Henriksen 108
Ptolemy, Claudius 77
Pushkin, Alexander 204

Racine, Jean 124
Rahbek, Kamma 118, 157, 188
Rahbek, Knud Lyne 108, 117-118, 157
Reenberg, Tøger 123-124
Ricoeur, Paul 8-9
Rifbjerg, Klaus 110, 216
Rosenkrantz, Jørgen 75-76
Rossel, Sven Hakon 10
Rothe, Tyge 117-118
Rousseau, Jean-Jacques 94, 100, 123, 127-128, 145, 172, 189

Sainte-Beuve, Charles Auguste 7, 211
Sand, George 208
Schack, Hans Egede 176, 208
Schack, May 102
Schandorph, Sophus 210
Schiller, Friedrich 144, 147, 173-174, 215
Schopenhauer, Arthur 213
Schrader, Johan Herman 120
Scott, Sir Walter 205
Seneca 74
Shelley, Percy Bysshe 204
Sibbern, F. C. 202
Skautrup, Peter 18
Skjold(king) 39
Skram, Amalie 149, 209-210, 213, 215
Skram, Erik 210-211
Skriver, Svend 144
Skúlason, Einar 33
Sneedorff, Jens Schielderup 95, 101-102, 104, 108, 118, 123, 127
Sophie 6, 79
Spielhagen, Friedrich 208
Spinoza, Baruch 101
St. Augustine 41, 56
Staffeldt, Schack 91-93, 95, 98, 139, 144, 147-148, 158, 163-169, 188, 199
Steffens, Henrich 144, 147, 160, 162-163, 168-171, 178, 181-182, 199
Steinsland, Gro 30

Sterne, Laurence 127-128, 145
Stjernfelt, Karoline 115
Strauss, David Friedrich 205
Strindberg, August 206, 214, 216
Struensee, Johann Friedrich 114-115, 117, 122
Stub, Ambrosius 125, 126*
Sturluson, Snorri 18, 27, 30
Suger, Abbot 48-49
Suhm, Peter Frederik 117-118
Sunesen, Anders 40-43, 45
Sørensen, Peder 35
Sørensen, Preben Meulengracht 30

Taine, Hippolyte 211
Tasso, Torquato 43
Tausen, Hans 72
Theodoric the Great 28
Therkelsen, Søren 78
Thomissøn, Hans 72
Thyra(queen) 21
Thyregod, C. A. 197
Tieck, Johann Ludwig 178-179
Tullin, Braunmann 96*, 125
Turgenev, Ivan 208

Ulfeldt, Corfitz 78,
Ulfeldt, Leonora Christina 74, 77-79, 79*, 80

Valdemar II 41, 61, 64
Valdemar IV 61
Vedel, Anders Sørensen 66
Verlaine, Paul 216, 218
Voltaire 99, 100, 106, 114, 126, 127
Von Goethe, Johann Wolfgang 127, 138-139, 144, 147, 160, 162, 172-174, 176-179, 202, 205, 215
Von Humboldt, Karl Wilhelm 172
Von Schelling, Friedrich Wilhelm Joseph 160, 169-171, 182, 205
Von Schlegel, Friedrich 170, 202
Von Zinzendorf, Nikolaus Ludwig 120

Wessel, Johan Herman 95, 108, 146*
Wiedewelt, Johannes 96*, 133*, 164*
Winther, Christian 188, 198
Wordsworth, William 209

Young, Edward 145

Zola, Émile 209-210

Ørsted, H. C. 160

Aakjær, Jeppe 198
Aarestrup, Emil 147, 149, 198-201, 201*, 202
Aarsleff, Carl 185*